Ja

THE BEAT
OFFICER'S
COMPANION

11th Edition

Gordon Wilson

BA (Law), MSc

Contents

Contents

Contents

Contents

Contents

Contents

Contents

Further titles available:

- Part I Promotion Crammer for Sergeants and Inspectors
- The Traffic Officer's Companion
- The Scottish Beat Officer's Companion

To order or for further details phone +44 (0) 20 8700 3700 or fax +44 (0) 20 8763 1006

By the same author
The Traffic Officer's Companion

© Gordon Wilson 2005

1st edition 1983
2nd edition 1986
3rd edition 1988
4th edition 1992
5th edition 1994
reprinted 1996
reprinted 1997
6th edition 1998
7th edition 2000
8th edition 2002
9th edition 2003
10th edition 2004
11th edition 2005

ISBN 07106 27343

Jane's Information Group

Sentinel House
163, Brighton Road
Coulsdon
Surrey CR5 2YH

Printed and bound in Great Britain by
Cambridge Printing

Preface

This book is presented in a manner similar to that adopted by 'The Traffic Officer's Companion'. The diagrammatic and pictorial format provides an easily read and understandable interpretation of those aspects of legislation, other than traffic laws, likely to be of practical value to the patrolling police officer. Readers wishing to avail themselves of a similar presentation of traffic legislation are referred to the 'Traffic Officer's Companion'.

The problems encountered by the present-day officer in memorising, interpreting, recalling and making decisions upon an ever-increasing field of legislation are not underestimated. The intention of this book has therefore been to provide a practical and speedy reference to those aspects likely to be of operational value.

Because the book is intended to serve merely as a guide to the operational police officer, the relevant legislation has been subjected to a practical interpretation. It has been necessary to be selective in the material used and the book should not, therefore, be regarded as a definitive work of reference. Specific technical details may require further research.

In this edition the main changes have been brought about by:

(a) **The Domestic Violence, Crime and Victims Act 2004**, which introduces a new offence of causing the death of a child or vulnerable person by a person who is a member of the same household;

(b) **The Non Commercial Movement of Pet Animals (England) Regulations 2004**, which, combined with Community Regulation 998/2003, amends regulations for the import of pet animals, so as to include a requirement for microchips, blood tests, certification and passports;

(c) **The Hunting Act 2004,** which makes it unlawful to hunt a wild animal with a dog unless the activity falls within one or more of defined exempt activities;

(d) **The Fireworks Regulations 2004**, which amend the previous regulations by restricting the persons by whom, and occasions on which, fireworks may be used;

(e) **S63B of the Police and Criminal Evidence Act 1984**, which allows the taking of samples from a person in police detention for the purpose of testing for Class A drugs;

(f) **The Football Spectators (Prescription) Order 2004**, which redefines a 'Regulated Football Match';

Preface

(g) **The Criminal Justice Act 1988 (Offensive Weapons) (Amendment) Order 2004**, which extends the definition of 'offensive weapon' to include a stealth knife and a truncheon;

(h) The revision of **PACE Codes of Practice**, which called for various amendments, introducing new provisions such as the recording of encounters. It also presented an opportunity to introduce expanded coverage of Code D, which deals with identification of suspects. This was thought to be useful because an identification officer may, in certain circumstances, delegate some methods of identification to officers of lower rank;

(i) **The Serious Organised Crime and Police Act 2005**, which, in addition to making a variety of amendments, introduced a number of new provisions and offences, including: a power to direct a person to leave a place following a prohibition order, a power to search for prohibited fireworks, the taking of intimate samples, and the offences of harassment in the home, trespassing and demonstrating on designated sites, and protection of animal research organisations;

(j) **The Prevention of Terrorism Act 2005** which introduces 'Control Orders' that impose obligations on individuals, the breach of which are arrestable offences; and

(k) **The Licensing Act 2003** which has not yet been fully brought into force but will repeal and re-enact most of the existing licensing laws including the whole of the Licensing Act 1964. In the meantime, an overview of the new Act has been included.

Gordon Wilson
Former Superintendent, Warwickshire Constabulary.

Chapter 1
Crime

Criminal Attempts

S 1 CRIMINAL ATTEMPTS ACT 1981

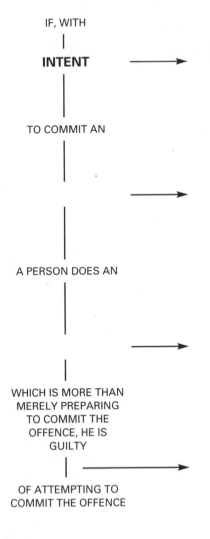

IF, WITH

INTENT ⟶ Even though the facts are such that the commission of the offence is impossible

TO COMMIT AN

Any offence which, if it were completed, would be triable as an indictable offence in England and Wales, except:

- conspiracy

- aiding, abetting, counselling or procuring or suborning an offence

- assisting offenders or agreeing not to disclose information about arrestable offences

A PERSON DOES AN

⟶ Where a person carries out acts in the *mistaken* belief that he is committing an offence, he will be guilty of an attempt to commit that offence

WHICH IS MORE THAN MERELY PREPARING TO COMMIT THE OFFENCE, HE IS GUILTY

⟶ The powers to arrest and search are the same as they would have been for the full offence

OF ATTEMPTING TO COMMIT THE OFFENCE

Theft

S 1 THEFT ACT 1968

`The essential ingredients of the offence of theft are outlined below and discussed in a little more depth in the following pages

A person will be guilty of theft if he:

- **DISHONESTLY**

- **APPROPRIATES**

- **PROPERTY**

- **BELONGING TO ANOTHER**

- **WITH THE INTENTION TO PERMANENTLY DEPRIVE**

It is immaterial whether the appropriation is made with a view to gain, or is made for the thief's own benefit.

THIS IS AN ARRESTABLE OFFENCE

ADVERTISING REWARDS for the return of stolen goods and using words like "no questions will be asked", "safe from apprehension or enquiry" or "money paid for their purchase will be repaid" constitutes an offence (S 23).

Dishonestly

S 2 THEFT ACT 1968

The appropriation of property will not be regarded as 'dishonest' if:

- he believed he had the right in law to take it, or

- he believed he would have had the owner's consent, had the owner known about it, or

- the owner cannot be discovered by taking reasonable steps (except where the property came to him as trustee or personal representative)

but even if he intended to pay for it, it could amount to dishonesty.

Appropriates

S 3 THEFT ACT 1968

An appropriation is any assumption of the rights of an owner.

This includes the case where he comes by the property without stealing it (even if he does so innocently) and later treats it as his own.

But where he gives value for the property in good faith, any later assumption by him of the rights he believed he was acquiring shall not, because of any defect in the vendor's title to the property, amount to theft.

Property

S 4 THEFT ACT 1968

The term 'property' includes money and all other property, real or personal (including things in action and other intangible property) – but special provisions relate to the following:

Personal property includes the printed paper on which a cheque is written or upon which an examination or other confidential information is written; and other intangible property such as debts and shares in a company.

Land and things forming part of land and severed from it cannot be stolen except:

- by a trustee, personal representative, etc by dealing with it in breach of the confidence reposed in him

- by a person not in possession of it who appropriates something forming part of the land by severing it

- by a person in possession under a tenancy who takes fixtures or structures let with

Mushrooms or flowers, fruit or foliage from a plant (but not the plant itself) growing wild cannot be stolen unless for reward, sale or commercial use.

Electricity cannot be stolen but see S 13 later.

Wild creatures or the carcass of wild creatures cannot be stolen if not tamed and not ordinarily kept in captivity unless they have been caught and not since lost or abandoned.

Belonging to Another S 5 THEFT ACT 1968

In normal situations it is obvious who is the owner of the property but sometimes there are complications. The law has therefore defined certain categories of people from whom property may be stolen: **Property belongs to any person who has possession or control of it, or who has in it any proprietary right or interest.**

Proprietary right or interest
eg The owner of a vehicle being repaired

Control
eg The garage proprietor

Possession
eg The person repairing the vehicle

Particular types of property will be regarded as belonging to:	
Type of property	**Belongs to**
Subject to a trust	Any person having a right to enforce the trust
Person receiving is under an obligation to retain and deal with it in a particular way	The person he received it from
Obtained by mistake and obliged to make restoration	Person entitled to restoration
Property of corporation sole	The corporation, not withstanding any vacancy in it

Intention to Permanently Deprive S 6 THEFT ACT 1968

If a person takes property belonging to another, but does not mean the other to be permanently deprived of it, he will still be regarded in law as having such an intention if he means to treat the property as his own to dispose of regardless of the other's rights – such as:

- borrowing or lending in such a way that it is equivalent to an outright taking or disposal

- parting with the property (obtained legally or not) under a condition as to its return which he may not be able to perform, eg pawning

Removal of Articles from Places Open to the Public

S 11 THEFT ACT 1968

Where the public have access to a building (or part of a building) in order to view the building or a collection housed in it, any person who without lawful authority removes from the building or its grounds any article kept for display to the public, shall be guilty of an offence.

Collection
Includes a temporary collection, but not one intended to promote sales or commercial dealings.

Public access
May be limited to a particular period or occasion but anything removed which is not part of a permanent exhibition must be done on a day when the public have access (but may be guilty of theft).

> THIS IS AN ARRESTABLE OFFENCE

Unlike theft, it is not necessary to prove an intention permanently to deprive.

Taking a Conveyance without Authority

S 12(1) THEFT ACT 1968

This offence is committed by a person:

without having the consent of the owner or other lawful authority, **taking** a conveyance for his own or another's use	knowing that a conveyance has been taken without the consent of the owner or other lawful authority, **drives** it or allows himself to be **carried** in or on it

or

The conveyance must be moved, however short the distance may be; merely trying to start an engine will not suffice. Also, it must be taken for use as a conveyance, merely pushing it around the corner for a prank will not satisfy this offence.

CONVEYANCE

Constructed or adapted for the carriage of a person by land, water or air.

THIS IS AN ARRESTABLE OFFENCE

A similar offence exists in relation to pedal cycles but it is not an arrestable offence. S 12(5)

AGGRAVATED VEHICLE-TAKING ACT 1992 adds S 12A to the Theft Act 1968. Provides for obligatory disqualification and endorsement where the above offence under S 12(1) has been committed and, before the vehicle was recovered, the vehicle was driven dangerously or was damaged or was driven in a way which led to personal injury or damage to other property.

Vehicle Interference

S 9 CRIMINAL ATTEMPTS ACT 1981

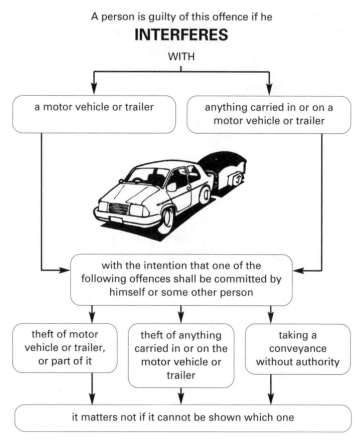

A person is guilty of this offence if he

INTERFERES

WITH

| a motor vehicle or trailer | anything carried in or on a motor vehicle or trailer |

with the intention that one of the following offences shall be committed by himself or some other person

| theft of motor vehicle or trailer, or part of it | theft of anything carried in or on the motor vehicle or trailer | taking a conveyance without authority |

it matters not if it cannot be shown which one

**Any arrest must be in accordance with the
Police and Criminal Evidence Act 1984**

Note: A person may still be guilty of an offence under S 25 of the Road
Traffic Act 1988, if, while a motor vehicle is on a road or local
authority parking place, he gets onto the vehicle or tampers with
the brakes or other parts of its mechanism.

Abstracting Electricity

S 13 THEFT ACT 1968

This offence is committed by any person who dishonestly uses electricity without authority, or dishonestly causes it to be wasted or diverted.

THIS IS AN ARRESTABLE OFFENCE

It is not necessary to prove that personal benefit was gained. An employee who leaves on the lights of his employer's premises throughout the night because of a grudge, would be guilty of the offence.

A common way of committing the offence is to unlawfully reconnect an officially disconnected meter.

See also 'fraudulent use of telecommunications system' later.

Robbery

S 8 THEFT ACT 1968

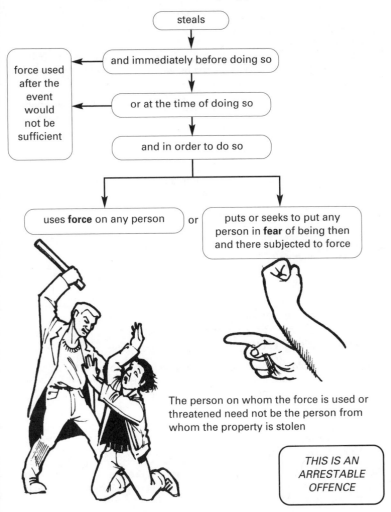

This offence is committed by any person who

steals

and immediately before doing so

or at the time of doing so

force used after the event would not be sufficient

and in order to do so

uses **force** on any person

or

puts or seeks to put any person in **fear** of being then and there subjected to force

The person on whom the force is used or threatened need not be the person from whom the property is stolen

THIS IS AN ARRESTABLE OFFENCE

Burglary

S 9 THEFT ACT 1968

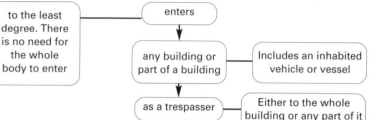

Burglarly is committed by any person who

to the least degree. There is no need for the whole body to enter	**enters**

any building or part of a building — Includes an inhabited vehicle or vessel

as a trespasser — Either to the whole building or any part of it

with intent to

steal; inflict grievous bodily harm on any person therein; or cause unlawful damage to the building or anything therein

and steals or attempts to steal anything in the building or that part of it; or inflicts or attempts to inflict on any person therein grievous bodily harm — Need not have the intention at the time of entry

THIS IS AN ARRESTABLE OFFENCE

Aggravated Burglary S 10 THEFT ACT 1968

The punishment for the above offence may be increased from 14 years imprisonment (if a dwellinghouse, 10 years otherwise) to life imprisonment if, at the time of committing the offence, the offender has with him any of the following:

Explosive (article manufactured for exploding, or intended by the person for that purpose)

Firearm (including air guns and air pistols)

Weapon of offence (made or adapted, or intended by the person, to injure or incapacitate)

Imitation firearm (anything having the appearance whether capable of being fired or not)

Obtaining Property by Deception
S 15 THEFT ACT 1968

It is an offence by any deception dishonestly to obtain property belonging to another with the intention to permanently deprive the other of it.

THIS IS AN
ARRESTABLE
OFFENCE

Deception
Means by words or conduct as to fact or law (made either deliberately or recklessly) including a deception as to the present intentions of himself or another. The deception need not be practised on the person from whom the property is obtained.

Obtaining
Means obtaining ownership, possession or control, or enabling another to do so.

Successful
If the other person did not part with the property, or was not deceived, or would have parted with it regardless of the deception, the elements of the offence have not been fulfilled.
But consider an attempt.

See also S 1 1978 Act later.

Obtaining a Money Transfer by Deception

SS 15A, 15B THEFT (AMENDMENT) ACT 1996, THEFT ACT 1968

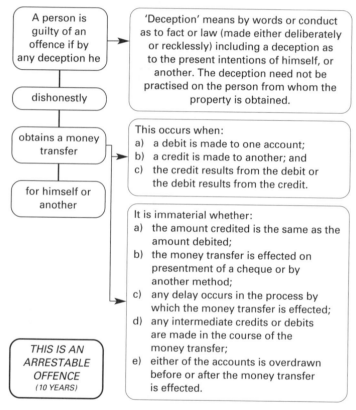

A person is guilty of an offence if by any deception he

'Deception' means by words or conduct as to fact or law (made either deliberately or recklessly) including a deception as to the present intentions of himself, or another. The deception need not be practised on the person from whom the property is obtained.

dishonestly

obtains a money transfer

This occurs when:
a) a debit is made to one account;
b) a credit is made to another; and
c) the credit results from the debit or the debit results from the credit.

for himself or another

It is immaterial whether:
a) the amount credited is the same as the amount debited;
b) the money transfer is effected on presentment of a cheque or by another method;
c) any delay occurs in the process by which the money transfer is effected;
d) any intermediate credits or debits are made in the course of the money transfer;
e) either of the accounts is overdrawn before or after the money transfer is effected.

THIS IS AN ARRESTABLE OFFENCE
(10 YEARS)

'Account' means an account kept with: a) a bank; or b) a person carrying on a business of receiving deposits to lend to others or to finance other activities of the business.

Retaining a Wrongful Credit

S 24A THEFT ACT 1968

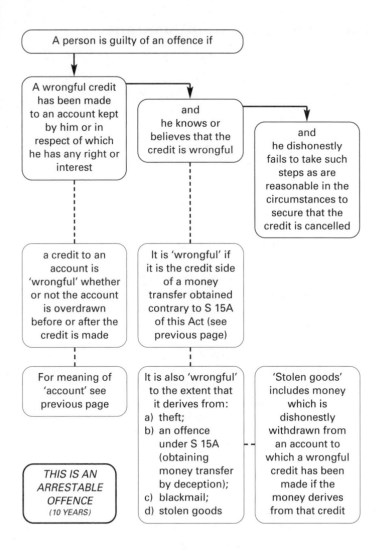

A person is guilty of an offence if

A wrongful credit has been made to an account kept by him or in respect of which he has any right or interest

and he knows or believes that the credit is wrongful

and he dishonestly fails to take such steps as are reasonable in the circumstances to secure that the credit is cancelled

a credit to an account is 'wrongful' whether or not the account is overdrawn before or after the credit is made

It is 'wrongful' if it is the credit side of a money transfer obtained contrary to S 15A of this Act (see previous page)

For meaning of 'account' see previous page

It is also 'wrongful' to the extent that it derives from:
a) theft;
b) an offence under S 15A (obtaining money transfer by deception);
c) blackmail;
d) stolen goods

'Stolen goods' includes money which is dishonestly withdrawn from an account to which a wrongful credit has been made if the money derives from that credit

THIS IS AN ARRESTABLE OFFENCE (10 YEARS)

Obtaining Pecuniary Advantage

S 16 THEFT ACT 1968

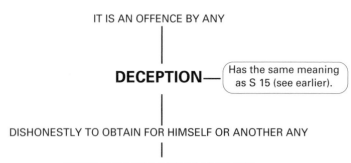

IT IS AN OFFENCE BY ANY

DECEPTION— Has the same meaning as S 15 (see earlier).

DISHONESTLY TO OBTAIN FOR HIMSELF OR ANOTHER ANY

PECUNIARY ADVANTAGE

A pecuniary advantage may be gained by:

Overdraft
If he is allowed to borrow by overdraft or to obtain an improvement in existing terms

Insurance
If he is allowed to take out a policy of insurance or annuity contract, or to obtain an improvement of existing terms

Remuneration
If he is given the opportunity to earn remuneration or greater remuneration in an office or employment, or to win money by betting

THIS IS AN ARRESTABLE OFFENCE

See also 1978 Act later.

Obtaining a Service by Deception

S 1 THEFT ACT 1978
AS AMENDED BY THE THEFT (AMENDMENT) ACT 1996, S 4(1)

The Theft Act 1978 was introduced to cover additional areas of obtaining by deception which were not adequately dealt with by the 1968 Act.

It is an offence by any deception

dishonestly to obtain

SERVICE FROM ANOTHER

Someone must be induced to confer a benefit by doing some act, or causing or permitting some act to be done, on the understanding that the benefit has been or will be

It will also be an obtaining of a service where the other is induced to make a loan, or to cause or permit a loan to be made, on the understanding that any payment (whether by way of interest or otherwise) will be or has been made in respect of the loan

PAID FOR

Obtaining a free service by deception will not be an offence under this provision

THESE ARE ARRESTABLE OFFENCES

Note that there is some overlap with S 15 of the 1968 Act but it is usually better to charge under S 1 of the 1978 Act.

Evading Liability by Deception

S 2 THEFT ACT 1978

It is an offence by deception dishonestly to:

SECURE REMISSION
of the whole or part of
an existing liability to
make payment, whether
his own or another's

OR

induce the creditor to
WAIT FOR OR FORGO
payment with intent
that he or some other
person may make
permanent default of
the whole or part of a
liability to make a
payment

———————

A person induced to take
a cheque or other security
for money by way of
conditional satisfaction of
a liability is treated as an
inducement to wait for
payment

OR

obtain (for himself or
another or allow
another to obtain)
**EXEMPTION OR
ABATEMENT**
of liability to
make payment

———————

'Obtain' includes
obtaining for another or
enabling another to obtain

> *THIS IS AN
> ARRESTABLE OFFENCE*

Deception may be by an act of commission or omission

Note that the obligation to pay must be legally enforceable; thus evading an unenforceable debt (eg a gambling debt or payment for the services of a prostitute) will not fall within the section.

False Accounting

S 17 THEFT ACT 1968

An offence is committed if a person:

THIS IS AN
ARRESTABLE
OFFENCE

DISHONESTLY

WITH A VIEW TO GAIN

FOR HIMSELF OR ANOTHER

OR WITH INTENT TO CAUSE LOSS TO ANOTHER

| destroys, defaces, conceals or falsifies any account or any record or document made or required for any accounting purpose | OR | in furnishing information for any purpose, produces or makes use of any account, or any such record or document made or required for accounting purposes, which to his knowledge is or may be misleading, false or deceptive in a material particular |

Notes

'Falsifying' means to make (or concur in making) in an account or other document an entry which is or may be misleading, false or deceptive in a material particular, or to omit (or concur in omitting) from an account or other document, a material particular.

'Gain or loss' means in money or other property, whether temporary or permanent. **'Gain'** includes keeping what one has as well as getting what one has not. **'Loss'** includes not getting what one might get as well as parting with what one has.

'Record' may include, for example, a taximeter or turnstile meter.

Liability of Company Officers

S 18 THEFT ACT 1968

Where an offence of

- obtaining goods by deception,
- obtaining pecuniary advantage by deception, or
- false accounting

(SS 15, 16 OR 17)

|
is committed by a body corporate
|
with the consent or connivance of
|
any director, manager, secretary or other similar officer of the body corporate, or any person who was purporting to act in such a capacity (including, where the body corporate is managed by its members, a member, in connection with his management functions)
|
that person will also be guilty of that offence

False Statements by Company Directors

S 19 THEFT ACT 1968

Where an officer of a body corporate or unincorporated association (or person purporting to act as such) (including, where the body corporate is managed by its members, a member, in connection with his management functions)
|
with intent to deceive members or creditors
of the body corporate or association about its affairs
|
publishes or concurs in publishing a written statement or account
|
which to his knowledge is or may be
misleading, false or deceptive in a material particular
|
he will commit an offence punishable with 7 years imprisonment
(AN ARRESTABLE OFFENCE)

Blackmail

S 21 THEFT ACT 1968

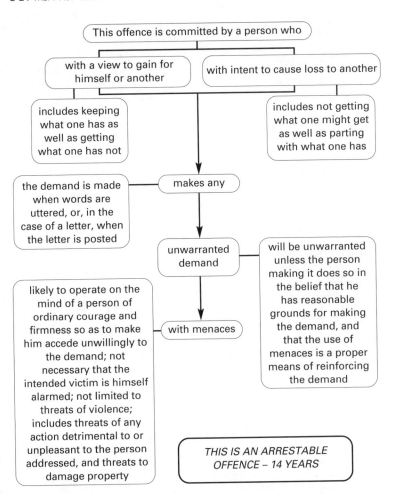

This offence is committed by a person who

with a view to gain for himself or another

with intent to cause loss to another

includes keeping what one has as well as getting what one has not

includes not getting what one might get as well as parting with what one has

makes any

the demand is made when words are uttered, or, in the case of a letter, when the letter is posted

unwarranted demand

will be unwarranted unless the person making it does so in the belief that he has reasonable grounds for making the demand, and that the use of menaces is a proper means of reinforcing the demand

with menaces

likely to operate on the mind of a person of ordinary courage and firmness so as to make him accede unwillingly to the demand; not necessary that the intended victim is himself alarmed; not limited to threats of violence; includes threats of any action detrimental to or unpleasant to the person addressed, and threats to damage property

THIS IS AN ARRESTABLE OFFENCE – 14 YEARS

Suppression etc of Documents

S 20 THEFT ACT 1968

DESTRUCTION, CONCEALMENT, ETC

A person who, dishonestly, with a view to gain for himself or another or with intent to cause loss to another

- destroys
- defaces, or
- conceals

any

- valuable security
- will or other testamentary document, or
- original document of or belonging to, or filed or deposited in any court of justice or any government department

shall be guilty of an offence punishable with 7 years imprisonment (**ARRESTABLE OFFENCE**).

EXECUTION

A person who, dishonestly, with a view to gain for himself or another or with intent to cause loss to another, by any deception procures the execution of a valuable security shall be guilty of an offence punishable with 7 years imprisonment (**ARRESTABLE OFFENCE**).

'**Execution**' includes making, acceptance, indorsement, alteration, cancellation or destruction in whole or in part of a valuable security; and the signing or sealing of any paper or other material in order that it may be made or converted into, or used or dealt with as, a valuable security

---

'**Deception**' has the same meaning as in S 15 (see earlier).
'**Valuable security**' means any document creating, transferring, surrendering or releasing
- any right to, in or over property, or
- authorising the payment of money or delivery of any property, or evidence of the creation, transfer, surrender or release of any such right, or
- the payment of money or delivery of any property, or
- the satisfaction of any obligation.
'**Gain or loss**' means in money or other property, whether temporary or permanent. '**Gain**' includes keeping what one has as well as getting what one has not. '**Loss**' includes not getting what one might get as well as parting with what one has.

Making Off Without Paying

S 3 THEFT ACT 1978

A person who, knowing that payment

ON THE SPOT
for any goods supplied or service done is
required or is expected of him

> Includes payment at the
> time of collecting goods
> on which work has been
> done or a service
> provided. It would not
> be an offence under this
> section if the supply of
> goods or services is
> contrary to law or not
> legally enforceable

DISHONESTLY MAKES OFF
without having paid as required or
expected and

WITH INTENT TO AVOID PAYMENT
of the amount due, shall be guilty of
an offence

> It must be proved that
> the intention was to
> make permanent default

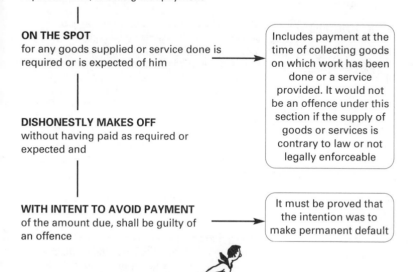

Any person may arrest, without warrant, anyone who is or is reasonably
suspected to be committing or attempting to commit an offence under
this section.

Handling Stolen Goods

S 22 THEFT ACT 1968

This offence is committed by a person who
(otherwise than in the course of stealing)

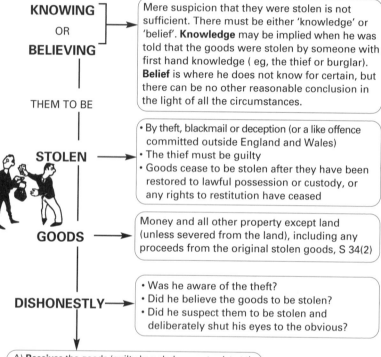

KNOWING
OR
BELIEVING

Mere suspicion that they were stolen is not sufficient. There must be either 'knowledge' or 'belief'. **Knowledge** may be implied when he was told that the goods were stolen by someone with first hand knowledge (eg, the thief or burglar). **Belief** is where he does not know for certain, but there can be no other reasonable conclusion in the light of all the circumstances.

THEM TO BE

STOLEN

- By theft, blackmail or deception (or a like offence committed outside England and Wales)
- The thief must be guilty
- Goods cease to be stolen after they have been restored to lawful possession or custody, or any rights to restitution have ceased

GOODS

Money and all other property except land (unless severed from the land), including any proceeds from the original stolen goods, S 34(2)

DISHONESTLY

- Was he aware of the theft?
- Did he believe the goods to be stolen?
- Did he suspect them to be stolen and deliberately shut his eyes to the obvious?

A) **Receives** the goods (guilty knowledge must exist at the time of receiving, not formed afterwards)

B) **Undertakes** the retention, removal, disposal or realisation of the goods by or for the benefit of another person

C) **Assists** in the retention, removal, disposal or realisation of the goods by or for the benefit of another person, or

D) **Arranges** to do A to C above

THIS IS AN ARRESTABLE OFFENCE

Going Equipped

S 25 THEFT ACT 1968

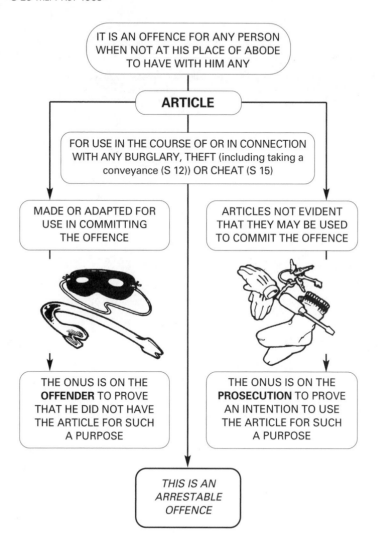

IT IS AN OFFENCE FOR ANY PERSON WHEN NOT AT HIS PLACE OF ABODE TO HAVE WITH HIM ANY

ARTICLE

FOR USE IN THE COURSE OF OR IN CONNECTION WITH ANY BURGLARY, THEFT (including taking a conveyance (S 12)) OR CHEAT (S 15)

MADE OR ADAPTED FOR USE IN COMMITTING THE OFFENCE

ARTICLES NOT EVIDENT THAT THEY MAY BE USED TO COMMIT THE OFFENCE

THE ONUS IS ON THE **OFFENDER** TO PROVE THAT HE DID NOT HAVE THE ARTICLE FOR SUCH A PURPOSE

THE ONUS IS ON THE **PROSECUTION** TO PROVE AN INTENTION TO USE THE ARTICLE FOR SUCH A PURPOSE

THIS IS AN ARRESTABLE OFFENCE

Assault

In the case of Fagan v Metropolitan Police Commissioner, 1968, 'assault' was defined as:

> **'Any act which intentionally or recklessly causes another person to apprehend immediate and unlawful personal violence.'**

A person is responsible for injuries which result from inducing into another's mind an immediate sense of danger which causes that person to injure himself in trying to escape.

There are varying degrees of assault which are governed by the seriousness of the injury, the harm done and the attendant circumstances.

Specific offences are discussed on the following pages and reflect the charging standards in assault cases issued by the Crown Prosecution Service in August 1994.

Common Assault

S 39 CRIMINAL JUSTICE ACT 1988

An incident is referred to as being a common assault where the injury is either non-existent or of a negligible nature, eg grazes, minor bruising, black eye, etc. The police do not normally institute proceedings for this type of occurrence, thus affording the aggrieved person the choice of taking proceedings either criminally or by civil action to obtain damages. Common assault and battery are two separate summary offences. Both require a mental element of an intention, or recklessness, causing another person to apprehend immediate and unlawful violence.

Actual Bodily Harm

S 47 OFFENCES AGAINST THE PERSON ACT 1861

This includes any hurt or injury calculated to interfere with the health or comfort of the victim. It need not be a permanent injury but must be more than something which is only momentary and trifling, eg lost teeth, minor fractures, loss of consciousness. It may include shock which causes injury to the victim's state of mind. 'Harm' also includes psychological harm but does not include mere emotions such as fear, distress or panic. The making of a telephone call could amount to this offence if the victim was apprehensive and was caused psychological damage. No foresight or foreseeability of the consequences is required.

> THIS IS AN
> ARRESTABLE
> OFFENCE

Defences to Assault

Consent
But only a defence if:
a) An illegal purpose is not involved, eg a duel or injecting illegal drugs

b) Violence or injury is not excessive

c) Consent is not obtained by fear, fraud or ignorance or the facts

Lawfully justified
For example:

Defence of oneself, a close relative or one's property. But only sufficient force may be used to repel the attack

Legal right
For example:

In the course of a lawful arrest, prevention of a breach of the peace, or serious crime.

But only such force as is necessary to achieve the result may be used

Wounding or Inflicting Grievous Bodily Harm

S 20 OFFENCES AGAINST THE PERSON ACT 1861

IT IS AN OFFENCE TO
UNLAWFULLY AND MALICIOUSLY

WOUND OR INFLICT ANY GRIEVOUS BODILY HARM

WITH OR WITHOUT ANY
WEAPON OR INSTRUMENT

These charges should be used for injuries involving permanent disability, serious permanent disfigurement, loss of sensory function, broken bones, substantial loss of blood or lengthy treatment, including psychiatric injury.

The defendant must have foreseen that his act would cause harm, even if not of the seriousness which actually resulted.

*THESE ARE
ARRESTABLE
OFFENCES*

Wounding or Causing Grievous Bodily Harm With Intent

S 18 OFFENCES AGAINST THE PERSON ACT 1861

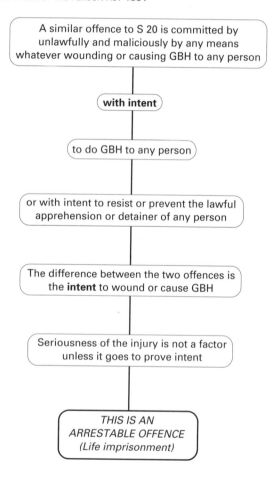

A similar offence to S 20 is committed by unlawfully and maliciously by any means whatever wounding or causing GBH to any person

with intent

to do GBH to any person

or with intent to resist or prevent the lawful apprehension or detainer of any person

The difference between the two offences is the **intent** to wound or cause GBH

Seriousness of the injury is not a factor unless it goes to prove intent

THIS IS AN ARRESTABLE OFFENCE (Life imprisonment)

Assault on the Police

S 89 POLICE ACT 1996

IT IS AN OFFENCE TO ASSAULT
OR TO RESIST OR WILFULLY
OBSTRUCT A POLICE CONSTABLE

IN THE EXECUTION OF HIS DUTY

OR A PERSON ASSISTING HIM

'In the execution of duty' covers a range of activities
in which the constable may be involved, eg:

Arrest
Must be in accordance with the Police
and Criminal Evidence Act 1984.

On premises
Unless specifically authorised, when on premises the constable is not acting
in the execution of his duty once he has been requested to leave (but he
must be given time to leave).

Stopping vehicles
This power must be exercised lawfully
eg not just to get a lift

Disturbances
If it is believed that a breach of the peace
is about to occur, a constable may use
reasonable force to prevent it.

Questioning suspects
There is no power to detain short of an
arrest, and any attempt forcibly to restrain
cannot amount to execution of duty.

It is also an offence to assault ANY PERSON with intent to resist or prevent
the lawful apprehension or detainer of himself or another for any offence
(S 38 Offences Against the Person Act 1861).

Female Genital Mutilation

FEMALE GENITAL MUTILATION ACT 2003

A person is guilty of an offence if he-

(a) excises, infibulates or otherwise mutilates the whole or any part of a girl's labia majora, labia minora or clitoris (S 1(1));

(b) aids, abets, counsels or procures a girl to excise, infibulate or otherwise mutilate the whole or any part of her own labia majora, labia minora or clitoris (S 2);

(c) aids, abets, counsels or procures a person who is not a United Kingdom national or permanent United Kingdom resident to do an act of female genital mutilation outside the U.K. which would, if done in the U.K., amount to an offence under S 1. (S 3)

Acts done outside the United Kingdom

Sections 1 to 3 above extend to any act done outside the United Kingdom by a United Kingdom national or permanent United Kingdom resident. In such cases, proceedings may be taken, and the offence may be treated as having been committed, in any place in England and Wales or Northern Ireland. (S 4)

Exemptions

1. No offence is committed by –

(a) a registered medical practitioner who performs a surgical operation which is necessary for the girl's physical or mental health (S 1(2)(a)), (it is immaterial whether she or any other person believes the operation is required as a matter of custom or ritual) (S 1(5);

(b) a registered medical practitioner, a registered midwife or a person undergoing training to become such a practitioner or midwife, who performs a surgical operation on a girl in any stage of labour or birth, for purposes connected with the labour or birth (S 1(2)(b)); or

(c) a person who performs a surgical operation as in (a) or (b) above outside the United Kingdom and who exercises functions corresponding to those of such an approved person (S 1(4)).

THIS IS AN ARRESTABLE OFFENCE – 14 YEARS

Homicide

THESE ARE
ARRESTABLE
OFFENCES

As far as the criminal law is concerned, there are four types of unlawful killing.

MURDER COMMON LAW

This is committed when a sane person over 10 years of age, through some deliberate act or omission causes the death of a human being, either intending to kill that person or some other person, or to cause grievous bodily harm, or to expose someone to a known serious risk of death or grievous bodily harm resulting from acts committed deliberately and without lawful excuse. It does not matter whether those consequences were intended or not.

Threats

It is also an offence to threaten to kill some person, intending that the person to whom the threat is made will fear that the threat will be carried out.

MANSLAUGHTER S 5 OFFENCES AGAINST THE PERSON ACT 1861, COMMON LAW

This is the unlawful killing of another without the intention to kill or cause grievous bodily harm. Manslaughter is usually described as being voluntary or involuntary:

Voluntary

Where death follows an intended injury (but if the injury is serious, then this may be murder). It normally occurs as a result of a sudden 'fraying of temper' or following some degree of provocation.

Involuntary

Where injury is not intended, but is nevertheless caused through gross negligence or an unlawful act.

INFANTICIDE S 1 INFANTICIDE ACT 1938

Committed by a mother who, by any wilful act or omission, causes the death of her child (under 12 months old) whilst being mentally unbalanced through childbirth or milk fever.

CHILD DESTRUCTION S 1 INFANT LIFE (PRESERVATION) ACT 1929

Committed by any person who, by any wilful act, intentionally causes the death of a child capable of being born alive (this is presumed after 28 weeks pregnancy) before it has had a life independent of its mother.

CONCEALING THE BIRTH OF A CHILD S 60 OFFENCES AGAINST THE PERSON ACT 1861

Although not one of the above offences of unlawful killing, this offence is akin and worth a mention. It is committed by any person who endeavours to conceal the birth of a child by any secret disposition of the dead body of the child, whether it died before, at, or after its birth. The concealment must be with the intention to keep the world at large ignorant of the birth and not just to escape individual anger.

Causing Death of Child or Vulnerable Adult

S 5 DOMESTIC VIOLENCE, CRIME AND VICTIMS ACT 2004

A person (D) is guilty of an offence if –

a) a **child or vulnerable adult** (V) dies as a result of the **unlawful act** of a person who-
   i) was a **member of the same household** as V, and
   ii) had frequent contact with him,
b) D was such a person at the time of that act,
c) at that time there was a significant risk of **serious physical harm** being caused to V by the unlawful act of such a person, and
d) either D was the person whose act caused V's death, or
   i) D was, or ought to have been, aware of the risk mentioned in paragraph (c),
   ii) D failed to take such steps as he could reasonably have been expected to take to protect V from the risk, and
   iii) the act occurred in circumstances of the kind that D foresaw or ought to have foreseen.

> *THIS IS AN ARRESTABLE OFFENCE – 14 YEARS*

The prosecution does not have to prove whether it is the first alternative in paragraph (d), or the second in sub-paragraphs (i) – (iii) that applies.

If D was not the mother or father of V-

a) D may not be charged with this offence if he was under the age of 16 at the time of the act which caused the death; and
b) for the purposes of sub-paragraph (d)(ii) above, D could not have been expected to take any such step as is referred to there before attaining that age.

Member of the same household includes a person who does not live in that household if he visits it so often and for such periods of time that it is reasonable to regard him as a member of it. Where V lived in different households at different times, 'the same household' means that in which V was living at the time of the act which caused his death.

Unlawful act means one which (a) constitutes an offence, or (b) (except for an act of D), would constitute an offence but for being the act of a person under the age of 10, or a person entitled to rely on a defence of insanity.

Act includes a course of conduct as well as an omission.

Child means a person under the age of 16.

Serious harm means harm amounting to grievous bodily harm for the purposes of the Offences against the Person Act 1861.

Vulnerable adult means a person aged 16 or over whose ability to protect himself from violence, abuse or neglect is significantly impaired through physical or mental disability or illness, through old age or otherwise.

Damage

S 1(1) CRIMINAL DAMAGE ACT 1971

> THIS IS AN
> ARRESTABLE
> OFFENCE

DAMAGE
IS THE OFFENCE
COMMITTED BY ANY
PERSON WHO WITHOUT

LAWFUL EXCUSE

He will be treated as having a lawful excuse if he believed he had consent of a person entitled to consent, or he would have consented had he known of the circumstances; or if he caused, or threatened to cause damage in protection of his own or another's property

If a building: to pull down or demolish

If growing things: to lay waste

If machinery: to break up

If animals: to kill

DESTROYS

OR

Nothing need be actually broken or deformed, eg uncoupling the brake pipe on a car; tampering with machinery so that it will not work; watering milk

DAMAGES

Whether real or personal. Including wild animals which have been tamed or are ordinarily kept in captivity but does not include mushrooms growing wild on any land or flowers, fruit or foliage from wild plants

PROPERTY

Property belongs to any person having custody or control of it, having a right or interest in it, or having a charge on it

BELONGING TO ANOTHER

If he intends or foresees damage to property, he may be liable where he in fact causes damage to other property which he had not intended or foreseen

INTENDING

**TO DESTROY OR DAMAGE ANY SUCH PROPERTY
OR BEING RECKLESS AS TO WHETHER ANY
SUCH PROPERTY WOULD BE DESTROYED OR DAMAGED.
IF THIS OFFENCE IS COMMITTED BY FIRE, IT WILL BE ARSON.**

Damage With Intent to Endanger Life

S 1(2) CRIMINAL DAMAGE ACT 1971

This offence is committed by a person who:

> without lawful excuse destroys
> or damages any property,
> whether belonging to himself
> or another

> intending to destroy or
> damage any property or
> being reckless as to whether
> any property would be
> destroyed or damaged

> intending by the destruction or
> damage to endanger the life of
> another or being reckless as to
> whether the life of another
> would be thereby endangered

> *THESE ARE
> ARRESTABLE
> OFFENCES*

Arson

S 1(3) CRIMINAL DAMAGE ACT 1971

An offence of damage or endangering life by damage,
by destroying or damaging property by fire
shall be charged as 'arson'.

THESE ARE
ARRESTABLE
OFFENCES

Threats to Damage

S 2 CRIMINAL DAMAGE ACT 1971

THIS OFFENCE IS COMMITTED BY A PERSON WHO WITHOUT
LAWFUL EXCUSE MAKES TO ANOTHER A

THREAT
INTENDING THAT THE OTHER WOULD FEAR
THAT IT WOULD BE CARRIED OUT

to destroy or damage any
property belonging to that
other or a third person

OR

to destroy or damage his
own property in a way
which he knows is likely
to endanger the life of that
other or a third person

Possession With Intent to Damage

S 3 CRIMINAL DAMAGE ACT 1971

THIS OFFENCE IS COMMITTED BY A PERSON WHO HAS
ANYTHING
IN HIS CUSTODY OR CONTROL INTENDING
WITHOUT LAWFUL EXCUSE
TO USE OR CAUSE OR PERMIT ANOTHER TO USE IT

to destroy or damage any
property belonging to
some other person

OR

to destroy or damage his
own or the user's property
in a way which he knows
is likely to endanger the
life of some other person

Sale of Paint Aerosols to Children

S 54 ANTI-SOCIAL BEHAVIOUR ACT 2003

A person commits an offence if he sells an aerosol paint container to a
person under 16.

Drugs

The Misuse of Drugs Act 1971 creates a number of offences relating to

Controlled drugs

This means any substance or product listed in one of the three classes (A, B or C) in Sched 2 to the Act. The main significance in classifying drugs as 'A', 'B' or 'C' lies in the punishment to which the offender is liable (and consequently the power of arrest). NB Possession of cannabis is now an arrestable offence (see S 24 PACE)

Whilst drugs are listed in their basic form it is clear that other forms of the drug and esters or salts are also included. Both the natural substances and any substance resulting from chemical transformation are controlled drugs.

S 28 of the Act contains a general defence which applies to the following sections referred to later: S 4 (production and supply), S 5 (possession), S 6 (cultivation of cannabis), and S 9 (opium). It will be a defence for the defendant to prove that he neither knew of, nor suspected, nor had reason to suspect, the existence of some fact which the prosecution must prove.

Powers to arrest are contained in the Police and Criminal Evidence Act 1984. It also provides wide powers of search, and contains specific defences.

A variety of aspects are listed below and dealt with in more detail in the following pages:

Import & Export

S 3 MISUSE OF DRUGS ACT 1971

The import or export of controlled drugs is prohibited unless authorised under the regulations.

Sched 5 of the Misuse of Drugs Regulations 2001 lists certain substances and preparations to which this section does not apply.

Being concerned with the improper import or export, and the fraudulent evasion of prohibition or restriction are all offences under the Customs and Excise Management Act 1979, S 50 and are all arrestable offences.

> *THESE ARE*
> *ARRESTABLE*
> *OFFENCES*

Production

S 4(2) MISUSE OF DRUGS ACT 1971

IT IS AN OFFENCE TO

UNLAWFULLY

(to be lawful it must be authorised
by regulations, eg manufacturers)

PRODUCE

by manufacture, cultivation
or any other method, eg
cultivating or growing

**BE CONCERNED IN THE
PRODUCTION BY ANOTHER OF**

(actual participation is not
necessary. All that needs to be
proved is an interest, eg hiring
premises)

A CONTROLLED DRUG

Supply of Articles

S 9A Misuse of Drugs Act 1971

It is an offence for a person to supply or offer to supply any article which may be used or adapted to be used in the administration of a controlled drug to himself or another, believing that the article is to be so used in circumstances where the administration is unlawful.

The above does not apply to a hypodermic syringe or part of one.

An offence is also committed if the article supplied or offered may be used to prepare a controlled drug for administration.

Any administration of a controlled drug is unlawful except:
• where the production or supply of the drug is not unlawful under S 4(1); or
• possession of the drug is not unlawful under S 5(1).

Supplying Drugs

S 4(3) MISUSE OF DRUGS ACT 1971

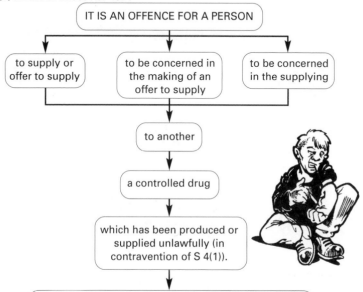

IT IS AN OFFENCE FOR A PERSON

- to supply or offer to supply
- to be concerned in the making of an offer to supply
- to be concerned in the supplying

to another

a controlled drug

which has been produced or supplied unlawfully (in contravention of S 4(1)).

It will be a defence to prove that he neither knew of, nor suspected, nor had reason to suspect, the existence of some fact which the prosecution must prove (S 28).

Notes

Lawful supply: The Misuse of Drugs Regulations 2001 contains a list of persons who may lawfully supply, etc, controlled drugs, eg pharmacists, vets and masters of ships who do not carry a doctor. It also lists the drugs which they may possess and the circumstances in which they may possess them. **'Supplying'** includes distributing. **'Offer to supply'** includes where the substance in possession is not a controlled drug. It also includes where an offer is made regardless of whether he intends to actually supply the drug. **'Concerned in'** is designed to include the "trafficker" and persons who connive in the supply, as well as persons who may be some distance from the actual making of the offer. **Exemption:** This offence does not include the supply of poppy-straw.

Possession

S 5(2) MISUSE OF DRUGS ACT 1971

IT IS AN OFFENCE TO

UNLAWFULLY ➤ The Misuse of Drugs Regulations 2001 define the persons who may have lawful possession, eg police constables, post office, Customs & Excise, etc

Includes things subject to his control but in the possession of another ◄ **POSSESS**

'Control' means knowledge of its control or shutting the eyes to the obvious

A CONTROLLED DRUG ➤ Possession of a quantity too minute to smoke or to have any effect will not justify a conviction

THIS IS AN ARRESTABLE OFFENCE
UNLESS THE DRUG CONCERNED IS A
CLASS 'C' DRUG. NB – CANNABIS IS NOW
A CLASS 'C' DRUG

Defence

S 5(4) MISUSE OF DRUGS ACT 1971

It is a defence to a charge of possession to prove that, knowing or suspecting it to be a controlled drug, he took possession of it for the purpose of:

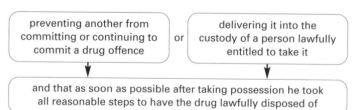

| preventing another from committing or continuing to commit a drug offence | or | delivering it into the custody of a person lawfully entitled to take it |

and that as soon as possible after taking possession he took all reasonable steps to have the drug lawfully disposed of

Possession With Intent to Supply

S 5(3) MISUSE OF DRUGS ACT 1971

IT IS AN OFFENCE FOR A PERSON
|

**TO HAVE A CONTROLLED DRUG
IN HIS POSSESSION**
|

WHETHER LAWFULLY OR NOT ➤ The offence may be
committed by a person
who has lawful possession,
eg a chemist
|

**WITH INTENT TO SUPPLY IT
UNLAWFULLY TO ANOTHER**

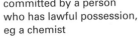

> *THESE ARE
> ARRESTABLE
> OFFENCES*

Cannabis – Cultivating

S 6(2) MISUSE OF DRUGS ACT 1971

IT IS AN OFFENCE TO

UNLAWFULLY ➤ Cultivation may be lawful
only under licence of the
Secretary of State
|

CULTIVATE ➤ Knowingly tending to
the plant at any stage
of its maturity
|

ANY PLANT OF THE GENUS 'CANNABIS'
by whatever name, eg hashish, gunjah, bhang, marijuana. It also includes any part of
the plant after it has been separated from the rest of the plant except mature stalk,
mature stalk fibre or seed.

THIS IS AN
ARRESTABLE
OFFENCE

Use of Premises

S 8 MISUSE OF DRUGS ACT 1971

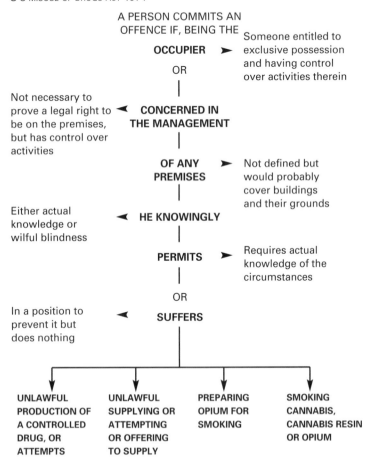

A PERSON COMMITS AN
OFFENCE IF, BEING THE

OCCUPIER ➤ Someone entitled to exclusive possession and having control over activities therein

OR

Not necessary to prove a legal right to be on the premises, but has control over activities ◄ **CONCERNED IN THE MANAGEMENT**

OF ANY PREMISES ➤ Not defined but would probably cover buildings and their grounds

Either actual knowledge or wilful blindness ◄ **HE KNOWINGLY**

PERMITS ➤ Requires actual knowledge of the circumstances

OR

In a position to prevent it but does nothing ◄ **SUFFERS**

UNLAWFUL PRODUCTION OF A CONTROLLED DRUG, OR ATTEMPTS

UNLAWFUL SUPPLYING OR ATTEMPTING OR OFFERING TO SUPPLY

PREPARING OPIUM FOR SMOKING

SMOKING CANNABIS, CANNABIS RESIN OR OPIUM

Opium

S 9 MISUSE OF DRUGS ACT 1971

IT IS AN OFFENCE

TO SMOKE OR OTHERWISE USE PREPARED OPIUM

Opium prepared for smoking, including dross and any other residues remaining after opium has been smoked

TO FREQUENT A PLACE USED FOR THE PURPOSE OF OPIUM SMOKING

Not restricted to premises

TO HAVE IN POSSESSION

ANY PIPES OR OTHER UTENSILS MADE FOR USE IN CONNECTION WITH THE SMOKING OF OPIUM

BEING PIPES OR UTENSILS WHICH HAVE BEEN USED BY HIM OR WITH HIS KNOWLEDGE AND PERMISSION

OR WHICH HE INTENDS TO USE OR PERMIT OTHERS TO USE

ANY UTENSILS WHICH HAVE BEEN USED BY HIM OR WITH HIS KNOWLEDGE AND PERMISSION IN CONNECTION WITH THE PREPARATION OF OPIUM FOR SMOKING

THIS IS AN ARRESTABLE OFFENCE

Police Powers

SEARCH

S 23(2) MISUSE OF DRUGS ACT 1971

If a constable has reasonable grounds to suspect that any person is unlawfully in possession of a controlled drug, he may:

Search that person
and detain him for the purpose of searching him

Search any vehicle or vessel in which the constable suspects that the drug may be found
and require the vehicle to be stopped for that purpose
and seize and detain anything found in the course of the search which appears to the constable to be evidence of an offence under this Act

> It is an offence to intentionally obstruct a person exercising these powers

Note should be made of the following provisions of the Police and Criminal Evidence Act 1984.

Where the power is exercised to search a person or vehicle without making an arrest, then **before** the search is commenced:

THE FOLLOWING INFORMATION SHOULD BE BROUGHT TO THE ATTENTION OF THE APPROPRIATE PERSON

- Constable's name and his police station. If not in uniform, documentary evidence of being a constable
- Object and grounds of proposed search
- Where a record of the search is made, his entitlement to a copy within 12 months if he asks for it

Where an unattended vehicle is searched, a notice should be left stating that it has been searched and giving the officer's name and station, the right to apply for compensation for any damage caused and his right to a copy of the search record. The notice is to be left inside the vehicle unless not practicable.

For power to test a detained person for drugs see under 'Testing for Drugs' later.

Closure of Premises used for Drugs

Ss 1 – 11 ANTI-SOCIAL BEHAVIOUR ACT 2003

A Closure Notice may be issued by a Superintendent or above in relation to premises (including land and outbuildings) if he has reasonable grounds for believing:

(a) that at any time during the preceding 3 months the premises have been used in connection with the **unlawful use, production or supply of a Class A drug**; and
(b) the use of the premises is associated with **disorder or serious nuisance** to members of the public.

The local authority must be consulted and reasonable steps must be taken to attempt to identify the person who lives on or has control of the premises.

The notice is served by affixing it to the premises and serving it on the person having control over the building or living there.

Within 48 hours of serving the notice, an application must be made to a Magistrates' Court for the issue of a **Closure Order**.

A Closure order prohibits the entry of all persons to the premises for a maximum period of 3 months (extendable to not more than 6 months). The order is subject to such provisions relating to access and parts of the building as the court thinks fit. It authorises constables to enter the premises by force if necessary.

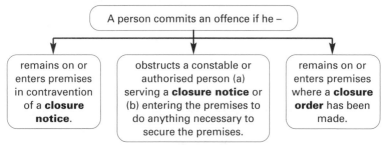

A person commits an offence if he –

| remains on or enters premises in contravention of a **closure notice**. | obstructs a constable or authorised person (a) serving a **closure notice** or (b) entering the premises to do anything necessary to secure the premises. | remains on or enters premises where a **closure order** has been made. |

A constable in uniform may arrest any person he reasonably suspects to be committing any of the above offences.

Chapter 2
Sexual Offences

Rape

S 1 SEXUAL OFFENCES ACT 2003

THIS IS AN ARRESTABLE OFFENCE – LIFE

A person (A) commits an offence if –

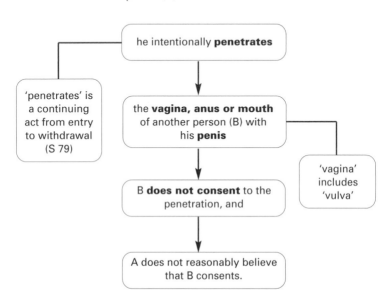

he intentionally **penetrates**

'penetrates' is a continuing act from entry to withdrawal (S 79)

the **vagina, anus or mouth** of another person (B) with his **penis**

'vagina' includes 'vulva'

B **does not consent** to the penetration, and

A does not reasonably believe that B consents.

Reasonable belief

Whether a belief is reasonable is to be determined having regard to all the circumstances, including any steps A has taken to ascertain whether B consents.

Consent

A person consents if he agrees by choice, and has the freedom and capacity to make that choice. (S 74)

Presumptions about consent

The absence of the complainant's consent and/or the absence of the defendant's reasonable belief that the complainant consented may be presumed, depending on the circumstances (Ss 75 & 76). See later under 'Presumptions about Consent'.

Assault by Penetration

S 2 SEXUAL OFFENCES ACT 2003

THIS IS AN ARRESTABLE OFFENCE – LIFE

A person (A) commits an offence if-

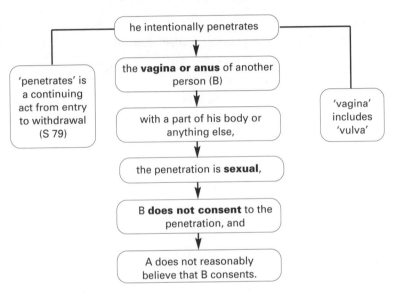

he intentionally penetrates

the **vagina or anus** of another person (B)

with a part of his body or anything else,

the penetration is **sexual**,

B **does not consent** to the penetration, and

A does not reasonably believe that B consents.

'penetrates' is a continuing act from entry to withdrawal (S 79)

'vagina' includes 'vulva'

Reasonable belief

Whether a belief is reasonable is to be determined having regard to all the circumstances, including any steps A has taken to ascertain whether B consents.

Consent

A person consents if he agrees by choice, and has the freedom and capacity to make that choice. (S 74)

Presumptions about consent

The absence of the complainant's consent and/or the absence of the defendant's reasonable belief that the complainant consented may be presumed, depending on the circumstances (Ss 75 & 76). See later under 'Presumptions about Consent'.

Sexual

See later under 'Sexual Offences – Interpretation'

Sexual Assault

S 3 SEXUAL OFFENCES ACT 2003

> THIS IS AN
> ARRESTABLE OFFENCE
> – 10 YEARS

A person (A) commits an offence if-

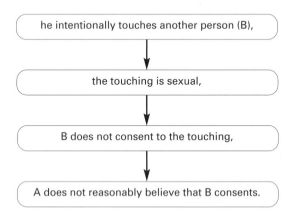

he intentionally touches another person (B),

⬇

the touching is sexual,

⬇

B does not consent to the touching,

⬇

A does not reasonably believe that B consents.

Touches

Includes touching with any part of the body, with anything else, and through anything. In particular it includes touching amounting to penetration. (S 79)

Reasonable belief

Whether a belief is reasonable is to be determined having regard to all the circumstances, including any steps A has taken to ascertain whether B consents.

Presumptions about consent

The absence of the complainant's consent and/or the absence of the defendant's reasonable belief that the complainant consented may be presumed, depending on the circumstances (Ss 75 & 76). See later under 'Presumptions about Consent'.

Sexual

See later under 'Sexual Offences – Interpretation'

Engaging in Sexual Activity Without Consent

S 4 SEXUAL OFFENCES ACT 2003

THIS IS AN ARRESTABLE OFFENCE – 10 YEARS (or LIFE if the offence involves penetration)

A person (A) commits an offence if-

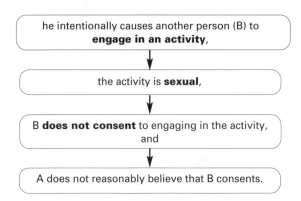

he intentionally causes another person (B) to **engage in an activity**,

the activity is **sexual**,

B **does not consent** to engaging in the activity, and

A does not reasonably believe that B consents.

Reasonable belief

Whether a belief is reasonable is to be determined having regard to all the circumstances, including any steps A has taken to ascertain whether B consents.

Presumptions about consent

The absence of the complainant's consent and/or the absence of the defendant's reasonable belief that the complainant consented may be presumed, depending on the circumstances (Ss 75 & 76). See later under 'Presumptions about Consent'.

Sexual

See later under 'Sexual Offences – Interpretation'

Exposure

S 66 SEXUAL OFFENCES ACT 2003

2 YEARS BUT ARRESTABLE BY VIRTUE OF S24 P.A.C.E.

A person commits an offence if-

a) he intentionally exposes his genitals, and
b) he intends that someone will see them and be caused alarm or distress.

Offences Against Children Under 13

Ss 5 – 8 SEXUAL OFFENCES ACT 2003

Rape (S 5)

A person commits an offence if-

(a) he intentionally penetrates the vagina, anus or mouth of another person with his penis, and

(b) the other person is under 13. (Life)

Assault of a child under 13 by penetration (S 6)

A person commits an offence if-

(a) he intentionally penetrates the vagina or anus of another person with a part of his body or anything else,

(b) the penetration is sexual, and

(c) the other person is under 13. (Life)

Sexual assault of a child under 13 (S 7)

A person commits an offence if-

(a) he intentionally touches another person,

(b) the touching is sexual, and

(c) the other person is under 13. (14 years)

Causing or inciting a child under 13 to engage in sexual activity (S 8)

A person commits an offence if-

(a) he intentionally causes or incites another person (B) to engage in an activity,

(b) the activity is sexual, and

(c) B is under 13. (14 years, unless the offence involves penetration, in which case, life)

N.B.

It will be noted that the main difference between these offences and those against Sections 1 to 4 is that consent is irrelevant.

Touches

Includes touching with any part of the body, with anything else, and through anything. In particular it includes touching amounting to penetration. (S 79)

Penetration

See under Ss 1-4.

Sexual

See later under 'Sexual Offences – Interpretation'

IN EACH CASE THESE ARE ARRESTABLE OFFENCES

Child Sex Offences

> *THESE ARE ALL ARRESTABLE OFFENCES*

Ss 9 – 12 SEXUAL OFFENCES ACT 2003

The following offences are committed by a person aged 18 or over (A)-

Sexual Activity with a child (S 9)

(a) if he intentionally touches another person (B),

(b) the touching is sexual, and

(c) either
  (i) B is under 16 and A does not reasonably believe that B is 16 or over, or
  (ii) B is under 13.
(14 years)

Causing or inciting a child to engage in sexual activity (S10)

(a) if he intentionally causes or incites another person (B) to engage in an activity,

(b) the activity is sexual, and

(c) either
  (i) B is under 16 and A does not reasonably believe that B is 16 or over, or
  (ii) B is under 13.
(14 years)

Engaging in sexual activity in the presence of a child (S 11)

(a) if he intentionally engages in an activity,

(b) the activity is sexual,

(c) for the purpose of obtaining sexual gratification, he engages in it
  (i) when another person (B) is present or is in a place from which A can be observed, and
  (ii) knowing or believing that B is aware, or intending that B should be aware, that he is engaging in it, and

(d) either
  (i) B is under 16 and A does not reasonably believe that B is 16 or over, or
  (ii) B is under 13.
(10 years)

Causing a child to watch a sexual act (S12)

(a) if for the purpose of obtaining sexual gratification, he intentionally causes another person (B) to watch a third person engaging in an activity, or to look at an image of any person engaging in an activity,

(b) the activity is sexual, and

(c) either
  (i) B is under 16 and A does not reasonably believe that B is 16 or over, or
  (ii) B is under 13.
(10 years)

Child Sex Offences

Ss 14 – 15 SEXUAL OFFENCES ACT 2003

> *THESE ARE ALL ARRESTABLE OFFENCES*

Arranging or facilitating commission of a child sex offence (S 14)

A person commits an offence if –

(a) he intentionally arranges or facilitates something that he intends to do, intends another person to do, or believes that another person will do, in any part of the world, and

(b) doing it will involve the commission of an offence under any of sections 9 to 13 of this Act.

Defence – he arranged or facilitated the act without intending it to be carried out, and he was acting for the protection of a child.

Protection of a child – means one of the following acts-

(a) protecting the child from sexually transmitted infection,

(b) protecting the physical safety of the child,

(c) preventing the child from becoming pregnant, or

(d) promoting the child's emotional well-being by the giving of advice,

and not for the purpose of obtaining sexual gratification or for the purpose of causing or encouraging the activity constituting the offence under sections 9 to 13.

(14 years)

Meeting a child following sexual grooming etc. (S 15)

A person aged 18 or over (A) commits an offence if-

(a) having met or communicated with another person (B) on at least 2 earlier occasions, he –
  (i)   intentionally meets (B), or
  (ii) travels with the intention of meeting B in any part of the world,

(b) at the time, he intends to do anything to or in respect of B, during or after the meeting and in any part of the world, which if done will involve the commission by A of a relevant offence,

(c) B is under 16, and

(d) A does not reasonably believe that B is 16 or over.
(10 years)

Met means in any part of the world.

Communicated means from, to or in any part of the world by any means.

Relevant offence means –

(a) an offence under this part of the Act (Sections 1 – 79)

(b) an offence under paragraphs 61 – 92 of Sched. 3 (mainly sexual offences in Northern Ireland), or

(c) anything done outside England and Wales and Northern Ireland which is not an offence in (a) or (b) but would be an offence under (a) if done in England and Wales.

Abuse of Position of Trust

Ss 16 – 19 SEXUAL OFFENCES ACT 2003

The following offences are very similar in nature to Ss 9 – 12 committed by persons aged 18 or over (see earlier). The main difference is that they are **committed by a person who is in a position of trust** (described on the following page). The effect in each case is to reduce the maximum penalty to 5 years. They are all, therefore, still arrestable offences.

Sexual activity with a child (S 16)

Committed where a person in a position of trust (A) intentionally touches another person (B) and the touching is sexual. Unlike the related offence (S 9), this offence requires that either-

a) B is under 18 and A does not reasonably believe that B is 18 or over, or
b) B is under 13.

There is a presumption that A did not reasonably believe that B was 18 or over unless sufficient evidence to the contrary is adduced.

Causing or inciting a child to engage in sexual activity (S 17)

Committed where a person in a position of trust (A) intentionally causes or incites another person (B) to engage in sexual activity. As with S 16, unlike the corresponding offence (S 10) this offence requires that either-

a) B is under 18 and A does not reasonably believe that B is 18 or over, or
b) B is under 13.

There is a similar presumption that A did not reasonably believe that B was 18 or over unless sufficient evidence to the contrary is adduced.

Sexual activity in the presence of a child (S 18)

Committed where a person in a position of trust (A) intentionally, and for the purpose of obtaining sexual gratification, engages in a sexual activity when another person (B) is present or is in a position to see. Again, unlike the similar offence (S 11), either-

a) B is under 18 and A does not reasonably believe that B is 18 or over, or
b) B is under 13.

Similarly, there is a presumption that A did not reasonably believe that B was 18 or over unless sufficient evidence to the contrary is adduced.

Causing a child to watch a sexual act (S 19)

Committed where a person in a position of trust (A) intentionally, and for the purpose of obtaining sexual gratification, causes another person (B) to watch a third person engaging in a sexual activity, or to look at an image of a person so engaging. In line with the above offences, this offence differs from the comparable offence (S 12) in that either-

a) B is under 18 and A does not reasonably believe that B is 18 or over, or
b) B is under 13.

A like presumption exists that A did not reasonably believe that B was 18 or over unless sufficient evidence to the contrary is adduced.

Defences

No activity will constitute an offence contrary to sections 16 – 19 above where-

a) B is 16 or over and A and B are **lawfully married**, or
b) immediately before a position of trust arose **a sexual relationship existed** between A and B (provided it was lawful).

Position of Trust – Meaning

S 21 SEXUAL OFFENCES ACT 2003

For the purposes of sections 16 – 19 a person (A) is in a position of trust in relation to another person (B) if any of the following apply-

B's situation	A's activity	Location
Detained by a court order or enactment	Looks after persons under 18 so detained	Institution
Resident in a home etc	Looks after persons under 18 who are resident	Accommodation and maintenance provided by a local authority or voluntary organisation
Accommodated and cared for	Looks after persons under 18 accommodated and cared for	Hospital, independent clinic, care home etc, community home etc, children's home, or residential family centre
Receiving education	Looks after persons receiving education	Educational institution
Under guardianship	Guardian	Northern Ireland
Training for employment	Looks after B on an individual basis in the provision of services	–
Accommodated by local authority	Regularly has unsupervised contact with B	Local authority accommodation
Subject to a court welfare report	Reporting on B and has regular unsupervised contact	–
Subject to local authority assessment	Appointed as personal adviser to B on an individual basis	–
Subject of care order, supervision order or education supervision order	Exercising the functions of the order and looks after B on an individual basis	–
Interests being safeguarded by the court or an enactment	Appointed to safeguard B's interests and has regular unsupervised contact with him	–
Subject to requirements on release from detention for a criminal offence, or a court order made in criminal proceedings	Looks after B on an individual basis in pursuance of the requirements	–

Familial Child Sex Offences

Ss 25 & 26 SEXUAL OFFENCES ACT 2003

Sexual Activity with Child Family Member (S 25)

A person commits an offence if –

(a) he intentionally touches another person (B),
(b) the touching is sexual,
(c) the relation of A to B is within S 27 (see following page),
(d) A knows or could reasonably be expected to know that his relation to B is of such a description, and
(e) either –
  (i)   B is under 18 and A does not reasonably believe that B is 18 or over, or
  (ii) B is under 13.

> *THIS IS AN ARRESTABLE OFFENCE (5 YEARS, OR 14 YEARS WHERE A IS OVER 18)*

Inciting a Child Family Member to Engage in Sexual Activity (S 26)

A person (A) commits an offence if –

(a) he intentionally incites another person (B) to touch, or allow himself to be touched by, A,
(b) the touching is sexual,
(c) the relation of A to B is within S 27 (see following page),
(d) A knows or could reasonably be expected to know that his relation to B is of such a description, and
(e) either –
  (i)   B is under 18 and A does not reasonably believe that B is 18 or over, or
  (ii) B is under 13.

Touches
Includes touching with any part of the body, with anything else, and through anything. In particular it includes touching amounting to penetration. (S 79)

> *THIS IS AN ARRESTABLE OFFENCE (5 YEARS, OR 14 YEARS WHERE A IS OVER 18)*

Sexual
See later under 'Sexual Offences – Interpretation'

Defences
No activity will constitute an offence contrary to sections 25 or 26 above where–

(a) B is 16 or over and A and B are lawfully married, or
(b) the relationship between A and B is not one of parent, grandparent, brother, sister, half-brother, half sister, aunt, uncle or foster parent, and immediately before the relation between them fell within S 27, a sexual relationship existed between A and B (provided it was lawful). (Ss 28 & 29)

Presumptions
The defendant is to be taken not to have reasonably believed the other was 18 or over, and to have reasonably believed that his relation to B was within S 27 (see following page), unless, in either case, evidence is adduced to the contrary.

Family Relationships – Meaning

S 27 SEXUAL OFFENCES ACT 2003

(1) The relation of one person (A) to another (B) is within this section if–
  (a) it is within one of the subsections below, or
  (b) it would be within one of those subsections but for S 67 of the Adoption and Children Act 2002 (which states that the adopted person is treated in law as if born as the child of the adopter(s)).

(2) The relation of A to B is within this subsection if–
  (a) one of them is the other's parent, grandparent, brother, sister, half-brother, half-sister, aunt or uncle, or
  (b) A is or has been B's foster parent.

(3) The relation of A to B is within this subsection if A and B live or have lived in the same household, or A is or has been regularly involved in caring for, training, supervising or being in sole charge of B, and–
  (a) one of them is or has been the other's step-parent,
  (b) A and B are cousins,
  (c) one of them is or has been the other's stepbrother or stepsister, or
  (d) the parent or present or former foster parent of one of them is or has been the other's foster parent.

(4) The relation of A to B is within this subsection if–
  (a) A and B live in the same household, and
  (b) A is regularly involved in caring for, training, supervising or being solely in charge of B.

Aunt
Means the sister or half-sister of a person's parent.

Uncle
Has a corresponding meaning to 'aunt'.

Cousin
Means the child of an aunt or uncle.

Foster parent
Means the person with whom the child has been placed by a local authority or voluntary organisation; or the person who fosters the child privately.

Step-parent
Includes a parent's partner.

Stepbrother and stepsister
Includes the child of a parent's partner.

Partner
Persons (whether of the same sex or different sexes) who live together as partners in an enduring family relationship.

Offences Against Persons with a Mental Disorder Impeding Choice

Ss 30–33 SEXUAL OFFENCES ACT 2003

A person (A) commits an offence if–

Sexual activity with mentally disordered person (S 30).
he intentionally touches another person (B) and the touching is sexual,

OR

Causing a person with mental disorder to engage in sexual activity (S 32).
he intentionally causes or incites another person (B) to engage in an activity and the activity is sexual,

OR

Engaging in sexual activity in presence of mentally disordered person (S 32).
(a) he intentionally engages in an activity and the activity is sexual,
(b) for the purpose of obtaining sexual gratification, he engages in it-
  (i) when another person (B) is present or is in a place from which A can be observed, and
  (ii) knowing or believing that B is aware, or intending that B should be aware, that he is engaging in it,

OR

Causing a person with mental disorder to watch a sexual act (S 33).
(a) for the purpose of obtaining sexual gratification, he intentionally causes another person (B) to watch a third person engaging in an activity, or to look at an image of any person engaging in an activity,
(b) the activity is sexual

AND

(a) B is unable to refuse because of or for a reason related to a mental disorder, and
(b) A knows or could reasonably be expected to know that B has a mental disorder and that because of it or for a reason related to it B is likely to be unable to refuse.

B is unable to refuse if –

(a) he lacks the capacity to choose whether to agree to the touching (whether he lacks sufficient understanding of the nature or reasonably foreseeable consequences of what is being done, or for any other reason), or
(b) he is unable to communicate such a choice to A.

THESE ARE ALL ARRESTABLE OFFENCES

Inducements etc to Persons with a Mental Disorder

Ss 34–37 SEXUAL OFFENCES ACT 2003

A person (A) commits an offence if-

by means of an **inducement** offered or given, a **threat** made or a **deception** practiced by A for the purpose, he-

Sexual activity with person with mental disorder (S 34).

with the agreement of another person (B), intentionally sexually touches that person

OR

Causing person with mental disorder to engage in sexual activity (S 35).

intentionally causes another person (B to engage in, or to agree to engage in, a sexual activity

Engaging in sexual activity in the presence of a person with a mental disorder (S 36).

procures another person (B) to be in a place and then intentionally engages in a sexual activity and for the purpose of sexual gratification he engages in it-
  (a) when B is present or is in a place from which A can be observed, and
  (b) knowing or believing that B is aware, or intending that B should be aware, that he is engaging in it

OR

Causing a person with a mental disorder to watch a sexual act (S 37).

for the purpose of sexual gratification, intentionally causes another person (B) to watch a third person engaging in a sexual activity, or to look at an image of any person engaging in a sexual activity

AND

B has a mental disorder, and A knows or could reasonably be expected to know that B has a mental disorder.

THESE ARE ALL ARRESTABLE OFFENCES

Care Workers for Persons with a Mental Disorder

Ss 38–41 SEXUAL OFFENCES ACT 2003

The following offences are very similar to Ss 30 – 33 (see earlier). The main differences are that they are **committed by care workers** (described below) and there is no need to prove that the mental disorder impeded choice. Although the effect in each case is to reduce the maximum penalty, **they are all still arrestable offences.**

Each of the offences are committed where a person (A) is involved in another person's care (B), B has a mental disorder, and A knew, or could reasonably be expected to know, that B had a mental disorder. Unlike the related offences, these offences presume that A knew or could reasonably have been expected to know that A had a mental disorder unless contrary evidence is adduced.

Care workers: sexual activity with a person with a mental disorder (S 38)
Committed when A intentionally touches B and the touching is sexual.

Care workers: causing or inciting sexual activity (S 39)
Committed where A intentionally causes or incites B to engage in sexual activity.

Care workers: sexual activity in the presence of a person with a mental disorder (S 40)
Committed where A intentionally, and for the purpose of obtaining sexual gratification, **engages in a sexual activity when B is present** or is in a position from which A can be observed, knowing or believing that B is aware, or intending that B should be aware, that he is engaging in it.

Care workers: causing a person with a mental disorder to watch a sexual act (S 41)
Committed where A intentionally, and for the purpose of obtaining sexual gratification, causes B to watch a third person engaging in a sexual activity, or to look at an image of a person so engaging.

Defences (Ss 43 & 44)
No activity will constitute an offence contrary to sections 38 – 41 above where –

(a) B is 16 or over and A and B are **lawfully married**, or

(b) immediately before the position of care arose **a sexual relationship existed** between A and B (provided it was lawful).

Care workers – meaning (S42)
A person (A) is involved in the care of another person (B) if –

1. B is accommodated and cared for in a care home, community home, voluntary home or children's home, and A regularly has face to face contact with B in the home in the course of A's employment, or

2. B is a patient for whom services are provided by a National Health service body, an independent medical agency, or in an independent clinic or independent hospital, and A regularly has face to face contact with B in the course of A's employment, or

3. whether or not in the course of employment, A provides care, assistance or services to B in connection with his mental disorder and has regular face to face contact with him.

Abuse of Children through Prostitution or Pornography

Ss 47–50 SEXUAL OFFENCES ACT 2003

A person (A) commits an offence in any of the circumstances listed below if either –

(a) the other person (B) is under 18 and B does not reasonably believe that A is 18 or over, or

(b) B is under 13.

Paying for sexual services of a child (S 47)
If he intentionally obtains for himself the sexual services of another person, and before obtaining those services he has made or promised payment for those services to B or a third person, or knows that another person has made or promised such payment.

Causing or inciting child prostitution or pornography (S 48)
If he intentionally causes or incites another person (B) to become a prostitute, or to be involved in pornography, in any part of the world.

Controlling a child prostitute or a child involved in pornography (S 49)
If he intentionally controls any of the activities of another person (B) relating to B's prostitution or involvement in pornography in any part of the world.

Arranging or facilitating child prostitution or pornography (S 50)
If he intentionally arranges or facilitates the prostitution or involvement in pornography in any part of the world of another person (B).

Involvement in photography means the recording of an indecent image of that person. (S 51)

Prostitute means a person (A) who on at least one occasion, and whether or not compelled to do so, offers or provides sexual services to another person in return for payment or a promise of payment to A or a third person. (S 51)

Payment means any financial advantage, including the discharge of an obligation to pay, or the provision of goods or services (including sexual services) gratuitously or at a discount. (S 51)

> *THESE ARE ALL ARRESTABLE OFFENCES*

Indecent Photographs

S 1 PROTECTION OF CHILDREN ACT 1978 AS AMENDED BY S 84 CRIMINAL JUSTICE AND PUBLIC ORDER ACT 1994 AND S 45 SEXUAL OFFENCES ACT 2003

IT IS AN OFFENCE TO

→ **TAKE, MAKE** OR PERMIT TO BE TAKEN

→ **SHOW** OR DISTRIBUTE

→ **POSSESS** WITH A VIEW TO DISTRIBUTION

→ **PUBLISH** AN ADVERTISEMENT OF A SHOWING OR DISTRIBUTION OF

ANY

INDECENT PHOTOGRAPH OR PSEUDO – PHOTOGRAPH

OF A **CHILD**

There is also an offence of possession under S 160 Criminal Justice Act 1988 which does not require the purpose for which the photograph is held to be proved. In this case, in addition to the defences mentioned below, there is a defence if it was sent to him by post without prior request, and he did not keep it for an unreasonable time.

Includes negatives, films, copies, video recordings, images including a computer graphic or data stored on a disc

In relation to the offences of distributing, showing, or possessing with a view to doing so, it shall be a **defence** if the accused proves that:

- there is a legitimate reason for distribution or possession
- he had not seen the photographs and neither knew nor suspected they were indecent
- at the time of the offence the child was 16 or over and they were married or living together as partners in an enduring family relationship, or
- it was for the purposes of crime prevention, detection or investigation

A person under the age of 18. But, irrespective of the actual age, if the impression conveyed by a pseudo-photograph is that of a child, it will be treated as showing a child, even if some of the characteristics shown are those of an adult.

THESE ARE ARRESTABLE OFFENCES

'Distribution' means parting with possession of it to, or exposes it for acquisition by, another person.

Indecent Displays

S 1 INDECENT DISPLAYS (CONTROL) ACT 1981

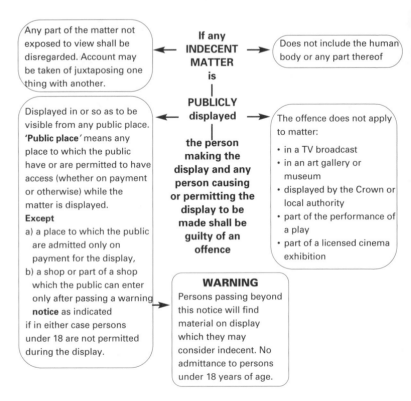

If any
**INDECENT
MATTER**
is

Any part of the matter not exposed to view shall be disregarded. Account may be taken of juxtaposing one thing with another.

Does not include the human body or any part thereof

**PUBLICLY
displayed**

Displayed in or so as to be visible from any public place. **'Public place'** means any place to which the public have or are permitted to have access (whether on payment or otherwise) while the matter is displayed.

Except

a) a place to which the public are admitted only on payment for the display,

b) a shop or part of a shop which the public can enter only after passing a warning **notice** as indicated

if in either case persons under 18 are not permitted during the display.

The offence does not apply to matter:

• in a TV broadcast
• in an art gallery or museum
• displayed by the Crown or local authority
• part of the performance of a play
• part of a licensed cinema exhibition

**the person
making the
display and any
person causing
or permitting the
display to be
made shall be
guilty of an
offence**

WARNING

Persons passing beyond this notice will find material on display which they may consider indecent. No admittance to persons under 18 years of age.

Police Powers

A constable may seize any article which he has reasonable grounds for believing to be indecent matter used in the commission of an offence.

Obscene Publications

OBSCENE PUBLICATIONS ACTS 1959 & 1964

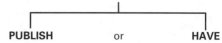

IT IS AN OFFENCE TO

PUBLISH or **HAVE**

(to distribute, circulate, sell, let on hire, give, lend; show, play or project matter to be looked at or a record; or transmit electronically stored data)

(ownership, possession or control)

FOR PUBLICATION FOR GAIN

(to the offender or any other person accruing benefit either directly or indirectly)

WHETHER OR NOT FOR GAIN

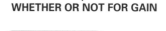

THESE ARE ARRESTABLE OFFENCES

ANY

OBSCENE → A tendency to deprave or corrupt those who are likely to read, see or hear the matter contained in it.

ARTICLE → Anything containing matter to be read or looked at; any sound, record, film, or other record of a picture or pictures, whether intended to be used alone or as one of a set, or for the reproduction or manufacture of such articles, eg negatives, printing blocks, etc.

DEFENCES

The offender had not examined the article and had no reasonable cause to suspect that his having it was an offence, or

its publication was justifiable as being for the public good in the interests of science, literature, art or learning, or of other objects of public concern. In the case of a moving picture film or soundtrack, its publication was justified as being for the public good in the interests of drama, opera, ballet or any other art, or of literature or learning.

Harmful Publications

CHILDREN AND YOUNG PERSONS (HARMFUL PUBLICATIONS) ACT 1955

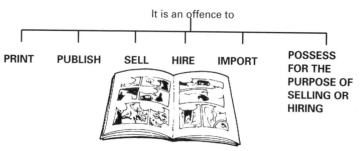

It is an offence to

PRINT **PUBLISH** **SELL** **HIRE** **IMPORT** **POSSESS FOR THE PURPOSE OF SELLING OR HIRING**

any book, magazine or other like work which is likely to fall into the hands of a child (under 14 years) or young person (under 18 years) and which consists wholly or mainly of stories told in pictures (with or without written material)

PORTRAYING

commission of crimes or acts of violence or cruelty

incidents of a repulsive or horrible nature

such that the whole work would tend to

CORRUPT

A CHILD OR YOUNG PERSON

into whose hands it might fall

DEFENCE (applies only to selling or hiring, or having in possession for that purpose.) That the accused had not examined the work and had no reasonable cause to suspect that it constituted an offence.

Prostitution

S 1 STREET OFFENCES ACT 1959 AS AMENDED BY THE SEXUAL OFFENCES ACT 2003

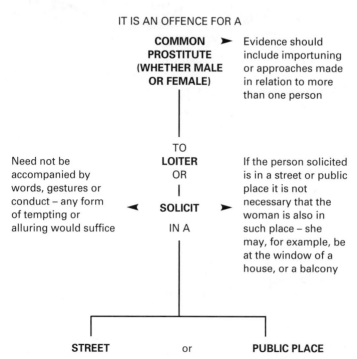

IT IS AN OFFENCE FOR A

COMMON PROSTITUTE (WHETHER MALE OR FEMALE) ➤ Evidence should include importuning or approaches made in relation to more than one person

TO **LOITER** OR **SOLICIT** IN A

Need not be accompanied by words, gestures or conduct – any form of tempting or alluring would suffice

If the person solicited is in a street or public place it is not necessary that the woman is also in such place – she may, for example, be at the window of a house, or a balcony

STREET or **PUBLIC PLACE**

(includes any bridge, road, lane, footway, subway, square, court, alley or passage, whether a thoroughfare or not, which is for the time being open to the public; and the doorways and entrances of premises abutting on a street, and any ground adjoining and open to a street)

(any highway and any other premises or place to which at the material time the public are permitted to have access whether on payment or otherwise, eg parks, libraries, railway stations, buses, etc)

FOR THE PURPOSE OF PROSTITUTION

A constable may arrest without warrant anyone he finds in a street or public place and suspects, with reasonable cause, to be committing this offence.

Kerb-Crawling

S 1 SEXUAL OFFENCES ACT 1985 AS AMENDED
BY THE SEXUAL OFFENCES ACT 2003

An offence is committed by a

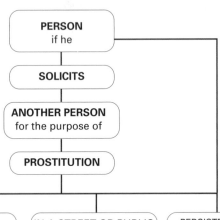

PERSON
if he

SOLICITS

ANOTHER PERSON
for the purpose of

PROSTITUTION

FROM A

MOTOR VEHICLE

(has the same meaning
as in the Road Traffic Act)

WHILE IT IS IN A

STREET OR PUBLIC PLACE

(has the same meaning
as in the Street Offences Act
(see previous page))

IN A STREET OR PUBLIC
PLACE WHILE IN THE

IMMEDIATE VICINITY

OF A

MOTOR VEHICLE

WHICH HE HAS JUST
GOT OUT OF OR OFF

PERSISTENTLY
SOLICITS
ANOTHER PERSON
IN A STREET OR
PUBLIC PLACE FOR
THE PURPOSE OF
PROSTITUTION
(S 2)

*THIS IS AN
ARRESTABLE
OFFENCE*

persistently or in such
circumstances as to be
likely to cause
annoyance to the
person solicited, or
nuisance to other
persons in the
neighbourhood

Advertising Prostitution

S 46 CRIMINAL JUSTICE AND POLICE ACT 2001

A person commits an offence if he places on, or in the immediate vicinity of,

a public telephone

an advertisement relating to prostitution

and he does so with the intention that the advertisement should come to the attention of any other person or persons

THIS IS AN ARRESTABLE OFFENCE

It will relate to prostitution if it:

(a) is for the services of a prostitute, whether male or female; or
(b) indicates that premises are premises at which such services are offered.

Any advertisement which a reasonable person would consider to be an advertisement relating to prostitution shall be presumed to be such an advertisement unless it is shown not to be.

Means:

(a) any telephone which is located in a public place and made available for use by the public, or a section of the public, and
(b) where such a telephone is located in or on, or attached to, a kiosk, booth, acoustic hood, shelter or other structure, that structure.

'Public place' means any place to which the public have or are permitted to have access, whether on payment or otherwise, other than:

(a) any place to which children under the age of 16 years are not permitted to have access, whether by law or otherwise, and
(b) any premises which are wholly or mainly used for residential purposes.

Brothels

S 33 SEXUAL OFFENCES ACT 1956

IT IS AN OFFENCE FOR A PERSON TO KEEP A

A brothel is a place where people of opposite sexes are allowed to resort for illicit sexual intercourse. The women need not necessarily be prostitutes. However, S 6 of the Sexual Offences Act 1967 extended this to include premises to which people resort for lewd homosexual practices.

Evidence of sexual intercourse is not necessary to prove 'assisting in the management'. It is sufficient to prove that more than one woman offered herself for physical acts of indecency or sexual gratification.

To be 'assisting in the management' it is not necessary to show that some sort of control was exercised over the management, nor that there was a specific act of management.

or to manage, or act or assist in the management of, a brothel.

A new offence was inserted by S 55 Sexual Offences Act 2003 of managing etc. a brothel used for practices of prostitution, whether or not also used for other practices (S 33A). **THIS IS AN ARRESTABLE OFFENCE (7 YEARS)**

Circumstances where premises WILL NOT be a brothel

A house occupied by a woman and used by her for her own prostitution, but not used by other women, is not a brothel.

Two flats in one building separately let to two prostitutes will not be a brothel.

Circumstances where premises WILL be a brothel

Two women, one being the occupier, both used the premises.

A block of flats inhabited by different women for prostitution

Three rooms in close proximity separately let to prostitutes.

Premises used by a team of prostitutes but not more than one per day used them.

Premises Used for the Purposes of Sex

SEXUAL OFFENCES ACT 1956 AS AMENDED BY THE SEXUAL OFFENCES ACT 2003

Landlord Letting Premises for Use as Brothel (S 34)

It is an offence for the lessor or landlord of any premises or his agent to let the whole or part of the premises with the knowledge that it is to be used as a brothel, or, where it is being so used, to be a wilful party to that use continuing.

The premises must be used by more than one prostitute.

Tenant Permitting Premises to Be Used as a Brothel (S 35)

It is an offence for the tenant or occupier, or person in charge, of any premises knowingly to permit the whole or part of the premises to be used as a brothel.

Tenant Permitting Premises to Be Used for Prostitution (S 36)

It is an offence for the tenant or occupier of any premises knowingly to permit the whole or part of the premises to be used for the purposes of habitual prostitution (whether any prostitute involved is male or female).

A woman who is the sole occupier cannot be convicted of this offence if she uses the premises for her own habitual prostitution.

Exploitation of Prostitution

Ss 52–54 SEXUAL OFFENCES ACT 2003

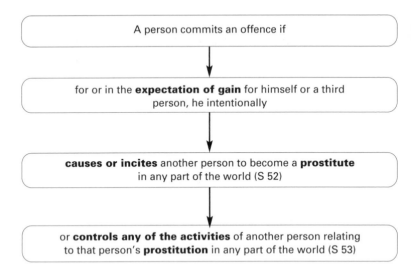

A person commits an offence if

for or in the **expectation of gain** for himself or a third person, he intentionally

causes or incites another person to become a **prostitute** in any part of the world (S 52)

or **controls any of the activities** of another person relating to that person's **prostitution** in any part of the world (S 53)

Gain means –

(a) any financial advantage, including the discharge of an obligation to pay or the provision of goods or services (including sexual services) gratuitously or at a discount, or

(b) the goodwill of any person which is or appears likely in time, to bring financial advantage. (S 54)

Prostitute means a person (A) who on at least one occasion, and whether or not compelled to do so, offers or provides sexual services to another person in return for payment or a promise of payment to A or a third person. (S 51)

Payment means any financial advantage, including the discharge of an obligation to pay, or the provision of goods or services (including sexual services) gratuitously or at a discount. (S 51)

THESE ARE
ARRESTABLE OFFENCES
(7 YEARS)

Trafficking for Sexual Exploitation

Ss 57–59 SEXUAL OFFENCES ACT 2003

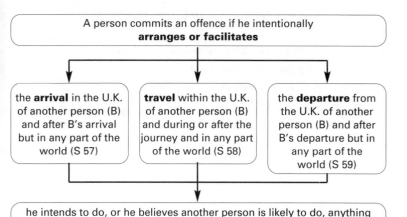

A person commits an offence if he intentionally **arranges or facilitates**

the **arrival** in the U.K. of another person (B) and after B's arrival but in any part of the world (S 57)

travel within the U.K. of another person (B) and during or after the journey and in any part of the world (S 58)

the **departure** from the U.K. of another person (B) and after B's departure but in any part of the world (S 59)

he intends to do, or he believes another person is likely to do, anything in respect of B which if done will involve the commission of a **relevant offence** (see below).

These offences apply to anything done –

(a) in the U.K., or

THESE ARE ALL ARRESTABLE OFFENCES (14 YEARS)

(b) outside the U.K., by a body incorporated under the law of a part of the U.K. or by an individual who is a British citizen, a British overseas territories citizen, a British National (Overseas), a British Overseas citizen, a person who is a British subject under the British Nationality Act 1981, or a British protected person within the meaning of S 50(1) of that Act.

Relevant offence means –

(a) any offence under Ss 1–72 of the Sexual Offences Act 2003,

(b) indecent photographs of children (S1(1) Protection of Children Act 1978),

(c) offences listed in Sched. 1 to the Criminal Justice (Children) (Northern Ireland) Order 1978,

(d) an offence under Art. 3(1)(a) of the Protection of Children (Northern Ireland) Order 1978, or

(e) anything done outside England and Wales and Northern Ireland which is not an offence in paras. (a) to (d) but would be if done in England and Wales and Northern Ireland.

Preparatory Offences

Ss 61–63 SEXUAL OFFENCES ACT 2003

Administering a substance with intent (S 61)

A person commits an offence if he intentionally administers a substance to, or causes a substance to be taken by, another person (B) –

(a) knowing that B does not consent and,

(b) with the intention of stupefying or overpowering B, so as to enable any person to engage in a sexual activity that involves B.
(10 years)

Committing an offence with intent to commit a sexual offence (S 62)

A person commits an offence under this section if he commits any offence with the intention of committing any offence under Ss 1–72 of this Act (including aiding, abetting, counselling or procuring such an offence).

Life (if the offence involves kidnapping or false imprisonment) or 10 years.

Trespass with intent to commit a sexual offence (S 63)

A person commits an offence if–

(a) he is a trespasser on any premises,

(b) he intends to commit any offence under Ss 1–72 of this Act on the premises, and

(c) he knows that, or is reckless as to whether, he is a trespasser.

Premises includes a structure or part of a structure.

Structure includes a tent, vehicle or vessel or other temporary or moveable structure. (10 years)

THESE ARE ALL ARRESTABLE OFFENCES

Sex with an Adult Relative

Ss 64 & 65 SEXUAL OFFENCES ACT 2003

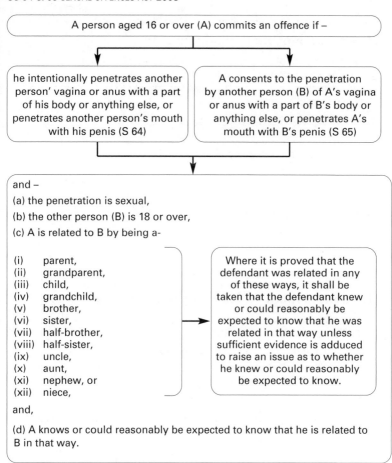

A person aged 16 or over (A) commits an offence if –

he intentionally penetrates another person' vagina or anus with a part of his body or anything else, or penetrates another person's mouth with his penis (S 64)

A consents to the penetration by another person (B) of A's vagina or anus with a part of B's body or anything else, or penetrates A's mouth with B's penis (S 65)

and –

(a) the penetration is sexual,

(b) the other person (B) is 18 or over,

(c) A is related to B by being a-

(i)   parent,
(ii)   grandparent,
(iii)   child,
(iv)   grandchild,
(v)   brother,
(vi)   sister,
(vii) half-brother,
(viii) half-sister,
(ix)   uncle,
(x)   aunt,
(xi)   nephew, or
(xii) niece,

Where it is proved that the defendant was related in any of these ways, it shall be taken that the defendant knew or could reasonably be expected to know that he was related in that way unless sufficient evidence is adduced to raise an issue as to whether he knew or could reasonably be expected to know.

and,

(d) A knows or could reasonably be expected to know that he is related to B in that way.

Uncle means the brother of the person's parent, and **aunt** has a corresponding meaning.

Nephew means the child of a person's brother or sister, and **niece** has a corresponding meaning.

Both offences are punishable with 2 years and are therefore not arrestable offences.

Voyeurism

S 67 SEXUAL OFFENCES ACT 2003

A person commits an offence if he is involved in any of the following activities-

Observing another person (Subs. 1)

(a) For the purpose of obtaining sexual gratification, he observes another person doing a private act, and

(b) he knows that the other person does not consent to being observed for his sexual gratification.

Operating equipment (Subs. 2)

(a) He operates equipment with the intention of enabling another person to observe, for the purpose of obtaining sexual gratification, a third person (B) doing a private act, and

(b) he knows that B does not consent to his operating equipment with that intention.

Recording another person (Subs. 3)

(a) He records another person (B) doing a private act,

(b) he does so with the intention that he or a third person will, for the purpose of obtaining sexual gratification, look at an image of B doing the act, and

(c) he knows that B does not consent to his recording the act with that intention.

Installing equipment (Subs. 4)

He installs equipment, or constructs or adapts a structure or part of a structure, with the intention of enabling himself or another person to commit an offence under subs. 1 above

Private act

A person is doing a private act if the person is in a place which, in the circumstances, would reasonably be expected to provide privacy, and –

(a) the person's genitals, buttocks or breasts are exposed or covered only with underwear,

(b) the person is using a lavatory, or

(c) the person is doing a sexual act that is not of a kind ordinarily done in public.

Structure includes a tent vehicle or vessel or other temporary or moveable structure.

PUNISHMENT FOR ANY OF THE ABOVE OFFENCES IS 2 YEARS BUT IS ARRESTABLE BY VIRTUE OF S24 P.A.C.E.

Intercourse with an Animal

S 69 SEXUAL OFFENCES ACT 2003

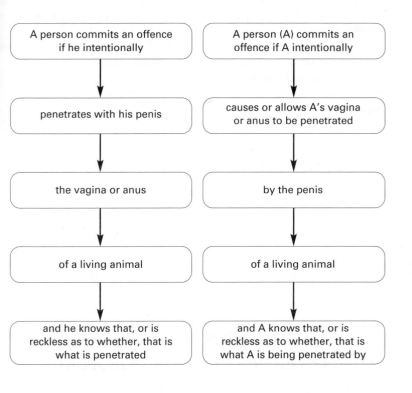

A person commits an offence if he intentionally	A person (A) commits an offence if A intentionally
penetrates with his penis	causes or allows A's vagina or anus to be penetrated
the vagina or anus	by the penis
of a living animal	of a living animal
and he knows that, or is reckless as to whether, that is what is penetrated	and A knows that, or is reckless as to whether, that is what A is being penetrated by

references to the vagina or anus include references to a similar part

**EITHER OFFENCE PUNISHABLE WITH 2 YEARS
BUT IS ARRESTABLE BY VIRTUE OF S 24 P.A.C.E.**

Sexual Penetration of a Corpse

S 70 SEXUAL OFFENCES ACT 2003

A person commits an offence if–

(a) he intentionally performs an act of penetration with a part of his body or anything else,

(b) what is penetrated is a part of the body of a dead person,

(c) he knows that, or is reckless as to whether, that is what is penetrated, and

(d) the penetration is sexual.

Sexual – see later under 'Sexual Offences – Interpretation'

Penetration – a continuing act from entry to withdrawal.

MAXIMUM PENALTY – 2 YEARS
BUT ARRESTABLE BY VIRTUE OF S 24 P.A.C.E.

Sexual Activity in a Public Lavatory

S 71 SEXUAL OFFENCES ACT 2003

A person commits an offence if–

(a) he is in a lavatory to which the public or a section of the public has or is permitted to have access, whether on payment or otherwise,

(b) he intentionally engages in an activity, and,

(c) the activity is sexual.

Sexual activity. The test for this is whether a reasonable person would, in all the circumstances but regardless of any person's purpose, consider it to be sexual.

TRIABLE SUMMARILY ONLY
BUT ARRESTABLE BY VIRTUE OF S 24 P.A.C.E.

Offences Outside the United Kingdom

S 72 SEXUAL OFFENCES ACT 2003

Any act done by a person in a country or territory outside the U.K. which–

(a) constituted an offence under the law in force in that country or territory, and

(b) would constitute an offence to which this section applies if it had been done in England and Wales or in Northern Ireland,

(c) constitutes that sexual offence under the law of that part of the U.K.

The sexual offences to which this section applies in England and Wales are–

(a) Ss 5–15 of this Act (offences against children under 13 or under 16),

(b) Ss 1–4, 16–41, 47–50, and 61 of this Act, where the victim was under 16,

(c) Ss 62 or 63 of this Act where the intended victim was under 16, or

(d) S1 Protection of Children Act 1978, or S 160 Criminal Justice Act 1988 (indecent photographs of children under 16).

Incitement to Commit Sexual Offences Outside the UK

SEXUAL OFFENCES (CONSPIRACY AND INCITEMENT) ACT 1996

A person will be guilty of incitement triable in England and Wales if each of the following conditions is satisfied:

1. The course of action involves:
   a) an act which would have been a listed sexual offence (see below) if committed in England or Wales,
   b) the whole or part of what he had in view was intended to take place outside the UK.
2. What he had in view is an offence in that other country or territory.

Any act of incitement by means of a message (however communicated) is to be treated as done in England and Wales if the message is sent or received in England or Wales.

Listed Sexual Offences

Indecency with Children Act 1960:

S 1   indecent conduct towards young child

Presumptions about Consent

Ss 75 & 76 SEXUAL OFFENCES ACT 2003

In proceedings for an offence to which this section applies (see below), **the complainant is to be taken not to have consented and the defendant is to be taken not to have reasonably believed that the complainant consented** (unless, in either case, sufficient contrary evidence is adduced to raise an issue), if –

(a) the defendant did the relevant act (see below), and

(b) any of the below circumstances existed, and the defendant knew they existed.

Offence	Relevant Act (in each case intentionally)
S 1 (Rape)	Penetrating, with his penis, the vagina, anus or mouth of another person
S 2 (Assault by penetration)	Sexually penetrating with part of his body or anything else the vagina or anus of another person
S 3 (Sexual assault)	Sexually touching another person
S 4 (Sexual activity without consent)	Causing another person to engage in a sexual activity
Circumstances	
Violence Any person was, at the time of the relevant act, or immediately before it began, using violence against the complainant or causing him to fear that immediate violence would be used against him.	
Fear of violence against another person Any person was, at the time of the relevant act or immediately before it began, causing the complainant to fear that violence was being used, or that immediate violence would be used, against another person.	
Unlawfully detained The complainant was, and the defendant was not, unlawfully detained at the time of the relevant act.	
Unconscious The complainant was asleep or unconscious at the time of the relevant act.	
Unable to consent through physical disability Because of the complainant's physical disability, he would not have been able at the time of the relevant act to communicate to the defendant whether he consented.	
Administering a stupefying or overpowering substance Any person had administered to or caused to be taken by the complainant, without the complainant's consent, a substance which, having regard to when it was administered or taken, was capable of causing or enabling the complainant to be stupefied or overpowered at the time of the relevant act.	

Conclusive presumptions about consent S 76
It is to be conclusively presumed that the complainant did not consent to the relevant act (as above)and that the defendant did not believe that the complainant consented if –

(a) the defendant intentionally deceived the complainant as to the nature or purpose of the relevant act, or

(b) the defendant intentionally induced the complainant to consent to the relevant act by impersonating a person known personally to the complainant.

Sexual Offences – Interpretation

Consent
A person consents if he agrees by choice, and has the freedom and capacity to make that choice (S 74).

Sexual
Penetration, touching or any other activity is sexual if a reasonable person would consider that–

(a) whatever its circumstances or any person's purpose in relation to it, it is because of its nature sexual, or

(b) because of its nature it may be sexual and because of its circumstances or the purpose of any person in relation to it (or both) it is sexual. (S 78)

This definition does not apply to S 71 (sexual activity in a public lavatory).

Penetration
This is a continuing act from entry to withdrawal. (S 79)

Part of the body
Includes a part surgically constructed (in particular through gender reassignment surgery). (S 79)

Image
A moving or still image and includes an image produced by any means and, where the context permits, a three dimensional image. (S 79)

Image of a person
Includes an image of an imaginary person. (S 79)

Mental disorder
Means the same as in S 1 Mental Health Act 1983 – "mental illness, arrested or incomplete development of mind, psychopathic disorder and any other disorder or disability of mind". (S 79)

Observation
However expressed, means either direct or by looking at an image. (S 79)

Touching
Includes touching with any part of the body, with anything else, or through anything, and in particular includes touching amounting to penetration. (S 79)

Vagina
Includes vulva. In relation to an animal, references to a vagina or anus includes reference to any similar parts. (S 79)

Notification Requirements

Ss 80–91 SEXUAL OFFENCES ACT 2003

Persons subject to notification requirements (S 80)

A person is subject to notification requirements if–

(a) convicted of a Sched. 3 offence (see later),

(b) found not guilty of such an offence by reason of insanity,

(c) found to be under a disability and to have done the act charged against him in respect of such an offence, or

(d) cautioned for such an offence.

Notification requirements: initial notification (S 83)

The offender must, within 3 days of the relevant date (see below), notify to the police–

(a) date of birth,

(b) national insurance number,

(c) name and any other names used on the relevant date,

(d) home address on the relevant date,

(e) name and any other names used on the date of notification,

(f) home address on the date of notification,

(g) address of any other premises in the U.K. where he regularly resides or stays

The period of 3 days will not include time– in court custody; imprisonment or service detention; detained in hospital; or outside the U.K.

Any changes to the above must be notified to the police within 3 days. (s 84)

Method of notification (S 87)

Notification is given by–

(a) attending a local police station prescribed by the Secretary of State, and

(b) giving oral notification to any police officer or other authorised person.

For the purpose of verifying the identity of the offender a photograph may be taken of any part of him and his fingerprints taken.

Young offenders; parental directions (S 89)

Where the offender is under 18, the court may direct that obligation for notification may be placed on the parent responsible for him and the offender must attend the police station with the parent.

Offences relating to notification (S 91)

A person commits an offence if he fails to comply with the above requirements or gives false information. (5 YEARS – ARRESTABLE OFFENCE).

Persons formerly subject to the Sex Offenders Act 1997 (S 81)

A person will still be subject to notification requirements if he was subject to the old law in respect of a Sched. 3 offence if the conviction, caution, etc. occurred before 1.9.97.

Relevant date (S 82)

This means

(a) the date of **conviction** (for person convicted of Sched. 3 offence),

(b) the date of the **finding** (for a person found not guilty by reason of insanity, or for a person suffering from a disability but to have done the act),

(c) the date of the **caution** for a person who has been cautioned for the offence, or

(d) the **corresponding relevant date** for a person subject to an order under the Sex Offenders Act 1997.

Notification Requirements – Schedule 3 Offences

SCHEDULE 3 SEXUAL OFFENCES ACT 2003

Listed below are the offences under the Sexual Offences Act 2003 for the purposes of notification of details to the police –

Section(s)	Circumstances of offence
1 or 2	Rape or assault by penetration
3	Sexual assault (and condition (a) below)
4 to 6	Causing sexual activity without consent, rape of under 13 or assault by penetration of under 13
7	Sexual assault child under 13– offender over 18 or sentenced 12 months
8 to 12	Sexual activity with child under 13 or child sex offences by adults
13	Child sex offences by child or young person & sentenced to 12 months
14	Arranging child sex– offender 18 or over, or sentenced to 12 months
15	Meeting child following grooming
16 to 19	Abuse of position of trust & imprisoned, detained in hospital, or community sentence for 12 months or more
25 or 26	Familial child sex, offender over 18 or sentenced to 12 months or more
30 to 37	Offences against persons with mental disorder
38 to 41	Care workers for persons with mental disorder (and condition (a) below)
47	Paying for sex with child (victim under 16 and offender either 18 or over, or sentenced to 12 months or more)
61	Administering substance with intent
62 or 63	Trespassing with intent to commit sexual offence (and condition (a) below)
64 or 65	Sex with adult relative (and condition (b) below)
66	Exposure (and condition (a) below)
67	Voyeurism (and condition (a) below)
69 or 70	Intercourse with animal or penetration of a corpse (and condition (b) below)

In addition, the following offences which were included in the (now revoked) Sex Offenders Act 1997 are also included in the Sched. 3 offences–

S 1 Protection of Children Act 1978 or S 160 of the Criminal Justice Act 1988	Indecent photographs of child under 16 (and condition (c) below)
S170 Customs and Excise Management Act	Importation of indecent photographs of child under 16 (and condition (c) below)

Conditions

(a) Either (i) offender under 18 and sentenced to at least 12 months imprisonment, or (ii) in any other case, either the victim under 18, or the offender sentenced to imprisonment, detained in hospital, or subject of a community sentence of at least 12 months.

(b) Either (i) offender under 18 and sentenced to at least 12 months imprisonment, or (ii) in any other case offender sentenced to imprisonment or detained in a hospital.

(c) Either (i) the conviction, finding or caution was before the commencement of this Act, or (ii) the offender was over 18 or sentenced to imprisonment for at least 12 months.

Chapter 3
Firearms and Explosives

Firearms – Definitions

S 57 FIREARMS ACT 1968

The term 'firearm' includes any:

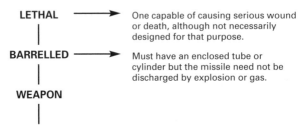

LETHAL ⟶ One capable of causing serious wound or death, although not necessarily designed for that purpose.

BARRELLED ⟶ Must have an enclosed tube or cylinder but the missile need not be discharged by explosion or gas.

WEAPON

of any description from which any shot, bullet or other missile can be discharged and including any:

• **Prohibited weapon** whether it is lethal or not.
• **Component part** of such lethal or prohibited weapon.
• **Accessory** to such weapons designed or adapted to diminish the noise or flash caused by firing the weapon.

'Ammunition' means ammunition for any firearm and includes grenades, bombs and other like missiles, whether capable of use with a firearm or not, and also includes prohibited ammunition.

The term **'imitation firearm'** means anything which has the appearance of being a firearm (other than a weapon designed or adapted for the discharge of any noxious liquid, gas or other thing) whether or not it is capable of discharging any shot, bullet or other missile.

Prohibited Weapons

S 5(1) FIREARMS ACT 1968

A person commits an offence if, without the authority of the Secretary of State, he has in his possession, or purchases or acquires, or manufactures, sells or transfers:

- any firearm which is so designed or adapted that two or more missiles can be successively discharged without repeated pressure on the trigger
- any self-loading or pump-action rifled gun other than one which is chambered for .22 rim-fire cartridges
- any firearm which either has a barrel less than 30cm or less than 60cm overall (disregarding any detachable, folding, retractable or other moveable butt-stock) other than an air weapon, a muzzle-loading gun or a firearm designed as signalling apparatus
- any self-loading or pump action smooth-bore gun which is not an air weapon or chambered for .22 rim-fire cartridges and either:
  a) has a barrel less than 24" in length, or an air weapon, or
  b) is less than 40" in overall length
- any smooth-bore revolver gun other than one which is chambered for 9mm rim-fire cartridges or a muzzle loading gun
- any rocket-launcher, or any mortar, for projecting a stabilised missile, other than a launcher or mortar designed for line-throwing or pyrotechnic purposes or as signalling apparatus
- any air rifle, air gun or air pistol which uses, or is designed or adapted for use with, a self-contained gas cartridge system
- any weapon of whatever description designed or adapted for the discharge of any noxious liquid, gas or other thing

(CONTINUED ON NEXT PAGE)

Prohibited Weapons – continued

• any cartridge with a bullet designed to explode on or immediately before impact, any ammunition containing or designed or adapted to contain any such noxious thing mentioned above and, if capable of being used with a firearm of any description, any grenade, bomb (or other like missile), or rocket or shell designed to explode on or immediately before impact

Prohibited Weapons Subject to Exemptions (S 5A)

Exemptions exist (but Firearm Certificate is still required) in relation to slaughtering instruments, humane killing of animals, starting pistols, trophies of war acquired before 1.1.46, part of a collection and manufactured before 1.1.19, firearms of rare or historic importance or firearms for shooting vermin or treating animals.

Exemptions also exist in relation to holders of certificates or authority, firearms collectors, bodies concerned in cultural or historical aspects of firearms, slaughtering instruments, and registered firearms dealers.

Other Prohibitions (S 5(1A))

Subject to S 5A above, a person commits an offence if, without the authority of the Secretary of State he has in his possession, or purchases or acquires, or sells or transfers:

• Any firearm which is disguised as another object
• Any rocket or ammunition which consists in or incorporates a missile designed to explode on or immediately before impact and is for military use
• Any launcher or other projecting apparatus designed to be used with any rocket or ammunition for the discharge of any noxious gas, liquid or other thing
• Any ammunition for military use which consists of or incorporates a missile designed so that a substance contained in the missile will ignite on or immediately before impact, or which is designed, on account of its having a jacket or hardcore, to penetrate armour plating, armour screening or body armour
• Any ammunition which incorporates a missile designed or adapted to expand on impact
• Anything which is designed to be projected as a missile from any weapon and is designed to be, or had been, incorporated in any ammunition as mentioned above

The expressions 'prohibited weapons' and 'prohibited ammunition' mean weapons and ammunition specified in this page and the preceding page, including anything designed to be projected as a missile from any weapon and designed to be, or has been, incorporated in any ammunition.

Prohibited Weapons and Ammunition – Exemptions

S 5A FIREARMS ACT 1968

The following exemptions apply only to those weapons listed under 'Prohibited Weapons Subject to Exemptions' (see facing page).

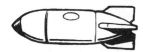

The authority of the Secretary of State is not required for:

a) possession, purchase or acquisition for activities recognised by another member state as a collector of firearms, or a body concerned in the cultural or historical aspects of weapons;

b) possession, purchase, acquisition, sale or transfer of any expanding ammunition or the missile for such ammunition if he is authorised by a firearm certificate or visitor's firearm permit for it, but restricted to the following uses:

- lawful shooting of deer;
- shooting of vermin;
- shooting other wildlife in the course of managing an estate;
- humane killing of animals; or
- shooting animals for the protection of other animals or humans;

c) possession of any expanding ammunition or missile for such ammunition designed to be used with a slaughtering instrument, if he is entitled under S 10 of this act to possess a slaughtering instrument and ammunition;

d) sale or transfer of expanding ammunition or the missile for such ammunition to any person authorised to purchase or acquire it; or

e) a firearms dealer or his servant to possess, purchase, acquire, sell or transfer, any expanding ammunition or the missile for such ammunition.

'Expanding ammunition' means any ammunition which incorporates a missile designed to expand on impact.

Firearms Certificates

S 1(1) FIREARMS ACT 1968 AS AMENDED BY THE FIREARMS (AMENDMENT) ACT 1988

Subject to any exemption under the act, it is an offence for a person to **purchase**, or **acquire** (to hire, accept as a gift or borrow), or **possess** (to have ultimate control over it, and not necessarily in physical possession):

1) any AMMUNITION except:
- **cartridges** containing 5 or more shot, none of which exceeds .36" diameter
- ammunition for an **air weapon**
- **blank cartridges** not more than 1" diameter

2) a FIREARM except:
- a **shotgun** (not being an air gun) which is a smooth-bore gun:
  - having a barrel not less than 24" in length nor more than 2" in diameter;
  - having either no magazine or a non-detachable magazine incapable of holding more than 2 cartridges (if adapted to have such a magazine, it must bear an approval mark); and
  - not being a revolver gun

- an **air weapon** (air rifle, air gun, air pistol not being a prohibited weapon and not declared by the Secretary of State to be specially dangerous). It will be specially dangerous if it:
  - (a) is capable of discharging a missile so that it has, on being discharged from the muzzle, kinetic energy in excess, in the case of an air pistol, of 6ft lb or, in the case of an air weapon other than an air pistol, of 12ft lb, or
  - (b) which is disguised as another object

without holding an in-force firearm certificate, or otherwise than as authorised by such a certificate. It is an offence to fail to comply with a condition subject to which the certificate is held.

Imitation firearms

FIREARMS ACT 1982

S 1 of the 1968 Act will apply to an imitation firearm if it has the appearance of a S 1 firearm and it is constructed or adapted as to be readily convertible into such a firearm.

Exemptions

In addition to registered firearms dealers, operators of miniature rifle ranges, and persons in the service of the Crown, who may be authorised to possess, purchase and acquire firearms, shotguns and ammunition, provision is made for the following exemptions:

- **Police permit:** The holder of a **police permit** may possess a firearm and ammunition in accordance with the terms of his permit (S 7(1))

- **Firearms dealers:** If registered, the dealer and his servant may possess, purchase or acquire firearms and ammunition in the course of the business. (Not restricted to the place of business)

- **Auctioneer:** An **auctioneer, carrier** or **warehouseman**, or servant of such may possess or deliver a firearm and ammunition in the course of his business (S 9(1)). The auctioneer may also **sell** if he holds a police permit (S 9(2))

- **Slaughterman:** A **licensed slaughterman** may possess a slaughtering instrument and ammunition in a slaughterhouse or knackers yard where he is employed. (Also applies to the **proprietor**). (S 10(1) & (2))

- **Sport:** A person may **carry for another** a firearm or ammunition, under instruction from, and for the use of, that other person for sporting purposes only (S 11(1))

- **Starter: A starter at an athletic** meeting may possess a firearm for starting races (S 11(2))

- **Persons temporarily in GB:** for not more than 30 days in the preceeding 12 months may possess, purchase or acquire a shot gun certificate (S 14)

- **Ranges:** User of air rifles and miniature rifles at a **miniature rifle range** or shooting gallery may possess such weapons (S 11(4))

- **Clubs:** A **member of a rifle club** or miniature rifle club approved by the Secretary of State (certain types of weapons may be specified in the approval) (S 15 1988 Act)

(CONTINUED ON NEXT PAGE)

Exemptions – continued

- **Private premises:** A person may borrow a **shotgun** from the occupier of **private premises** and use it on those premises in the occupier's presence (S 11(5)). A person over 17 years of age may borrow a **rifle** from the occupier of **private premises** if the occupier holds a certificate and he or his servant is present (S 16 1988 Act)

- **Approved:** A person may use a shotgun at police-approved meetings for **shooting at artificial targets** (S 11(6))

- **Theatres:** Persons taking part in **theatrical performances** or rehearsals, or production of films, may possess firearms and, if approved by the Secretary of State, prohibited weapons (S 12(1) & (2))

- **Signalling equipment: Signalling apparatus** on an aircraft or at an aerodrome, or firearms or ammunition on board a ship, as equipment of such (S 13(1))

- **Northern Ireland:** The holder of a **Northern Ireland firearm certificate** (S 15)

- **Crown service:** Persons in the **service of the Crown** (includes police officers in their capacity as such) (S 54)

- **Proof houses:** Possession of a firearm going to, at, or coming from a specified **proof house** where they are tested (S 58).

- **Visitor's permit:** The holder of a **visitor's firearms or shotgun permit** (S 17 1988 Act)

- **Antique firearms:** See page 87

Shotguns

S 2(1) FIREARMS ACT 1968

IT IS AN OFFENCE FOR A PERSON TO

Means to have ultimate
control over it ◄ **POSSESS**

PURCHASE

Means to hire, accept as
a gift or borrow ◄ **ACQUIRE**

A SHOTGUN

(A smooth-bore gun with a barrel not less than 24" in length, not being an air
gun. But component parts and sound moderators are
not included. It must be a complete shotgun. A certificate would
not be required for a part, eg a barrel)

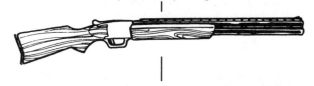

**WITHOUT HOLDING A CERTIFICATE AUTHORISING
HIM TO POSSESS SHOTGUNS**

IT IS AN OFFENCE TO FAIL TO COMPLY WITH A CONDITION SUBJECT TO
WHICH A SHOT GUN CERTIFICATE IS HELD

Antiques

S 58(2) FIREARMS ACT 1968

Nothing in the Act relating to firearms shall apply to an antique rifle or
shotgun which is sold, transferred, purchased, acquired or possessed **as a
curiosity or ornament.**

The term 'antique' is not defined. But for practical purposes, a breach-loading
weapon capable of firing a metallic cartridge would probably not be an antique.

A genuine antique used for target practice would not be possessed as a
curio and, therefore, would require a certificate.

Criminal Use of Firearms

FIREARMS ACT, 1968

The law attempts to prevent the criminal
use and possession of firearms and imitation
firearms in the following provisions,
all of which are arrestable offences:

SECTION 16

Possession of a firearm or ammunition with
intent to endanger life or enable another
to do so (injury not essential)

*THESE ARE
ARRESTABLE
OFFENCES*

SECTION 16A

Possession of a firearm or imitation firearm with intent by means thereof,
or to enable another by means thereof, to cause any person to believe that
unlawful violence will be used against him or another person.

SECTION 17(1)

Making use or attempting to make use of a firearm or imitation firearm
with **intent to resist or prevent arrest** of self or another

SECTION 17(2)

Possession of a firearm or imitation firearm **at time of committing or of
arrest for schedule 1 offence** (see following page)

SECTION 18(1)

Having with him a firearm or
imitation firearm with **intent to
commit an indictable offence**
or to resist or prevent arrest of
self or another

Schedule 1 to the Firearms Act 1968

The offences listed below are those referred to in section 17(2) of the
FIREARMS ACT 1968

1   Offences under S 1 of the Criminal Damage Act 1971

2   Offences under any of the following provisions of the Offences Against
    the Person Act 1861:
    • Ss 20-22 (Inflicting bodily injury; garroting; criminal use of stupefying
      drugs)
    • S 30 (Laying explosive to building, etc)
    • S 32 (Endangering railway passengers by tampering with track)
    • S 38 (Assault with intent to commit felony or resist arrest)
    • S 47 (Criminal assaults)

3   Offences under the Child Abduction Act 1984, Pt 1

4   Theft, robbery, burglary, blackmail and any offence under S 12(1) (taking
    of motor vehicle or other conveyance without the owner's consent) of the
    Theft Act 1968

5   Offences under S 89(1) of the Police Act 1996 or S 41 Police (Scotland) Act
    1967 (assaulting a constable in the execution of his duty)

6   An offence under S 90(1) of the Criminal Justice Act 1991 (assaulting a
    prisoner custody officer)

7   An offence under S 13(1) of the Criminal Justice and Public Order Act
    1994 (assaulting a secure training centre custody officer)

8   Offences under any of the following provisions of the Sexual Offences
    Act 2003:
    • S 1 (rape)
    • S 2 (assault by penetration)
    • S 4 (sexual activity without consent, involving penetration)
    • S 5 (rape of child under 13)
    • S 6 (Assault of child under 13 by penetration)
    • S 8 (causing or inciting child under 13 to engage in sexual activity
      involving penetration), and
    • S 30 & S 31 (sexual activity with a person with a mental disorder
      impeding choice, involving penetration)

9   Aiding and abetting the commission of any offence specified in the
    foregoing sections, and attempts to commit them

Firearms Dealers

S 3(1) FIREARMS ACT 1968

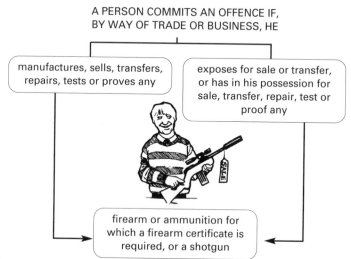

A PERSON COMMITS AN OFFENCE IF,
BY WAY OF TRADE OR BUSINESS, HE

manufactures, sells, transfers, repairs, tests or proves any

exposes for sale or transfer, or has in his possession for sale, transfer, repair, test or proof any

firearm or ammunition for which a firearm certificate is required, or a shotgun

Does not include air weapons, cartridges containing 5 or more shot, none of which exceeds .36" dia. But does include ammunition capable of being fired from a shotgun or smooth-bore gun for which a firearms certificate is required
(S 5 FIREARMS (AMENDMENT) ACT 1988)

unless he is registered as a firearms dealer

He must keep a register in which the prescribed particulars are recorded within 24 hours of the transaction. Inspection of the register must be allowed by a police officer authorised in writing by the chief constable

The main **exemptions** cover auctioneers, miniature rifle ranges and proof houses.

It is an **offence** for a person to sell or transfer to another person in the UK, or to repair, test or prove a firearm or ammunition to which S 1 applies unless that other person holds a certificate authorising his possession, or is exempt.

It is an **offence** for a pawnbroker to accept a S 1 firearm or ammunition, or a shotgun, as pawn.

Possession of Firearms

FIREARMS ACT 1968

A person commits an offence if, without lawful authority or reasonable excuse (the proof whereof lies on him), he has with him in a **public place**:

- a loaded shotgun
- an air weapon, whether loaded or not
- any other firearm, whether loaded or not, together with ammunition suitable for use in that firearm; or
- an imitation firearm (S 19)

'Public place' includes any highway and any other premises or place to which at the material time the public have, or are permitted to have, access, whether on payment or otherwise.

A person commits an offence if, while he has a firearm or imitation firearm with him, he enters or is in any **building** or part of a building as a **trespasser** and without reasonable excuse (the proof whereof lies on him) (S 20(1)). For **'imitation firearm'** see beginning of this chapter.

Trespassing

A person commits an offence if, while he has a firearm or imitation firearm with him, he enters or is on any **land** as a **trespasser** and without reasonable excuse (the proof whereof lies on him) (S 20(2)). **'Land'** includes land covered with water.

A person who has been sentenced to serve 3 years or more **imprisonment** or detention, shall not have a firearm or ammunition in his possession **at any time.** A person who has been sentenced to borstal training, to corrective training, or to imprisonment for 3 months or more but less than 3 years, shall not have a firearm or ammunition in his possession for **5 years** from the date of his release. A child or young person convicted of a serious crime and who has been released on licence; or a person who is bound over to keep the peace or be of good behaviour, or is subject to a probation order, a condition of which in any of those cases prohibits him from possessing a firearm, shall not possess a firearm for the duration of the licence or is so subject (S 21).

Miscellaneous Offences

DRUNKENNESS
S 12 LICENSING ACT 1872

It is an offence to be drunk when in possession of any **loaded** firearm, and such a person may be apprehended. Includes air guns. **Note:** there is no mention of public place, highway, etc.

HIGHWAYS
S 161(2) HIGHWAYS ACT 1980
S 28 TOWN POLICE CLAUSES ACT 1847 (IF ADOPTED IN THAT LOCALITY)

It is an offence, without lawful authority or excuse, to discharge any firearm within 50 feet of the centre of a highway if a user of the highway is injured, interrupted or endangered.

A constable may arrest without warrant any person who, within his view, wantonly discharges any firearm in any street to the obstruction, annoyance or danger of the residents or passengers.

SHORTENING BARRELS, ETC
S 4(1) FIREARMS ACT 1968

It is an offence to shorten the barrel of a shotgun to a length less than 24" (except registered dealers, who may shorten it for the purpose of replacing a defective part, to produce a barrel of not less than 24"). It is also an offence to possess, purchase or acquire such a weapon. S 6 of the Firearms (Amendment) Act 1988 creates an offence (unless a dealer) to shorten to less than 24" the barrel of a smooth-bore gun for which a firearm certificate is required (other than one with bore exceeding 2").

CONVERTING
S 4(3) FIREARMS ACT 1968

It is an offence (other than as a registered dealer) to convert into a firearm anything which, though having the appearance of being a firearm, is so constructed as to be incapable of discharging any missile through its barrel, S 4(3). It is also an offence to possess, purchase or acquire such a weapon, S 4(4)

SUPPLYING TO DRUNK OR UNSOUND PERSON
S 25 FIREARMS ACT 1968

It is an offence to sell or transfer any firearm or ammunition to, or repair, prove or test any firearm or ammunition for another person whom he knows or has reasonable cause for believing to be drunk or of unsound mind.

Firearms – Ages

FIREARMS ACT 1968

	Under 17 but over 14	**Under 15**	**Under 14**
Firearms and ammunition	• May not purchase or hire • Offence to sell or let on hire to, S 22(1), S 24(1) • May accept as a gift or loan if both parties have firearms certificates		• May not possess except as gun bearer, member of rifle club or miniature rifle range or shooting gallery, S 22(2) • Offence to make a gift to, lend to, or part with possession to, S 24(4)
Shotguns	• May not purchase or hire • Offence to sell or let on hire to, S 22(1)	• May not have with him an assembled shotgun except: i) under supervision of a person over 21, or ii) when so covered with a securely fastened gun cover that it cannot be fired, S 22(3) • offence to make a gift to, S 24(3)	
Air weapons	• May not have with him an air weapon or ammunition unless under the supervision of a person over 21; but if on premises may not fire any missile beyond the premises • If over 14 may have with him on private premises with the consent of the occupier but may not fire any missiles beyond the premises • May have with him as a member of an approved rifle club • May use at a shooting gallery if an air rifle or miniature rifle not over .23" calibre • It is an offence to make a gift of an air weapon or ammunition to a person under 17 • It is an offence, except as mentioned above, to part with possession of an air weapon or ammunition to a person under 17		May not have with him an air weapon or ammunition unless under the supervision of a person over 21; but if on premises may not fire any missile beyond the premises

> **IT IS AN OFFENCE TO SELL OR LET ON HIRE ANY FIREARM OR AMMUNITION TO A PERSON UNDER THE AGE OF 17**

Police Powers

FIREARMS ACT **1968**

Stop and Search S 47

Where a constable has reasonable cause to suspect a person:

a) of having a firearm, with or without ammunition, with him in a public place or

b) to be committing or about to commit, elsewhere than in a public place, an offence of carrying firearms with criminal intent (S 18(1)) or trespassing with a firearm (S 20)

he may search that person and may detain him for the purpose of doing so. He may search any vehicle if he suspects it contains a firearm or ammunition and may require it to stop for that purpose. He may require the person to hand over the firearm and any ammunition for examination. It is an offence to fail to hand it over. The constable may enter any place for the purpose of exercising these powers.

Production of Certificate S 48(1)

A constable may demand from any person whom he believes to be in possession of a firearm or ammunition for which a certificate is required, or of a shotgun, the production of his firearm certificate or, as the case may be, his shotgun certificate.

Where appropriate the constable may demand the corresponding document issued by another European state (S 48(1A))

If he fails to produce the certificate or to permit the constable to read it, or to show that he is exempt from the requirement to hold one, the constable may seize and detain the firearm, ammunition or shotgun, and demand the person to declare to him immediately his name and address.

It is an offence for a person to fail to produce a certificate; or refuse to declare, or to fail to give, his true name and address.

Arrest

Where the person fails to satisfy the constable as to his identity, consider arrest under S 25 of the Police and Criminal Evidence Act 1984 (see later).

Chapter 4

Licensing

At the time of going to press, the Licensing Act 2003 had been made but very few provisions had been brought into force. However, the reader may appreciate advance notice of the following changes to licensing laws which may be brought into force in the near future:

1. All existing licensing legislation is to be replaced.

2. There is to be a single licensing system for all premises (including registered clubs).

3. Police powers will be extended to enter registered clubs where a drug offence is suspected, or to prevent a breach of the peace.

4. Licensing hours will be locally fixed.

Betting

BETTING, GAMING AND LOTTERIES ACT 1963

Although 'betting' is not defined in the statutes it is commonly taken to mean:

The staking of money or other value on the event of a doubtful issue

Betting is not in itself unlawful but becomes so in any one of four ways:

Unauthorised business S 2

A bookmaker is a person who carries on a business of betting and he must hold a bookmaker's permit.

The permit must be produced at the request of a constable.

A person acting as a servant or agent of a bookmaker must:
- be over 21
- be authorised in writing by the bookmaker

unless he acts only on the bookmaker's premises.

The bookmaker must keep a register of persons authorised to act as his servant or agent.

With young persons S 21

It is an offence to have a betting transaction with; to employ to effect betting transactions; or to receive or negotiate a bet through – a person under the age of 18.

Unauthorised premises S 1

Otherwise than on horse racecourses and dog tracks, premises may not be used for betting transactions.
(See betting offices on following page)

But premises may be used if all persons involved in the transaction either reside or work there.

An offence is committed by any person who resorts to unauthorised premises for the purpose of betting (proof that he was on the premises will be sufficient until he proves otherwise).

But **'pool betting transactions'** will be allowed if consisting of the delivery of completed coupons or other entry forms promoted by a registered pool promoter, and associated stake money for a qualifying competition involving forecasts for at least four association football games (S 1(4A)).

In a street or public place S 8

It is an offence to frequent or loiter in a street or public place for betting except on a racecourse.

Betting Offices

S 10 & SCHED 4 BETTING, GAMING AND LOTTERIES ACT 1963, LICENSED BETTING OFFICE REGULATIONS 1986

Licensed betting offices must be managed in accordance with the following rules:

Under 18s Not permitted. A notice to this effect must be displayed.

Licence The betting office licence must be displayed on the premises.

Hours Must remain closed Good Friday, Christmas Day, and daily between 6.30pm and 7am (10pm to 7am between April and August inclusive).

Access Except for the licensee and his servant, no access must be available to premises used for other purposes.

Refreshments Refreshments may be provided except intoxicating liquor.

Notice A notice must be displayed inside the premises but not capable of being read from outside setting out the terms of betting (including deductions from winnings, maximum amount of bets and the procedure for resolving disputes).

Apparatus Sound or visual apparatus may only provide information about betting on sporting events and incidental advertisements. Images received must be intended for the general public or other licensees generally. If video recordings are used, they must be available to other licensees generally.

Advertisements See later.

Entertainment No music, dancing or other entertainment may be provided or allowed except as authorised above. The premises shall not be used for any purpose other than betting transactions.

Gaming Machines may be used but only if for cash prizes and no more than two machines.

Publications may be sold if racing periodicals or specialist betting publications.

Lottery Tickets may be sold if not a private lottery or other prohibited lottery.

Enforcement

BETTING, GAMING AND LOTTERIES ACT 1963

Licensee, etc S 10(2)

The licensee, his servant or agent,
may refuse to admit to, or may expel
from premises any person who is:

- drunk
- violent
- quarrelsome
- disorderly
- likely to subject the licensee to a penalty

Any person who fails to leave when requested commits an offence.

Constable S 10(3)

A constable may, at the request of the licensee,
his servant or agent, help to expel from the
premises any person whom the constable has
reasonable cause to suspect to be liable to be
expelled, and such force as may be required
may be used for that purpose.

Power of Entry S 10(4)

A constable may enter a licensed
betting office for the purpose of
ascertaining whether provisions are
being complied with, and any
person who obstructs the constable
commits an offence.

Advertisements and Notices

S 10(5) BETTING, GAMING AND LOTTERIES ACT 1963,
LICENSED BETTING OFFICE REGULATIONS 1986

Betting office licence to be displayed on the premises.

Under 18s not admitted notice(s) must be displayed (a) near the entrance, and (b) where practicable, in a window so it can be read from the outside.

Terms of betting

A conspicuous notice must be displayed inside the premises, but not so that it can be read from the outside, setting out the terms on which persons are invited to bet on the premises including the amount of deductions made from winnings, the maximum limit on the amount of winnings and the procedure for the resolution of disputed bets.

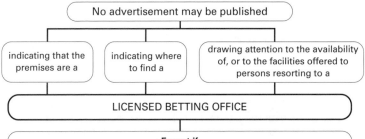

No advertisement may be published

| indicating that the premises are a | indicating where to find a | drawing attention to the availability of, or to the facilities offered to persons resorting to a |

LICENSED BETTING OFFICE

Except if

(a) it is published inside but not outside the licensed betting office; or
(b) it is published outside the office:
  (i) from a place inside the office; or
  (ii) in premises giving access to the office;

and is restricted to text as follows:

- the expression "Licensed Betting Office" or similar, not exceeding 3 words and included in the name of the licensee;
- where premises give access to a betting office, an indication as to where the office may be found;
- the hours of opening;
- facilities available to persons resorting to the premises;
- an indication of the range of bets available; and
- betting events and odds available.

Gaming

S 52(1) GAMING ACT 1968

MEANS THE PLAYING OF A **GAME OF CHANCE** FOR WINNINGS IN MONEY OR MONEY'S WORTH, WHETHER ANY PERSON PLAYING THE GAME IS AT RISK OF LOSING ANY MONEY OR MONEY'S WORTH OR NOT

GAME OF CHANCE
DOES NOT INCLUDE ANY ATHLETIC GAME OR SPORT BUT, WITH THAT EXCEPTION, INCLUDES A GAME OF CHANCE AND SKILL COMBINED AND A PRETENDED GAME OF CHANCE OR OF CHANCE AND SKILL COMBINED

Bingo, card games and dominoes are all gaming because they all involve an element of chance

Any money staked would be gaming

Darts would not be gaming because it is pure skill

Any money staked would be betting

'Lotteries' not constituting 'Gaming'. Where the playing of a game of chance constitutes a 'small lottery incidental to certain entertainments' (S 3), a 'private lottery' (S 4), a 'societies' lottery' (S 5) or a 'local lottery' (S 6), and the winner is ascertained by reference to not more than 3 determining factors, the playing of the game will not constitute 'gaming' (S 52(3)).

The Gaming Act 1968 controls gaming
The four parts into which the Act is divided are as follows:

Part 1   Gaming other than on premises licensed or registered under the Act

Part 2   Gaming on premises which have been licensed or registered under this Act

Part 3   Gaming machines

Part 4   Gaming at entertainment not held for private gain

These are now discussed in turn on the following pages.

Gaming Elsewhere than on Premises Licensed or Registered Under the Act

GAMING ACT **1968**

This part of the Act does not apply to gaming machines, entertainment not for private gain, or amusements with prizes.

Certain restrictions are imposed on the gaming which is allowed:

THE NATURE OF THE GAME S 2

This restriction does not apply to domestic occasions in a private dwelling, in a hostel, hall of residence or similar place not used as a business, and the players are all inmates or residents

The game shall not involve playing or staking against a bank, whether or not a player holds the bank

The chances must be equally favourable to all players

Where the players are playing against some other person, the chances must not be more favourable to the other person than the players

CHARGES FOR TAKING PART S 3

Other than any stakes hazarded, no charge, in money or money's worth, may be made to take part (this would include an admission charge) but this restriction would not apply to member's clubs

LEVY ON STAKES OR WINNINGS S 4

A levy may not be charged on any of the stakes or winnings, whether by direct payment, deduction, exchange of tokens at a lower rate than of issue, or any other means

Public places S 5
No person may take part in gaming in a street or any place to which the public have access on payment or otherwise.

Street includes any bridge, road, lane, footway, etc, which is open to the public, and the doorways and entrances of premises abutting upon, and any ground adjoining and open to, a street.

Licensed premises S 6
Dominoes and cribbage, and any other game authorised by the licensing justices may be played on premises for which a justices' on-licence is in force (other than a restaurant or guest house licence).

Persons Under 18
No person under the age of 18 years may take part in gaming on premises (S 7).

Gaming on Premises Which Have Been Licensed or Registered Under This Act

This part does not apply to gaming by way of gaming machines
S 12 GAMING ACT 1968

The following restrictions apply to gaming on premises which are either licensed under the Act, or which consist of a club or miners' welfare institute registered under the Act.

Who may take part?

- Only persons who are present on the premises at the time gaming takes place (applies to both Licensed or Registered clubs)
- They must be members of the club in question, or bona fide guests of such a member (applies to both Licensed or Registered clubs)
- Neither the licence holder nor any other person acting on his behalf may take part in the gaming except holding the bank (Licensed clubs only)
- At least 24 hours (for a Licensed club, 48 hours in the case of a Registered club) must have elapsed since application being made for membership and taking part in the gaming
- No person under 18 years shall be present whilst gaming is taking place (except on premises restricted to the playing of bingo) (S 17)

Games which may be played

In licensed clubs, in addition to any game which does not contravene the requirements of 'nature of the game' (see previous page), the following games may be played if they comply with the provisions of the Gaming Clubs (Banker's Games) Regs. 1994:

roulette, dice, baccarat (whether it is baccarat banque, chemin de fer, punto banco, punto 2000 or some other version), the big six, sic bo, three card poker, blackjack, casino stud poker and super pan 9.

In registered clubs, in addition to any game which does not contravene the requirements of 'nature of the game' (see previous page), pontoon and chemin de fer may be played

Charges for taking part

Charges to take part are generally prohibited by S 3 but may be made in the following circumstances:

- **Licensed Clubs** A fixed amount of money may be charged in respect of one or more facilities for 1 person. But if it is a recurring charge, it may not be incurred again by the same person within 1 hour of the last charge (except a series of games of chemin de fer).
- **Registered Clubs** One or more charges may be made in respect of a person if the amount of that charge, or charges in aggregate, does not exceed £2 for that person for that day.

Gaming on Sundays

In licensed premises gaming may not take place between 4am and 2pm on Sundays.

A constable may at any reasonable time enter any premises LICENSED under the Act and may inspect the premises, machines or other equipment, and any book or other document on the premises, for the purpose of ascertaining whether any contravention has been committed (S 43).

Bingo Clubs

S 20 GAMING ACT 1968

Application of section

This section applies to any club licensed under this Act where restrictions have been imposed which limit the gaming which may take place to bingo.

Simultaneous games of bingo

Where a game of bingo is played simultaneously on different bingo club premises, and:

a) all the players take part at the same time and all are present at that time on one or other of those premises;

b) the draw takes place on one or other of those premises while the game is being played; and

c) any claim by a player to have won is indicated to all the players before the next number is called,

then, if the following conditions are fulfilled,

a) the aggregate amount paid as winnings for that game does not exceed the aggregate amount staked by the players in that game, and

b) the aggregate amount paid as winnings for that game, together with the aggregate amount paid as winnings for all games in the same week (7 days beginning Monday) played on any of those premises does not exceed £2,000,000

the requirement for the player to be on the premises when the gaming takes place (S 12) shall have effect as if those different premises were the same premises.

And the requirement to:
• be a member of the club or bona fide guest; and
• the requirement for 24 hours to have elapsed since making the application for membership, and taking part in gaming,

will only apply to persons present on the individual premises.

Persons under 18

Where the gaming takes place on bingo club premises persons under 18 will be allowed on the premises while gaming takes place provided they do not take part in the gaming.

Maximum aggregate weekly winnings

Without prejudice to the above, the aggregate amount paid as winnings in respect of all games of bingo in any one week (7 days beginning Monday) on any bingo premises shall not exceed the aggregate amount of the players' stakes by more than £20,000.

Bingo with prizes

See following page.

Gaming With Prizes

S 21 GAMING ACT 1968

Application of this section

This provision deals with 'gaming' to which this part of the Act applies and in respect of which:

a) the amount paid for a chance to win a prize does not exceed 50p;

b) the aggregate amount of the sale of chances in any 1 game does not exceed £500, and the sale of chances and the declaration of results take place on the same day and time as when the game is played, and on the same premises;

c) any money prize does not exceed £25;

d) the winning of a prize, or the purchase of a chance to win, does not entitle (whether subject to a further payment or not) any person to any further opportunity to take part in any other gaming or lottery; and

e) the aggregate amount or value of prizes on any one game does not exceed £500.

If the above conditions are fulfilled, the following 'relaxations' will apply:

Type of game

If the gaming takes place on licensed premises, the restrictions placed on which type of game may be played (see previous page) will not apply.

Where a condition of a licence for any premises includes a restriction as to the types of games which may be played, those restrictions will not apply.

Charges for taking part

If the gaming takes place on licensed premises, the restrictions on making charges for taking part will not apply (see previous page).

Bingo Clubs

Where the gaming takes place on bingo club premises persons under 18 will be allowed on the premises while gaming takes place provided they do not take part in the gaming.

Where a game of bingo is played for prizes on bingo club premises, the prizes won will be disregarded for the purposes of calculating the aggregate maximum amount paid to players as winnings in any one week.

Gaming Machines on Premises Licensed or Registered Under This Act

GAMING ACT 1968

For practical purposes, machines are of two types:

JACKPOT MACHINES S 31
- May only be used on premises which are either licensed or registered under the Act for the purpose of gaming or gaming machines (S 35)
- There is a limit to the charge for playing a single game on the machines (currently 50p)
- There is a maximum limit on the winnings which may be paid out on a single game (which must be by way of coins):
  1) for registered premises (club or miners' welfare), £250;
  2) for bingo clubs, £500; and
  3) for any other premises which are licensed, £2,000
  (GAMING MACHINES (MAXIMUM PRIZES) REGS. 1998, S I 1998/2150 & 2001/3970)
- Where a percentage of the aggregate value of charges for play is prescribed for any machine on licensed premises, it must not pay out less than that percentage
- A statement must be displayed on the machine giving:
  1) the value of prizes which can be won by playing a single game;
  2) any special circumstances in which that prize cannot be won; and
  3) the percentage of the aggregate value of charges for play paid out as winnings
- The machines may not be used on the premises on any occasion when the public are admitted whether on payment or otherwise
- The maximum number of machines which may be available is:
  a) registered club or miners' welfare, three
  b) bingo clubs, four; and
  c) any other licensed premises, ten

AMUSEMENT MACHINES S 34
- May only be used on premises for which a permit has been granted; on premises used as a pleasure fair for which a permit has been granted; or at a travelling showmen's pleasure fair
- The charge for playing the machine once shall be by coins or tokens to a maximum value of 30p

CONTINUED ON NEXT PAGE

Gaming Machines - continued

- Prizes are restricted to one of the following:
  1) Money prize not exceeding £5 or tokens exchangeable for such amount;
  2) Non-money prize not exceeding £8 or tokens exchangeable for such non-money prize.
  3) A mixture of money and non-money prizes which do not exceed the above amounts;
  4) Tokens which can be either used to play further games or be exchanged as above
- In the case of a Betting Office, the maximum charge for playing the machine is 30p and the prize must be monetary, not exceeding £25, delivered by the machine.

USE AT NON-COMMERCIAL ENTERTAINMENTS S 33

Jackpot machines, amusement with prizes machines, or any other type of machine may be used as an incident to non-commercial entertainment if not on premises licensed or registered under the Act, without further authority and without limits on numbers or prizes. This would apply to bazaars, sales of work, fêtes, dinners, dances, sporting or athletic events, etc, whether limited to one day or extended over two or more days. In these cases the whole of the proceeds after deducting expenses must be devoted to other than private gain. The opportunity to win prizes shall not be the only, or only substantial, inducement to attend.

Gaming – Advertisements

S 42 GAMING ACT 1968 (AS AMENDED)

ADVERTISEMENTS

➤ Includes every form of advertising whether in publications, notices or circulars, photographs, film, sound broadcast, television or other means of sound broadcast.

are not allowed if they

(a) inform the public that premises in Great Britain are for gaming,

(b) invite the public to take part in gaming as such,

(c) invite the public to subscribe to gaming in Great Britain or elsewhere,

EXCEPT

- gaming incidental to S 33 machines at non-commercial entertainment;
- gaming not held for private gain under S 41;
- gaming with amusement machines under a S 34 permit

- amusements with prizes which constitute a lottery or gaming or both, with a permit under S 16 Lotteries and Amusements Act 1976;
- gaming at a travelling showman's pleasure fair;
- gaming in the form of playing bingo

But advertising is allowed if:

(a) a sign inside or outside of licensed premises indicating that gambling takes place, or

(b) a notice required by the Act, or

(c) a publication in a newspaper stating that a gaming licence has been granted (but must be within 14 days of the grant), or

(d) an advertisement in a publication (not published wholly or mainly for the purpose of promoting gaming premises), relating to licensed premises other than bingo clubs, and which contains no more than the name, logo, address, telephone, fax, ownership and facilities provided, or

(e) an advertisement published in a newspaper which circulates wholly or mainly outside GB.

Gaming at Non-commercial Entertainment

S 41 GAMING ACT 1968

Gaming which:

- is played at entertainment promoted otherwise than for private gain;
- is not gaming to which part 2 (gaming on premises licensed or registered under this Act) or part 3 (gaming machines) of the Act applies; and
- does not constitute 'amusements with prizes under S 15 or S 16 of the Lotteries and Amusements Act 1976 (see later)

must comply with the provisions listed below.

Provisions

1. **Nature of the game** It must not involve playing against a bank, whether held by one of the players or not; and chances must be equally favourable to all the players.
2. **Payment to take part** In respect of all games, not more than one payment (whether by entrance fee, stake or otherwise) shall be made by each player, and this shall not exceed £4.
3. **Total value of prizes** In respect of all games, the total value of prizes shall not exceed £400.
4. **Proceeds** The whole of the proceeds, less expenses and any cost of providing prizes, shall be applied for purposes other than private gain.
5. **Expenses** shall not exceed a reasonable cost of facilities provided.
6. **Multiple entertainments** Where 2 or more entertainments are provided by the same person on the same premises on the same day, the above provisions will apply to those entertainments collectively as if they were one.
7. **Series of entertainments** Where a series of entertainments is held otherwise than as in paragraph 6, the above provisions will have effect separately in relation to each one; and the total value of prizes is increased to £700 for the final game in a series, if the player qualified to take part by playing in another entertainment held the day before.

Offences

If gaming takes place in contravention of these provisions, every person concerned in the **organisation or management** of the gaming shall be guilty of an offence. A person who takes part in **procuring the assembly** of the players will have been involved in the organisation of the gaming.

Where gaming takes place on any **premises, vessel or vehicle** in contravention of these provisions, any person who knew or had reasonable cause to suspect that they would be used in contravention of the provisions and **allowed them to be used** for gaming, or **let, let on hire or made them available** for gaming, will be guilty of an offence.

Lotteries

S 1 LOTTERIES AND AMUSEMENTS ACT 1976
READERS DIGEST ASS V WILLIAMS (1976) 3 ALL ER 737

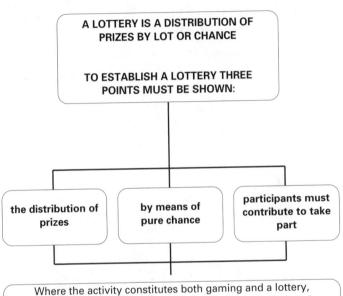

A LOTTERY IS A DISTRIBUTION OF PRIZES BY LOT OR CHANCE

TO ESTABLISH A LOTTERY THREE POINTS MUST BE SHOWN:

- **the distribution of prizes**
- **by means of pure chance**
- **participants must contribute to take part**

Where the activity constitutes both gaming and a lottery, it shall not be gaming (and therefore not subject to the gaming restrictions) if it is one of the five legal types (small lotteries incidental to certain entertainments, private lotteries, societies lotteries, local lotteries or the national lottery) and the winner is ascertained by reference to not more than three determining factors, eg bingo would be gaming because more than three numbers are called out

S 52(3) GAMING ACT 1968

Lotteries which do not constitute gaming are illegal unless they are one of the following types:

- **Small**
- **Private**
- **Societies**
- **Local**

These will be discussed in further depth on the following pages

Small Lotteries Incidental to Exempt Entertainments

S 3 LOTTERIES & AMUSEMENTS ACT 1976

Exempt Entertainment

Means a bazaar, sale of work, fête, dinner, dance, sporting or athletic event, or other entertainment of similar character, whether for one day or for two or more days.

A lottery promoted as an incident of exempt entertainment will not be unlawful if the conditions below are complied with. If any one of them is contravened, any person concerned in its promotion or conduct will be guilty of an offence.

The conditions are:

• All proceeds less expenses must be devoted to other than private gain
• Prizes must not be money
• Sale of tickets etc, and declaration or result must take place at the entertainment
• The lottery shall not be the only or substantial inducement to attend

Private Lotteries

S 4 LOTTERIES AND AMUSEMENTS ACTS 1976

*A **private lottery** means one which is promoted:

- for members of one society established and conducted for purposes other than betting, gaming and lotteries;
- for persons who all work on the same premises; or
- for persons who all reside on the same premises,

and the following conditions are met:

- the lottery must be promoted by a person for whom it is promoted and, in the case of a society, is authorised in writing by the governing body; and
- the sale of tickets or chances in the lottery is confined to persons for whom it is promoted and, in the case of a society, to any other person on the society's premises.

'Society' includes any club, institution, organisation or association of persons by whatever name called and any separate branch or section of such a club, etc.

Each local or affiliated branch of a society shall be regarded as a separate and distinct society.

*A **private lottery is not unlawful** but the following conditions must be observed:

a) the whole proceeds, less expenses for printing and stationery shall be devoted to the provision of prizes, or, in the case of a society, devoted either to the provision of prizes, or the purposes of the society, or part prizes and part purposes of the society;

b) no written notice or advertisement of the lottery shall be exhibited, published or distributed other than a notice of it exhibited on the premises of the society, or where they work or reside, or an announcement or advertisement of it on the ticket, if any;

c) the price of every ticket or chance shall be the same and the price of a ticket shall be stated on the ticket;

d) every ticket must show the name and address of each of the promoters; a statement of the persons to whom the sale of tickets is restricted; and a statement that no prize will be delivered to persons other than the one to whom the winning ticket is sold;

e) no ticket or chance shall be issued other than by sale and upon receipt of its full price which is non-returnable; and

f) no tickets shall be sent through the post.

Offences

If any of the above conditions is contravened, each of the promoters of the lottery, and any other person breaking a condition, shall be guilty of an offence.

Societies' and Local Lotteries

LOTTERIES & AMUSEMENTS ACT 1976 AND
LOTTERIES REGULATIONS 1993

SOCIETIES' LOTTERIES S 5

Promoted by a society established for: charitable purposes, athletic sports or games or culture, other purposes which are not for private gain or commercial

A society's lottery is not unlawful if the following conditions are met:
- Promoted in GB
- Society is registered under the Act and the name of the registration authority must appear on the ticket
- Scheme approved by the society
- Total value of tickets, etc sold is £10,000 or less, otherwise scheme to be registered with the Board before sale of tickets
- All proceeds less expenses to be applied to purposes of the society

LOCAL LOTTERIES S 6

These are lotteries promoted by the local authority

A local lottery is not unlawful if the following conditions are met:
- Promoted in GB
- Promoted in accordance with a scheme approved by the local authority
- Scheme registered with the Board before sale of tickets
- Publicity must be given to the objects of the lottery (S 7)
- All money accruing must be applied to the objects of the lottery (S 8)
- Tickets must specify the name of the promoting authority, the date of the lottery, and the fact that it has been registered with the Board

AND

- No more than 55% of proceeds to be spent on prizes (S 11)
- No ticket to exceed £2 (S 11)
- Full price must be paid for tickets and no refunds (S 11)
- No payment other than the price of a ticket or chance shall be required to take part
- Tickets, etc may not be sold by or to persons under 16 or by machine (Regs 3&5)
- Tickets not to be sold in a street except from a kiosk or shop front (Reg 4)
- Tickets must bear name and address of promoter (in the case of societies), the date of the lottery and the name of the society (S 11)
- The price of every ticket shall be the same and shall be stated on the ticket (S 11)
- The promoter of the lottery must be authorised in writing by the governing body (in the case of societies)
- No prize to exceed £25,000 or 10% of value of tickets sold, whichever is greater
- Total value of tickets sold not to exceed £2,000,000
- Total value of tickets sold in all lotteries in 1 year not to exceed £10,000,000

'Society' – see previous page
'Board' – the Gaming Board of Great Britain

Amusements with Prizes

S 15 & S 16 LOTTERIES AND AMUSEMENTS ACT 1976

An **'amusement with prizes'** may include activities which constitute 'gaming'.

There are basically two types, those which are provided at **'exempt entertainments'**, and those provided at certain **commercial entertainments**. In both cases, the conditions to which they are subject apply where amusement is provided which constitutes a lottery or gaming or both, but does not constitute:

• Gaming to which Part 2 of the Gaming Act 1968 applies; or

• Gaming by means of a machine to which Part 3 of that Act applies.

'Exempt entertainment' means a bazaar, sale of work, fete, dinner, dance, sporting or athletic event or other entertainment of a similar character, whether limited to one day or extending over two or more days.

Both types are subject to different conditions which are detailed below.

Exempt Entertainments (S 15)

Where such amusement constitutes a lottery, the 'lottery offences' under S 2 (see following page) do not apply. Whether it is a lottery or not, the below conditions must be observed:

a) the whole proceeds, less expenses, shall go to other than private gain; and

b) the facilities for winning prizes must not be the only, or the only substantial, inducement to attend.

Commercial Entertainments (S 16)

This section applies where the amusements are provided:

a) on premises for which a permit for the provision of commercial amusements with prizes has been granted under this Act;

b) on premises used mainly for amusements by way of machines and a permit has been granted under S 34 of the Gaming Act 1968 for the provision of machines for commercial purposes; or

c) at a pleasure fair consisting of amusements provided by travelling showmen, which is held on any day of the year on premises not previously used in that year on more than 27 days for such a purpose.

In these circumstances the 'lottery offences' under S 2 (see following page) do not apply. However, the following conditions must be observed:

a) the amount paid for any 1 chance to win must not exceed 50p;

b) the aggregate amount taken by the sale of chances for any 1 determination shall not exceed £90;

c) the sale of the chances and declaration of the result take place on the same day and on the same premises during the time when the amusement is provided;

d) no money prize may exceed £25;

e) the winning of a prize may not entitle the person, whether or not further payments are made by him, to any further opportunity to take part in any amusement with prizes or in any gaming or lottery; and

f) in the case of a pleasure fair, the opportunity to win prizes is not the only, or the only substantial, inducement to attend the fair.

Lottery Offences

S 2 LOTTERIES AND AMUSEMENTS ACT 1976

Where a lottery does not come within the aforementioned 'legalised' lotteries, every person who, in connection with any lottery promoted in GB or elsewhere, is involved in any of the following activities, commits an offence.

a) **Printing** Prints any tickets;

b) **Sale or distribution** Sells or distributes, or offers or advertises for sale or distribution, or has in his possession for the purpose of sale or distribution, any tickets or chances;

c) **Inducements** Prints, publishes or distributes or has in his possession for the purpose of publication or distribution, any advertisement, any list of prize winners or winning tickets, or any such matter relating to the lottery, as is calculated to act as an inducement to participate;

d) **Importation** Brings, or invites any person to send, into GB any ticket or advertisement from a place outside the British Islands and member states, for the purpose of sale or distribution;

e) **Exportation** Sends or attempts to send out of GB to a place outside the British Islands and member states, any money or valuable thing received in respect of the sale or distribution of any ticket or chance, or any document recording the sale or distribution or identity of the holder of a ticket or chance;

f) **Premises** Uses any premises, or knowingly causes or permits the use of premises for promoting or conducting the lottery; or

g) **Procuring others** Causes, procures or attempts to procure any person to do any of the above.

Licensing Act 2003

Commencement

At the time of going to press, commencement orders have brought into force the majority of provisions of the Act. However, these relate largely to enabling provisions, methods and forms of application for licences, and conditions which may be attached. The main parts of interest to the police, eg offences, powers of entry, etc. have not yet been brought into force. Nevertheless, the reader might appreciate a general overview of the purpose of the Act.

Licences and activities

The Act provides a unified system for the regulation of the sale and supply of alcohol, the provision of regulated entertainment and the provision of late night refreshment (referred to collectively as "the licensable activities"). The system of licensing is achieved through the provision of personal licences, premises licences, club premises certificates and temporary event notices. These are granted by the licensing authority – normally the local authority. **Personal licences** authorise individuals to sell or supply alcohol for consumption on or off premises for which a **premises licence** is in force. The premises licence details the operating conditions. **Club premises certificates** authorise qualifying clubs to use the premises for qualifying activities. In addition, the Act provides for **temporary event notices** to cater for occasional, temporary events, replacing the old system of "occasional permissions" and "occasional licences". A summary of the licence must be displayed prominently on the premises.

Licensing hours

In contrast to the existing law, the Act does not prescribe the days or the opening hours during which alcohol may be sold or supplied. Instead, the applicant will be able to choose the days and times during which they wish to be authorised to carry on activities. The licence will be granted on those terms, subject to representations being made, in which case the licence may be either rejected or varied.

Repeals

The Act repeals and replaces the existing licensing provisions relating to alcohol sales and supplies, public entertainment and late night refreshment. This includes the whole of the Licensing Act 1964.

(CONTINUED ON NEXT PAGE)

Licensing Act 2003 – continued

Offences

Numerous offences are created by the Act. These include-

1. Carrying on unauthorised licensable activities (S 136);
2. Exposing or keeping alcohol for unauthorised sale (S 137 &138);
3. Allowing disorderly conduct on licensed premises (S 140);
4. Sale of alcohol to, or obtaining for, a person who is drunk (S 141 & 142);
5. Being drunk or disorderly and failing to leave, or attempting to enter, premises (S 143);
6. Keeping smuggled goods on premises (S 144);
7. Admitting an unaccompanied child under 16 onto premises (S 145);
8. Sale of alcohol to, consumption by, provision to, or sale by, a child (S 146–153).

Police Powers

A constable may enter and search **any premises** in respect of which he has reason to believe that an **offence under this Act** has been, is being or is about to be committed. Reasonable force may be used if necessary (S 180). There is also an additional power to enter **club** premises where an offence of supplying a controlled drug is suspected, or if there is likely to be a breach of the peace there (S 97).

Justices' Licences

Ss 160 AND 167 LICENSING ACT 1964,
S 1 ALCOHOLIC LIQUOR DUTIES ACT 1979

It is an offence to sell or expose for sale any intoxicating liquor without holding a justices' licence, or canteen licence or occasional permission authorising that sale, or to do so except at the place where the licence authorises it.

'**Intoxicating liquor**' means spirits, wine, beer, cider and any fermented, distilled or spiritous liquor but does not include:

(a) any liquor which is of a strength not exceeding 0.5 per cent;

(b) perfumes;

(c) flavouring essences not intended for consumption as or with dutiable liquor;

(d) spirits, wine or made-wine intended for use as a medicine and not as a beverage.

A licence is not required for the sale, supply or purchase of **liqueur chocolates** provided that their alcoholic content is not more than 1/50 gall of liquor (spirit) per pound of confectionery and either consists of separate pieces weighing not more than 1.5 oz or designed to be broken into such pieces. But this chocolate must not be sold to a person **under the age of 16 years**.

'**Beer**' includes ale, porter, stout and any other description of beer, and any liquor which is made or sold as a beer or substitute for beer of a strength exceeding 0.5%, but does not include black beer the worts of which before fermentation were of a specific gravity of 1200° or more.

'**Spirits**' means:

a) spirits of any description with a strength over 1.2%;

b) any such mixture, compound or preparation made with spirits of a strength over 1.2%; or

c) liquors contained with any spirits, in any mixture with a strength over 1.2%.

'**Wine**' means any liquor with a strength over 1.2% and which is obtained from the fermentation of fresh grapes or the must of fresh grapes, whether or not the liquor is fortified with spirits or flavoured with aromatic extracts. The expression 'wine' also includes '**made wine**' which means any liquor which has a strength of over 1.2% and which is made from the alcoholic fermentation of any substance or by mixing a liquor so obtained with any other substance, but does not include wine, beer, black beer, spirits or cider.

'**Cider**' means cider (or perry) of a strength over 1.2% but less than 8.7% obtained from the fermentation of apple or pear juice without the addition of any disallowed alcoholic substance for colouring or flavour.

(CONTINUED ON NEXT PAGE)

Justices' Licences – continued

THERE ARE TWO TYPES OF LICENCE (S 1):

'OFF'

Authorises the sale of intoxicating liquor for consumption off the premises only, and may authorise the sale of:

• intoxicating liquor of all descriptions, or
• beer, cider and wine only

'ON'

Authorises the sale of intoxicating liquor for consumption either on or off the premises for which the licence is granted, and may authorise the sale of:

• intoxicating liquor of all descriptions, or
• beer, cider and wine only, or
• beer and cider only, or
• cider only, or
• wine only

Display of name, etc The licensee must keep painted on or affixed to the premises in a conspicuous place (usually above the entrance), his name, followed by the word "licensed", and the type of licence he holds (S 183).

Permitted Hours

S 60 LICENSING ACT 1964
REGULATORY REFORM (SPECIAL OCCASIONS LICENSING) ORDER 2001

'On licensed' premises
a) on weekdays other than Christmas Day, Good Friday or New Year's Eve, from 11am to 11pm;
b) on Sundays, other than Christmas Day or New Year's Eve, and on Good Friday, from 12 noon to 10.30pm;
c) on Christmas Day, from 12 noon to 10.30pm with a break of 4 hours beginning at 3pm; and
d) on New Year's Eve, except a Sunday, 11am to 11pm, and on New Year's Eve on a Sunday, from 12 noon to 10.30pm.

The above hours are known as the **'general licensing hours'**.

The licensing justices for a district may modify the hours in a) above to commence earlier than 11am, but not earlier than 10am.

Special Occasions Hours
Subject to any restriction order, on licensed premises (not 'off-licence') and registered clubs the 'special occasions' hours are between the end of permitted hours on New Year's Eve, and the beginning of permitted hours the following day.

'Off licensed' premises are the same as above except:
a) on weekdays other than Christmas Day, hours commence at 8am; and
b) on Sundays other than Christmas Day, hours commence at 10am.

Registered Clubs
a) on days other than Christmas Day, the general licensing hours (see above); and
b) on Christmas Day, the hours fixed by the club in accordance with the following-

   i) no more than 6 ½ hours beginning not earlier than 12 noon and ending not later than 10.30pm;
   ii) a break of not less than 2 hours, to include the hours from 3pm to 5pm; and
   iii) not more than 3 ½ hours after 5pm.

Sales etc Outside Permitted Hours

S 59(1) LICENSING ACT 1964

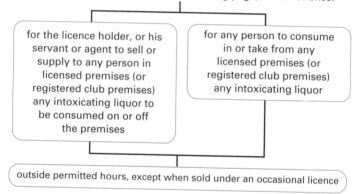

Subject to the exceptions on the following page, it is an offence:

for the licence holder, or his servant or agent to sell or supply to any person in licensed premises (or registered club premises) any intoxicating liquor to be consumed on or off the premises

for any person to consume in or take from any licensed premises (or registered club premises) any intoxicating liquor

outside permitted hours, except when sold under an occasional licence

Liability For the licensee or registered club to be liable, the acts of the servant or agent must be within the express or implied scope of his employment, even if it was contrary to express orders. The servant or agent will also be liable. Supply outside permitted hours to members of a registered club at a place other than the club premises is not an offence within this section. If consumption takes place on the premises, it is immaterial whether it was sold or supplied on the premises; it may have been brought into the premises by the consumer.

Permitted Hours – Exceptions

S 63 LICENSING ACT 1964

Where intoxicating liquor is supplied during permitted hours, sale, etc will not be prohibited in the following circumstances:

'Drinking-up time'
During the first 20 minutes after the end of permitted hours, consumption may take place and liquor may be removed from the premises, unless supplied or taken away in an open vessel.

After meals
During the first half hour following permitted hours, consumption of liquor is allowed by persons taking meals if the drink is ancillary to the meal.

Residents
Sale or supply to, or consumption by, any person who is residing in the premises (this also includes persons not residing there but in charge of or carrying on the business on the premises). Persons residing on licensed premises may take intoxicating liquor off the premises.

Off sales
The ordering or drinks for consumption off the premises, and the despatch of liquor so ordered.

Traders
Sale to a trader for the purposes of his trade, or to a registered club, canteen or mess.

Employees
Supply of drink for consumption on the premises to persons employed there if it is supplied at the expense of the employer.

Private friends
Supply for consumption on the premises to any private friends of a person residing there who are bona fide entertained by him at his own expense (this would include the licensee, but the persons entertained must be real personal friends and not merely customers).

Extension of hours, special hours certificate, extended hours, general order of exemption, special order of exemption – see later.

Permitted Hours – Restrictions

LICENSING ACT 1964 (AS AMENDED BY THE LICENSING ACT 1988)

SEASONAL LICENCES (S 64)

These are conditions inserted in the licence on application by the person applying for the grant of a licence, or a licence holder, that during certain parts of the year there shall be **no permitted hours** on the premises. These variations are to cater for the requirements of the district.

SIX DAY AND EARLY CLOSING LICENCES (S 65)

On application by the licensee the justices shall insert in the licence a condition that on **Sundays** there shall be **no permitted hours**; or that the **permitted hours** in the evening shall end one hour earlier than general licensing hours.

RESTRICTION ORDERS (S 67A) may be made by licensing justices (or magistrates' court in relation to registered clubs) on the ground that it is desirable to reduce disturbance or annoyance due to the use of the premises. They may be made in respect of registered clubs and licensed premises other than 'off licences' or premises subject to an 'occasional licence'. An order may restrict permitted hours to exclude any time between 2.30pm and 5.30pm on weekdays other than Good Friday, and any time between 3pm and 7pm on Sundays and Good Friday. They may specify particular days of the week and periods of the year. A notice must be displayed in licensed premises showing the effect of the order.

Extensions to Permitted Hours in Restaurants

S 68 LICENSING ACT 1964, AS AMENDED BY THE LICENSING (RESTAURANT MEALS) ACT 1987 AND THE LICENSING ACT 1988

Granted to the holder of a justices' 'ON' licence or to a registered club in respect of premises which are structurally adapted and bona fide used for the purpose of **habitually** providing for customers **substantial refreshment** to which the sale and supply of intoxicating liquor is ancillary.

Hours
The effect of the grant of this certificate is to extend general permitted hours by one hour in the evening, and on Christmas Day, between the first and second parts of the general licensing hours.

SALE OR SUPPLY OF
INTOXICANTS MAY BE MADE
TO PERSONS TAKING
|
TABLE MEALS ➤ Does not necessarily mean a table as such. It includes a counter serving the purpose of a table (but not used to serve refreshments to persons not seated at a table), but the customer must be seated
|
IN THE PREMISES,
PROVIDING THAT
CONSUMPTION TAKES PLACE
IN A PART OF THE PREMISES
|
SET APART ➤ In other parts of the premises, hours are still restricted to the normal general permitted hours
|
FOR THE SERVICE OF
SUCH PERSONS

Special Hours Certificates

S 77 & S 78 LICENSING ACT 1964

Licensed premises (S 77)
A certificate may be granted with or without limitations for:

• casino premises; or
• premises for which a music and dancing licence is in force,

and the premises or part of the premises is structurally adapted and bona fide used, or intended to be used, for the purpose of providing:

• in the case of casino premises, gaming facilities and substantial refreshment, and
• in the case of any other premises, music and dancing and substantial refreshment

to which the sale of intoxicants is ancillary.

'Music and dancing licence' means a licence granted under Sched 12 to the London Government Act 1963, or Sched 1 to the Local Government (Miscellaneous Provisions) Act 1982

Registered clubs (S 78)
A certificate may be granted with or without limitations for a registered club if:

• a certificate of suitability of club premises has been granted under S 79 of this Act, and
• the premises or part of the premises is structurally adapted and bona fide used, or intended to be used, for the purpose of providing for its members music and dancing and substantial refreshments to which the supply of intoxicants is ancillary.

Provisional certificates (S 77A & S 78ZA)
In either case, where premises are being altered or extended or (in the case of licensed premises) constructed, and in either case the relevant provisions above are satisfied, a provisional certificate may be granted.

Limitations (S 78A)
Certificates may be granted which are limited to:

• particular times of the day,
• particular days of the week,
• particular periods of the year,
• to days not including Sunday, or
• different times for Sundays and other days.

Special Hours Certificates – Permitted Hours

S 76 LICENSING ACT 1964

The following hours apply to licensed premises and registered clubs in respect of which a special hours certificate has been granted:

Weekdays The hours extend to 2am, except:

(a) they end at midnight on any day on which music and dancing (or in the case of a casino, gaming facilities) are not provided after midnight;

(b) when music and dancing (or in the case of a casino, gaming facilities) ends between midnight and 2am, the permitted hours end when the music and dancing (or gaming) ends; and

(c) where the certificate includes a limitation, the permitted hours shall not extend beyond those stipulated.

Summer time On the morning on which summer time begins, substitute 2am with 3am. In the case of a limitation, and the hours are stipulated to end between 1am and 2am, the hours will be extended by 1 hour.

In the metropolis outside the city of London, where authorised by the Secretary of State, except on the morning of the beginning of summer time, for 2am, read 3am, and, for the morning of summer time, read 4am.

Sundays The hours extend to 12.30am, except:

(a) they end at midnight on any Sunday on which music and dancing (or in the case of a casino, gaming facilities) are not provided after midnight;

(b) when music and dancing (or in the case of a casino, gaming facilities) ends between midnight and 12.30am, the permitted hours end when the music and dancing (or gaming) ends; and

(c) where the certificate includes a limitation, the permitted hours shall not extend beyond those stipulated.

These provisions will not apply to a certificate granted before they came into force, but they may be varied on application by the holder.

Sundays before bank holidays Where a Sunday (except Easter Sunday) falls immediately before a bank holiday in England and Wales, then permitted hours will be the same as for Sundays above except-

(a) in the case of premises in the metropolis, for 12.30am read 3am; and

(b) in the case of other premises, for 12.30am read 2am.

These provisions will not apply to a certificate granted before they came into force, but they may be varied on application by the holder.

Drinking up time 30 minutes is allowed.

Notice The licensee must display a notice on the premises, stating the effect of the special hours certificate.

Extended Hours in Restaurants etc Providing Entertainment

S 70 LICENSING ACT 1964

Qualifications for an order to be granted

An order may be granted under this section in respect of licensed premises and registered clubs which are structurally adapted and bona fide used, or intended to be used, for the purpose of habitually providing musical or other entertainment as well as substantial refreshment, and the sale and supply of intoxicating liquor is ancillary to that refreshment and entertainment.

Time added to the extension to permitted hours

If the extension of 1 hour to general licensing hours applies to the premises in accordance with S 68 of this Act (see earlier), and an order has been granted under this section, permitted hours shall be:

(a) until 1am for the purpose of sale and supply of intoxicating liquor before the end of the entertainment or refreshment, and its consumption (but not to persons admitted after midnight or less than half an hour before the entertainment is due to end, unless taking a table meal);
(b) if the order granted under this section applies to Sundays, for '1am' above read 12.30am, and for 'midnight' read 11.30pm.

Drinking up time Other than on Sundays, half an hour is allowed after the entertainment ends to consume intoxicating liquor supplied before then.

'Entertainment' does not include any form of entertainment given otherwise than by persons actually present and performing.

'Habitually providing refreshment and entertainment' means it is used or intended to be used, or is set apart, for the purpose of providing them after, and for a substantial period preceding, the end of the general licensing hours on every day or on particular days of the week, subject to any break for a period or periods not exceeding 2 weeks in any 12 successive months or on any special occasion or by reason of an emergency.

Orders of Exemption

S 74 LICENSING ACT 1964 AS AMENDED BY THE LICENSING ACT 1988

GENERAL ORDER

This may be granted to the holder of a justices 'on' licence, or to the secretary of a club, if the premises are situated in the immediate vicinity of a public market or place where people follow a lawful trade or calling, if the justices are satisfied that it is desirable to do so for the accommodation of a considerable number of persons attending the market, etc

SPECIAL ORDER

This may be granted to the holder of a justices 'on' licence on a specified **special occasion**. The order applies not only to the room in which the function is being held, but to the entire premises. The licence holder may, however, be requested to give an undertaking limiting the exemption to a particular room

In the City of London or the Metropolitan Police district the order may be made by the Commissioner of Police with the approval of the Lord Mayor (in the City of London) or the Secretary of State (in the Metropolitan district)

If granted, such hours as may be specified are added to permitted hours. This is exercised by adding any hour to permitted hours

In Martin v Spalding 1979 the Divisional Court gave guidance on interpreting a 'special occasion':

> The occasion must not be too frequent. The more often a thing takes place, the less special it becomes. It must be special in the local or national sense. The licensee may not make a special occasion in order to claim the benefit of an exemption order.

Occasional Licences

S 180 LICENSING ACT 1964

Granted to the holder of a justices' 'ON' licence to sell in some place other than his licensed premises such intoxicants as his justices' licence empowers him to sell between such hours as may be specified in the order

Such premises need not be licensed, or may have a restricted licence which does not cater for the needs of a particular function

The police have the same powers of entry as they have in relation to 'licensed premises'

There is no offence of children under 14 being present

Permitted hours applicable to the premises of the licensee do not apply

There is no offence of selling outside of permitted hours where there is an occasional licence

But consider an offence of selling without a licence if the occasional licence has expired

The licence cannot be granted for Xmas Day, Good Friday or any day of public fast or thanksgiving

The licence may not extend over more than three consecutive weeks at a time

Occasional Permissions

LICENSING (OCCASIONAL PERMISSIONS) ACT 1983

These licences are granted to a member of an 'eligible organisation' authorising him to sell intoxicating liquor during a period not exceeding 24 hours at a function held by the organisation.

The occasional permission is given in writing and specifies:

• the place where intoxicating liquor may be sold;
• the kind(s) of intoxicating liquor which may be sold;
• the hours between which it may be sold on the specified date; and
• any conditions, if any, as the justices may think proper.

Not more than 12 permissions may be granted to an organisation (or branch) in any 12 months.

'Eligible organisation' means any organisation not carried on for private gain.

'Private gain' A purpose which is calculated to benefit an organisation as a whole will not be private gain except where the organisation carries on a commercial undertaking.

Offences

1. **The holder or his agent** knowingly:
• selling intoxicating liquor to a person under 18;
• allowing such a person to consume intoxicating liquor in a bar; or
• allowing any person to sell intoxicating liquor to such a person.

2. **A person under 18** buying or attempting to buy intoxicating liquor or consuming it in a bar.

3. **Any person**:
• buying or attempting to buy intoxicating liquor for consumption in a bar by a person under 18;
• procuring or attempting to procure intoxicating liquor for consumption on the premises by a drunken person; or
• aiding a drunken person in obtaining or consuming intoxicating liquor on the premises.

4. **The holder**:
• allowing any person under 18 to sell or serve any intoxicating liquor;
• permitting drunkenness or any violent, quarrelsome or riotous conduct;
• selling intoxicating liquor to a drunken person;
• failing to comply with conditions attached to the permission;
• failing to produce the permission to a constable within a reasonable time.

Power to exclude The holder may refuse admission to, or expel any person from, the premises who is drunk, violent, quarrelsome or disorderly or whose presence would subject the holder to a penalty. A person who fails to do so commits an offence. A constable shall, on demand from the holder or his agent, help to expel any such person and may use such force as may be required to do so.

Power of entry For the purposes of preventing or detecting the above offences, a constable may enter the premises during the hours specified in the permission.

Restaurants and Residential Licences

LICENSING ACT 1964 AS AMENDED BY THE LICENSING (RESTAURANT MEALS) ACT 1987 AND THE LICENSING ACT 1988

The following licences may be granted:

RESTAURANT S 94(1)

This is granted for premises **structurally adapted and bona fide used** or intended to be used for the purpose of **habitually** providing a main meal at midday or in the evening, or both. But intoxicating liquor may not be sold or supplied on the premises other than to persons taking table meals where the drink is ancillary to the meal.

RESIDENTIAL S 94(2)

This is granted for premises **bona fide used** or intended to be used for the purpose of **habitually** providing, for reward, **board and lodging** including breakfast and one other main meal. But intoxicating liquor shall not be sold or supplied other than to persons residing there or their bona fide friends entertained by them at their own expense. There will normally be a condition that adequate sitting accommodation must be provided for the service of substantial refreshment, or the consumption of intoxicating liquor, in a room not used for sleeping accommodation (S 96).

RESTAURANT AND RESIDENTIAL S 94(3)

This is granted for premises falling within the conditions of both restaurant and residential licence, but intoxicating liquor may only be sold or supplied as permitted by the conditions of both licences.

Permitted hours

These are general permitted hours, the hour following those hours and the break between the first and second part of general licensing hours on Christmas Days (S 95).

Children in Bars
S 168 LICENSING ACT 1964 (AS AMENDED)

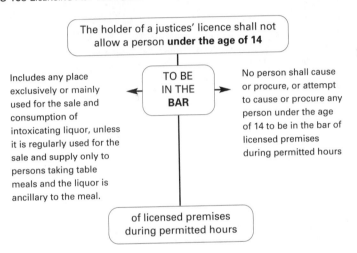

The holder of a justices' licence shall not allow a person **under the age of 14**

Includes any place exclusively or mainly used for the sale and consumption of intoxicating liquor, unless it is regularly used for the sale and supply only to persons taking table meals and the liquor is ancillary to the meal.

TO BE IN THE BAR

No person shall cause or procure, or attempt to cause or procure any person under the age of 14 to be in the bar of licensed premises during permitted hours

of licensed premises during permitted hours

But no offence will be committed if:

- The person under 14 was in the bar solely for the purpose of passing through to another part of the premises which was not a bar and there was no other convenient means of access
- The bar was part of a railway refreshment room or other premises for which the holding of a justices' licence was merely ancillary
- The licensee used due diligence to prevent under 14s being admitted
- The person under 14 had apparently attained that age
- The person under 14 was the licensee's child
- The person under 14 resided there but was not employed there, or
- The person under 14 was accompanied by a person over 18 and a 'Children's Certificate' was in force for that part of the premises. A notice must be displayed in a conspicuous place in the area to which the certificate relates, stating that a certificate is in force and explaining the effect of it.

Persons Under 18

LICENSING ACT 1964

Sale to under 18s (S 169A)
It is an offence for any person to sell intoxicating liquor to a person under 18 in licensed premises. Defences:

1. he believed the person not to be under 18, and, either he had taken all reasonable steps to establish the person's age, or that nobody could reasonably have suspected from his appearance that he was under 18. 'Reasonable steps' means asking for evidence of age unless no reasonable person would be convinced by it;
2. that he exercised all due diligence to avoid an offence committed by an act or default of some other person; or
3. the person is over 16 and the intoxicating liquor involved was beer, porter or cider for consumption with a meal in a place which is not a bar and is usually set apart for meals. 'Bar' includes any place exclusively or mainly used for the sale and consumption of intoxicating liquor (S 201) but, by S 171, does not include a bar which is set apart for table meals and not used for the sale or supply of intoxicating liquor other than to persons having a table meal, and the drink is ancillary to it.

Allowing sale to under 18s (S 169B)
It is an offence for a person to knowingly allow any person to sell intoxicating liquor to a person under 18. The offence applies to a person who works in licensed premises in a capacity, whether paid or unpaid, which gives him authority to prevent the sale. However, defence no. 3 above applies to this offence.

Purchase by or for under 18s (S 169C)
A person under 18 commits an offence if, in licensed premises, he buys or attempts to buy intoxicating liquor. The offence does not apply if he buys or attempts to buy at the request of a constable or weights and measures inspector.
An offence is committed if, in licensed premises, a person buys or attempts to buy intoxicating liquor on behalf of a person under 18, or for the consumption in a bar by such a person. It is a defence to prove that he had no reason to suspect that the person was under 18. Defence no. 3 above also applies.

Consumption by a person under 18 (S 169E)
A person under 18 will commit an offence if, in the bar of licensed premises, he consumes intoxicating liquor. A person who works in the licensed premises in a capacity, whether paid or unpaid, which gives him authority to prevent the consumption, will commit an offence if he knowingly allows such consumption.

Persons Under 18 – continued

LICENSING ACT 1964

Delivery to persons under 18 (S 169F)

A person who works in licensed premises, whether paid or unpaid, commits an offence if he knowingly delivers to a person under 18 intoxicating liquor sold in those premises for consumption off the premises.

A person who works in the licensed premises in a capacity, whether paid or unpaid, which gives him authority to prevent the delivery, will commit an offence if he knowingly allows such delivery.

Defences:
• the delivery is made to the residence or working place of the purchaser, or
• the person under 18 works in the licensed premises, whether paid or unpaid, in a capacity which includes the delivery of intoxicating liquor.

Sending a person under 18 to obtain intoxicating liquor (S 169G)

It is an offence to knowingly send a person under 18 to obtain intoxicating liquor sold in licensed premises for consumption off the premises. The offence is committed whether the liquor is to be obtained from licensed premises or from other premises from which it is delivered in pursuance of the sale.

Defences:
• the person under 18 works in the premises where the sale is to be made, in a capacity, whether paid or unpaid, which includes the delivery of intoxicating liquor; or
• the person under 18 is sent by a constable or weights and measures inspector.

Employment of under 18s in bars (S 170)

The licensee commits an offence if he employs a person under 18 in the bar of licensed premises when it is open for the sale of intoxicating liquor. However, no offence will be committed if the person is over 16 and is employed under an approved training scheme.

'Employed' includes working without wages. But it will not include being employed in some other part of the premises and entering the bar to give or receive a message, or to pass to another part of the premises where there is no other convenient means of access.

'Bar' includes any place exclusively or mainly used for the sale and consumption of intoxicating liquor (S 201) but, by S 171 does not include a bar which is set apart for table meals and not used for the sale or supply of intoxicating liquor other than to persons having a table meal, and the drink is ancillary to it.

Unsupervised off-sales by under 18s (S 171A)

In 'off-licensed' premises, or the 'off-licence' department of 'on-licensed' premises, the licensee commits an offence if he allows a person under 18 to sell intoxicating liquor, unless the sale is specifically approved by the licensee or by a person over 18 acting on his behalf.

Drunks in Licensed Premises

LICENSING ACT 1964

PERMITTING DRUNKENNESS S 172

The holder of a justices' licence shall not permit drunkenness or any violent, quarrelsome or riotous conduct to take place in the licensed premises. Where a person is drunk, the burden lies with the licensee to prove that he, or a person employed by him, took all reasonable steps to prevent it. The offence may also be committed by a person who works in the premises in a capacity, whether paid or unpaid, which gives him authority to prevent it.

SELLING TO DRUNKS S 172

The holder of a justices' licence shall not sell intoxicating liquor to a drunken person. The offence may also be committed by a person who works in the premises in a capacity, whether paid or unpaid, which gives him authority to sell it.

PROCURING ALCOHOL S 173

No person in licensed premises may procure or attempt to procure intoxicating liquor for consumption by a drunken person, nor aid a drunken person to obtain or consume it.

POWER TO EXPEL S 174

The holder of a justices' licence may refuse to admit to, or may expel from, the premises any person who is drunk, violent, quarrelsome or disorderly, or whose presence is in breach of an exclusion order or may subject the licensee to a penalty. A person who fails, without reasonable cause, to leave the premises when requested, commits an offence.

A constable is required to assist to expel any person as above on the request of the licensee, his servant or agent. He may use such force as is necessary for this purpose.

See also: S 3 LICENSED PREMISES (EXCLUSION OF CERTAIN PERSONS) ACT 1980 which grants similar powers in relation to persons in breach of an exclusion order imposed by a court as a result of committing an offence accompanied by violence on licensed premises.

Prostitutes in Licensed Premises

S 175(1) LICENSING ACT 1964

The license holder shall not knowingly allow the premises to be the habitual resort or place of meeting of reputed prostitutes

The object of their so resorting need not be prostitution (but they may be allowed for the purpose of obtaining reasonable refreshment)

Neither shall the licensee allow his premises to be used as a brothel (S 176)

Gaming in Licensed Premises

S 177 LICENSING ACT 1964

The licensee shall not allow any game to be played on the premises in such circumstances that an offence under the Gaming Act 1968 is committed (see earlier).

Constables in Licensed Premises

S 178 LICENSING ACT 1964

It is an offence for the licence holder to:

knowingly allow a constable to remain on the premises whilst on duty, except for the purposes of the execution of his duty

bribe or attempt to bribe any constable

supply any liquor or refreshment to any constable on duty except by authority of a superior officer of the constable

Power of Entry

S 186 LICENSING ACT 1964

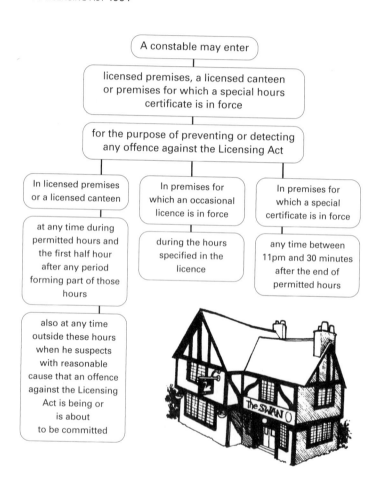

A constable may enter

licensed premises, a licensed canteen or premises for which a special hours certificate is in force

for the purpose of preventing or detecting any offence against the Licensing Act

In licensed premises or a licensed canteen

at any time during permitted hours and the first half hour after any period forming part of those hours

also at any time outside these hours when he suspects with reasonable cause that an offence against the Licensing Act is being or is about to be committed

In premises for which an occasional licence is in force

during the hours specified in the licence

In premises for which a special certificate is in force

any time between 11pm and 30 minutes after the end of permitted hours

An offence is committed by any person who fails to admit a constable who demands entry to the premises under the authority of this section.

Drunks in Public Places

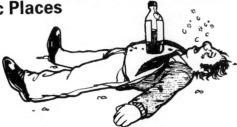

Drunkenness
S 12 LICENSING ACT 1872

It is an offence to be found drunk in any highway or other public place whether a building or not, or any licensed premises. (Public place includes all places where the public have access whether on payment or otherwise.) A power to apprehend is provided by the Licensing Act 1902.

Carriage, etc
S 12 LICENSING ACT 1872

It is an offence to be drunk whilst in charge on any highway or other public place of any horse, cattle, pig, sheep, carriage, motor vehicle, trailer, bicycle or steam engine. The offender may be arrested.

Firearms
S 12 LICENSING ACT 1872

It is an offence, whilst drunk, to be in possession of any loaded firearm (including an airgun). The offender may be arrested.

Children
S 2 LICENSING ACT 1902

It is an offence to be drunk in a highway or other public place, whether a building or not, or any licensed premises, while having the charge of a child apparently under the age of 7 years.

Disorderly
S 91(1) CRIMINAL JUSTICE ACT 1967

It is an offence in a public place to be guilty, whilst drunk, of disorderly behaviour. (Public place includes any highway and any other premises or place to which at the material time the public have, or are permitted to have, access whether on payment or otherwise.) The offender may be arrested without warrant by any person.

Alcohol Consumption in Designated Public Places

Ss 12 – 15 CRIMINAL JUSTICE AND POLICE ACT 2001

> Where a constable reasonably believes that a person is, or has been, or intends, consuming intoxicating liquor

> in a designated public place

> the constable may require the person:
>
> (a) not to consume in that place anything which the constable believes to be intoxicating liquor;
>
> (b) to surrender anything in his possession which he believes to be intoxicating liquor, or a container for such liquor.

> and may dispose of anything surrendered to him in such manner as he considers appropriate.

> It is an offence to fail without reasonable excuse to comply with such a requirement. This is an arrestable offence.

> The constable must inform the person concerned that failure to comply without reasonable excuse is an offence.

> A 'designated public place' is a public place which is identified in an order made by a local authority.

Public Charitable Collections

S 66 CHARITIES ACT 1992

At the time of going to press, this section was not in force.
See following page for current provisions.

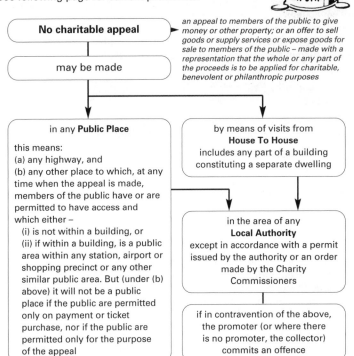

No charitable appeal

may be made

an appeal to members of the public to give money or other property; or an offer to sell goods or supply services or expose goods for sale to members of the public – made with a representation that the whole or any part of the proceeds is to be applied for charitable, benevolent or philanthropic purposes

---

in any **Public Place**

this means:
(a) any highway, and
(b) any other place to which, at any time when the appeal is made, members of the public have or are permitted to have access and which either –
  (i) is not within a building, or
  (ii) if within a building, is a public area within any station, airport or shopping precinct or any other similar public area. But (under (b) above) it will not be a public place if the public are permitted only on payment or ticket purchase, nor if the public are permitted only for the purpose of the appeal

---

by means of visits from
House To House
includes any part of a building constituting a separate dwelling

in the area of any
Local Authority
except in accordance with a permit issued by the authority or an order made by the Charity Commissioners

if in contravention of the above, the promoter (or where there is no promoter, the collector) commits an offence

---

Exceptions

Does not apply to a charitable appeal which:
(a) is made in the course of a public meeting; or
(b) is made –
  (i) on land within a churchyard or burial ground contiguous or adjacent to a place or public worship, or
  (ii) on other land occupied for the purposes of a place of public worship and contiguous or adjacent to it, being in each case land which is enclosed, or substantially enclosed; or
(c) is an appeal to the public to give money or other property by placing it in a receptacle

Street and House-to-house Collections

POLICE, FACTORIES ETC (MISCELLANEOUS PROVISIONS) ACT 1916; HOUSE TO HOUSE
COLLECTIONS ACT 1939; AND HOUSE TO HOUSE COLLECTIONS REGULATIONS 1947

Street collections
It is an offence for any person, in any street or public place, to collect
money or sell articles for the benefit of charitable or other purposes
otherwise than in accordance with regulations made by:

- the common council of the city of London;
- the police authority for the Metropolitan Police District; or
- the council of that district.

'Street' includes any highway and any public bridge, road, lane, footway,
square, court, alley, or passage, whether a thoroughfare or not.

House to house collections
It is an offence for a person to promote a collection for a charitable
purpose, or to act as a collector for such purpose, unless a licence,
certificate or order of exemption has been issued authorising such
activities.

'Collection' means an appeal to the public by means of visits from house to
house, to give, whether for consideration of not, money or other property.

The promoter must issue to each collector:
- a certificate of authority;
- a prescribed badge; and
- a collecting box or receipt book indicating the purpose of the collection
  and a distinguishing number.

The collector must:
- sign the certificate and badge and return them when the collection is
  completed;
- not be under the age of 16;
- not importune or annoy people; and
- only collect money which is placed in the collecting box, or issue a
  receipt for it.

A collection may be made by envelope if authorised by the Secretary
of State.

Police powers
A PC may require a person whom he believes is acting as a collector to
declare his name and address and to sign his name. Failure to do so is an
offence.

Chapter 5
Animals

Cruelty to Animals

S 1 PROTECTION OF ANIMALS ACT 1911

It is an offence for a person to cause, permit or be concerned with any of the following activities:

Physical Cruelty

To cruelly beat, kick, ill-treat, over-ride, over-drive, over-load, torture, infuriate or terrify any animal, or in any way to cause unnecessary suffering to any animal.

Conveyance

To convey or carry any animal in such a manner or position as to cause any unnecessary suffering.

Abandoning

S 1 ABANDONMENT OF ANIMALS ACT 1960
Without reasonable cause or excuse, whether temporarily or not, in circumstances likely to cause unnecessary suffering, eg leaving animals at home whilst on holiday.

Fighting

The fighting or baiting of any animal or keeping, using, managing, etc, any premises for such purpose. Any person present at such an event, or who advertises it will also commit an offence (see later).

Drugs

The administration of any poisonous or injurious drug or substance to any animal without reasonable cause or excuse.

Operations

To subject the animal to any operation which is performed without due care and humanity.

Tethering

To tether any horse, ass or mule under such conditions or in such a manner as to cause that animal unnecessary suffering.

Police Powers

A police constable may arrest without warrant any person whom he has reason to believe to be guilty of this offence either upon his own view or that of a third person. He may take charge of any animal or vehicle (S 12).

Cruelty to Animals – continued

S 15 PROTECTION OF ANIMALS ACT 1911

For the purposes of the offence of cruelty to animals,

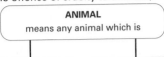

ANIMAL
means any animal which is

DOMESTIC

horse, ass, mule, bull, sheep, pig, goat, dog, cat, fowl, or any other animal which is tame or has been or is being sufficiently tamed to serve some purpose for the use of man

CAPTIVE

any animal (not being a domestic animal) including any bird, fish or reptile which is in captivity or confinement, or which is maimed, pinioned or subjected to any appliance for the purpose of hindering or preventing its escape

A wild animal temporarily unable to escape is not a captive animal

Does not include invertebrates eg worms

The offences created by this Act do not apply:

To anything done in the course of destruction, or preparation for destruction, of any animal as food for mankind unless unnecessary suffering is inflicted. S 1(3)

To the coursing or hunting of any captive animal, unless such animal is liberated in an injured, mutilated or exhausted condition, or if it is done in an enclosed space from which it has no reasonable chance of escape.

Fur Farming

FUR FARMING (PROHIBITION) ACT 2000

A person is guilty of an offence if he keeps animals solely or primarily:
(a) for slaughter (whether by himself or another) for the value of their fur; or
(b) for breeding progeny for such slaughter.

A person is guilty of an offence if he knowingly causes or permits another person to keep such animals.

Cruelty To Wild Mammals

WILD MAMMALS (PROTECTION) ACT **1996**

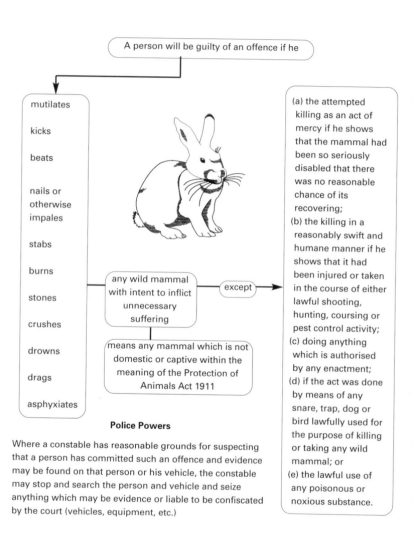

A person will be guilty of an offence if he

mutilates

kicks

beats

nails or otherwise impales

stabs

burns

stones

crushes

drowns

drags

asphyxiates

any wild mammal with intent to inflict unnecessary suffering

except

means any mammal which is not domestic or captive within the meaning of the Protection of Animals Act 1911

(a) the attempted killing as an act of mercy if he shows that the mammal had been so seriously disabled that there was no reasonable chance of its recovering;

(b) the killing in a reasonably swift and humane manner if he shows that it had been injured or taken in the course of either lawful shooting, hunting, coursing or pest control activity;

(c) doing anything which is authorised by any enactment;

(d) if the act was done by means of any snare, trap, dog or bird lawfully used for the purpose of killing or taking any wild mammal; or

(e) the lawful use of any poisonous or noxious substance.

Police Powers

Where a constable has reasonable grounds for suspecting that a person has committed such an offence and evidence may be found on that person or his vehicle, the constable may stop and search the person and vehicle and seize anything which may be evidence or liable to be confiscated by the court (vehicles, equipment, etc.)

Protection of Wild Animals

WILDLIFE AND COUNTRYSIDE ACT 1981

Schedule 5 to this Act lists certain wild animals which are protected. The list is too long to be reproduced here, but includes – adder, bat, beetle, butterfly, wildcat, cricket, dolphin, frog, grasshopper, moth, mussel, newt, otter, porpoise, red squirrel, toad, water vole, walrus and whale.

Offences relating to animals contained in Schedule 5:
1. To intentionally kill, injure or take any wild animal;
2. To have in possession or control any live or dead wild animals or anything derived from such an animal;
3. To intentionally or recklessly-
   • damage or destroy, or obstruct access to, any structure or place which a wild animal uses for shelter or protection, or
   • disturb any such animal while it is occupying a structure or place which it uses for that purpose,
but the above will not be an offence if it takes place in a dwelling house;
4. To intentionally or recklessly disturb a dolphin, whale or basking shark;
5. To sell, offer or expose for sale, or have in possession or transport for the purpose of sale, a live or dead wild animal, or any part of, or anything derived from, such an animal;
6. To publish or cause to be published any advertisement to buy or sell, or intend to buy or sell any such thing as is mentioned in '5' above.

Defences (S 10)
(a) Anything done as a requirement of the Minister of Agriculture, the Secretary of State or the Animal Health Act.
(b) The taking of a disabled animal solely for the purpose of tending it and releasing it when no longer disabled.
(c) The killing of an animal which was so seriously disabled that there was no reasonable chance of it recovering.
(d) The incidental result of a lawful operation and could not reasonably have been avoided.
(e) The killing or injuring of a wild animal by an authorised person, if done to prevent serious damage to livestock, foodstuffs for livestock, crops, vegetables, fruit, growing timber or any other form of property or to fisheries. This defence could only be relied upon if the events were not anticipated – otherwise a licence would be needed.

(CONTINUED ON NEXT PAGE)

Protection of Wild Animals – continued

Prohibited methods of taking and killing any wild animals (S 11(1))
(a) Setting self-locking snares calculated to cause injury to wild animals;
(b) Using self-locking snares (whether or not so calculated), or a bow, crossbow, or explosive;
(c) Using as a decoy any live mammal or bird;
(d) Knowingly causing or permitting any of the above.

Prohibited methods of taking and killing Schedule 6 wild animals (S 11(2)):
Schedule 6 lists certain animals which may not be killed or taken by certain methods. They are: badger, horseshoe bat, typical bat, wildcat, bottle-nosed dolphin, common dolphin, dormouse, hedgehog, pine martin, common otter, polecat, common porpoise, shrew and red squirrel.
The prohibited methods are:
(a) Setting any of the following articles calculated to cause injury: trap, snare, electrical device for killing or stunning or any poisonous, poisoned or stupefying substance;
(b) Using an automatic or semi-automatic weapon, target illuminating device or night sight, artificial light, mirror or dazzling device, or gas or smoke;
(c) Using a mechanically propelled vehicle in pursuit; or
(d) Using for the purpose of killing or taking a wild animal, any of the following articles whether or not calculated to cause injury: trap, snare, electrical device for killing or stunning or any poisonous, poisoned or stupefying substance; or net;
(e) Using as a decoy any sound recording; or
(f) Knowingly causing or permitting any of the above.

Snares (S 11(3))
It is an offence to fail to inspect at least once a day, any snare which has been set in position and which is of such a nature and is so placed as to be calculated to cause bodily injury to any wild animal.

Protection of Plants

S 13 WILDLIFE AND COUNTRYSIDE ACT 1981

Schedule 8 of the Act lists a variety of wild plants which are afforded protection. They are too numerous to list here, but include the following:

blackwort, purple colt's foot, wild cotoneaster, numerous forms of gentian, numerous forms of lichen and moss, numerous forms of orchid, fen ragwort and fen violet.

Offences

1. Intentionally picking, uprooting or destroying any wild plant included in the Schedule;
2. not being an authorised person, intentionally uprooting any wild plant not included in the Schedule;
3. selling, offering or exposing for sale, or having in possession or transporting for the purpose of sale any live or dead wild plant included in the Schedule; and
4. publishing or causing to be published an advertisement to buy or sell any of those things.

In relation to offences 1 and 2 above, it is a defence to show that the act was an incidental result of a lawful operation and could not reasonable have been avoided.

Police Powers

S 19 WILDLIFE AND COUNTRYSIDE ACT 1981

If a constable suspects with reasonable cause that any person is committing or has committed an offence under sections 1, 5, 6, 7 or 8 (protection of wild birds); sections 9 or 11 (protection of wild animals); or section 13 (protection of wild plants); he may, without warrant:

(a) stop and search that person if the constable suspects with reasonable cause that evidence of the commission of the offence is to be found on him;
(b) search or examine any thing which is in that person's possession if the constable suspects with reasonable cause that evidence of the commission of the offence is to be found on that thing;
(c) seize and detain any thing which may be evidence of the commission of the offence or may be liable to be forfeited (includes vehicles, animals, weapons, etc.).

For the purpose of exercising the above powers or for the purpose of arresting the person under S 25 of the Police and Criminal Evidence Act 1984, the constable may, if he has reasonable cause for suspecting that the person has committed one of the above offences, enter any land other than a dwelling house.

Animal Fights

Ss 5A, 5B PROTECTION OF ANIMALS ACT 1911
ADDED BY THE PROTECTION OF ANIMALS (AMENDMENT) ACT 1988
S 1 COCKFIGHTING ACT 1952

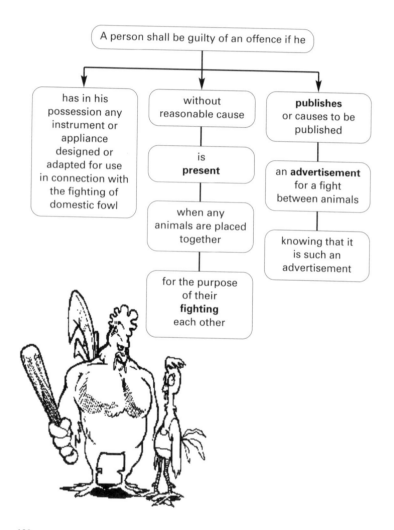

A person shall be guilty of an offence if he

has in his possession any instrument or appliance designed or adapted for use in connection with the fighting of domestic fowl

without reasonable cause

is **present**

when any animals are placed together

for the purpose of their **fighting** each other

publishes or causes to be published

an **advertisement** for a fight between animals

knowing that it is such an advertisement

Injured Animals

S 11 PROTECTION OF ANIMALS ACT 1911

If a police constable finds any animal

horse, mule, ass, bull, sheep, goat or pig

so diseased or so severely injured or in such a physical condition that in his opinion the animal cannot be removed without cruelty

then if the owner is absent or refuses to consent to its destruction the constable may summon a veterinary surgeon, if one resides within a reasonable distance

does not include dogs or cats

but although not included in this enactment, the main consideration should be the welfare of the animal

If the veterinary surgeon certifies that it is cruel to keep the animal alive the constable may, without the consent of the owner, cause the animal to be slaughtered in such a manner as to inflict as little suffering as possible and, if on a highway, cause the carcase to be removed

If the veterinary surgeon certifies that the animal **can** be removed, the person in charge of the animal shall forthwith cause it to be removed with as little suffering as possible and, if that person fails to do so, the constable may, without his consent, cause it to be removed

A veterinary surgeon should still be called and if the owner is not present or fails to meet his expenses it is usual for the police to seek the aid of a local voluntary organisation, or for the police authority to pay them

Sale of Pets

PET ANIMALS ACT 1951
AS AMENDED BY THE PET ANIMALS (AMENDMENT) ACT 1983

(See also 'Sale of Dogs' on following page)

No person shall keep a pet shop
except under the authority of a
licence granted by the local
authority (S 1).

If any person carries on a
business of selling animals as pets in any part of a street or public place, or
at a stall or barrow in a market, he shall be guilty of an offence (S 2).

If any person sells an animal as a pet to a person who he has reasonable
cause to believe to be under the age of 12 years, the seller shall be guilty of
an offence (S 3).

Sale of Dogs

BREEDING AND SALE OF DOGS (WELFARE) ACT 1999

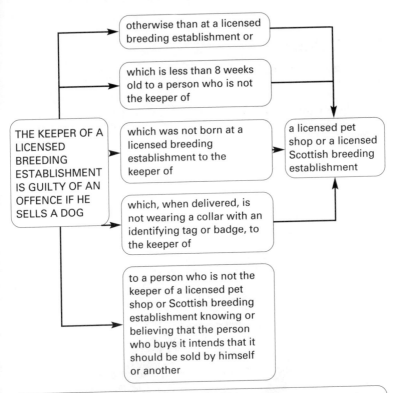

THE KEEPER OF A LICENSED BREEDING ESTABLISHMENT IS GUILTY OF AN OFFENCE IF HE SELLS A DOG

- otherwise than at a licensed breeding establishment or
- which is less than 8 weeks old to a person who is not the keeper of
- which was not born at a licensed breeding establishment to the keeper of
- which, when delivered, is not wearing a collar with an identifying tag or badge, to the keeper of

a licensed pet shop or a licensed Scottish breeding establishment

- to a person who is not the keeper of a licensed pet shop or Scottish breeding establishment knowing or believing that the person who buys it intends that it should be sold by himself or another

The keeper of a licensed pet shop is guilty of an offence if he sells a dog which, when delivered to him, was wearing a collar with an identifying tag or badge, but is not wearing such a collar when delivered to the person to whom he sells it.

The identifying tag or badge must clearly display the following information:
(a) the date of birth of the dog;
(b) an identifying number, if any, allocated to the dog by the licensed breeding establishment at which it was born; and
(c) the breeding establishment at which it was born.

Dogs

Dog Collars

ARTICLE 1 CONTROL OF DOGS ORDER 1992

Every dog while in a highway or in a place of public resort, shall wear a collar with the name and address of the owner inscribed on the collar or on a plate or badge attached thereto.

Exceptions

- Dogs used on official duties by the armed forces, HM Customs & Excise or the police.
- Dogs used for sporting purposes and packs of hounds
- Dogs used for the capture or destruction of vermin
- Dogs used for driving or tending cattle or sheep
- Guide dogs for the blind
- Dogs used for emergency rescue work

The owner of the dog and any person in charge of it, who, without lawful authority or excuse causes or permits the dog to be on the highway or place of public resort shall each be guilty of an offence. Dogs not wearing a collar may be seized as a stray dog. This order will be executed and enforced by officers of a local authority and not by the police.

Dogs Worrying Livestock

S 1 DOGS (PROTECTION OF LIVESTOCK) ACT 1953 AS AMENDED

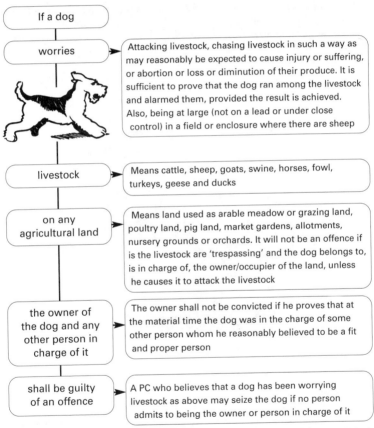

If a dog

worries → Attacking livestock, chasing livestock in such a way as may reasonably be expected to cause injury or suffering, or abortion or loss or diminution of their produce. It is sufficient to prove that the dog ran among the livestock and alarmed them, provided the result is achieved. Also, being at large (not on a lead or under close control) in a field or enclosure where there are sheep

livestock → Means cattle, sheep, goats, swine, horses, fowl, turkeys, geese and ducks

on any agricultural land → Means land used as arable meadow or grazing land, poultry land, pig land, market gardens, allotments, nursery grounds or orchards. It will not be an offence if is the livestock are 'trespassing' and the dog belongs to, is in charge of, the owner/occupier of the land, unless he causes it to attack the livestock

the owner of the dog and any other person in charge of it → The owner shall not be convicted if he proves that at the material time the dog was in the charge of some other person whom he reasonably believed to be a fit and proper person

shall be guilty of an offence → A PC who believes that a dog has been worrying livestock as above may seize the dog if no person admits to being the owner or person in charge of it

It is a defence to a charge of killing or injuring a dog to prove that it was done to protect the livestock and the police were informed with 48 hours

Orders for Controlling Dangerous Dogs

S 2 DOGS ACT 1871

Where a dog is regarded as being dangerous, either because it has attacked someone, or because it has worried livestock and is not kept under proper control, application may be made to the court for an order to be made for the dog to kept by the owner under proper control or destroyed. It is an offence to fail to comply with such an order.

S 28 TOWN POLICE CLAUSES ACT 1847

Where the Town Police Clauses Act applies, an offence is committed by any person who in any street, to the obstruction, annoyance or danger of residents or passengers, suffers to be at large any unmuzzled ferocious dog, or sets on or urges any dog or other animal to attack, worry or put in fear any person or animal.

Dangerous Dogs

S 1 DANGEROUS DOGS ACT 1991

This section applies to:

- PIT BULL TERRIERS
- JAPANESE TOSAS
- DOGS DESIGNATED BY THE SECRETARY OF STATE
  At the time of going to press, this includes the Dogo Argentina and the Fila Braziliero Dangerous Dogs (Designated Types) Order 1991

A person commits an offence if he:

has such a dog in his **POSSESSION** or **CUSTODY** except under a power of seizure or in accordance with an order for its destruction;

BREEDS
or breeds from, any of the above;

SELLS
or exchanges such a dog or offers, advertises or exposes such a dog for sale or exchange;

MAKES A GIFT
(or offers to do so) of such a dog or advertises or exposes such a dog as a gift;

ALLOWS
such a dog of which he is the owner or of which he is for the time being in charge to be in a **PUBLIC PLACE** without being **MUZZLED** and **KEPT ON A LEAD**;
('**Muzzled**' means sufficient to prevent it biting someone, and '**kept on a lead**' means securely held by a person not less than 16 years. S 7)

ABANDONS
such a dog of which he is the owner;

Allows such a dog to **STRAY**, being the owner or for the time being in charge.

Control of Dogs

S 3 DANGEROUS DOGS ACT 1991

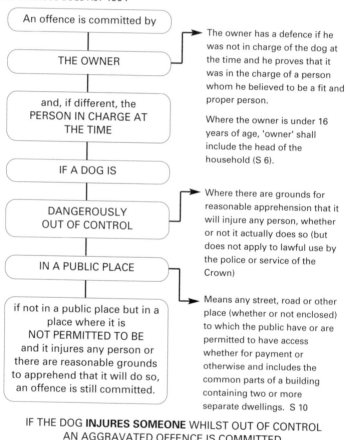

An offence is committed by

THE OWNER

The owner has a defence if he was not in charge of the dog at the time and he proves that it was in the charge of a person whom he believed to be a fit and proper person.

Where the owner is under 16 years of age, 'owner' shall include the head of the household (S 6).

and, if different, the PERSON IN CHARGE AT THE TIME

IF A DOG IS

DANGEROUSLY OUT OF CONTROL

Where there are grounds for reasonable apprehension that it will injure any person, whether or not it actually does so (but does not apply to lawful use by the police or service of the Crown)

IN A PUBLIC PLACE

Means any street, road or other place (whether or not enclosed) to which the public have or are permitted to have access whether for payment or otherwise and includes the common parts of a building containing two or more separate dwellings. S 10

if not in a public place but in a place where it is NOT PERMITTED TO BE and it injures any person or there are reasonable grounds to apprehend that it will do so, an offence is still committed.

IF THE DOG **INJURES SOMEONE** WHILST OUT OF CONTROL AN AGGRAVATED OFFENCE IS COMMITTED FOR WHICH HEAVIER PENALTIES ARE LIABLE

POLICE POWERS
S 5 DANGEROUS DOGS ACT 1991

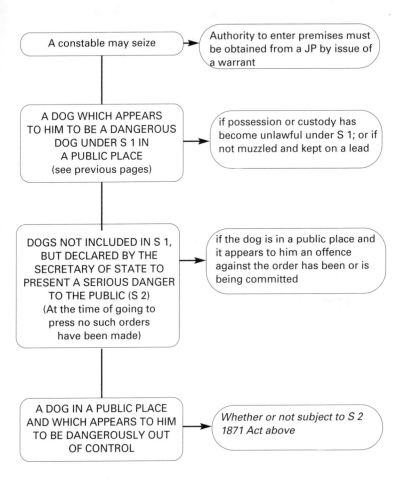

A constable may seize → Authority to enter premises must be obtained from a JP by issue of a warrant

A DOG WHICH APPEARS TO HIM TO BE A DANGEROUS DOG UNDER S 1 IN A PUBLIC PLACE (see previous pages) → if possession or custody has become unlawful under S 1; or if not muzzled and kept on a lead

DOGS NOT INCLUDED IN S 1, BUT DECLARED BY THE SECRETARY OF STATE TO PRESENT A SERIOUS DANGER TO THE PUBLIC (S 2) (At the time of going to press no such orders have been made) → if the dog is in a public place and it appears to him an offence against the order has been or is being committed

A DOG IN A PUBLIC PLACE AND WHICH APPEARS TO HIM TO BE DANGEROUSLY OUT OF CONTROL → Whether or not subject to S 2 1871 Act above

Guard Dogs
S 1 GUARD DOGS ACT 1975

A person shall not use or permit the use of a

guard dog

Means a dog which is being used to protect premises, or property kept on the premises, or a person guarding the premises or such property

at any premises

Means land other than agricultural land and land within the curtilage of a dwelling house. It also includes buildings and parts of buildings, other than dwelling houses

unless

A NOTICE

containing a warning that a guard dog is present is clearly exhibited at each entrance to the premises

and

A HANDLER

is present on the premises

and

at all times keeps the dog under his control

except where another handler has control of it or whilst the dog is secured so that it is not at liberty to go freely about the premises

Dangerous Wild Animals

S 1 DANGEROUS WILD ANIMALS ACT 1976

No person is allowed to keep a dangerous wild animal unless he has been granted a licence to do so by the local authority (S 1).

A 'dangerous wild animal' is one which is specifically mentioned in the Act. Many animals are mentioned but the following list gives a guide to the type of animal referred to:

Alligators, crocodiles, ostriches, apes, poisonous snakes, lions, tigers, leopards, bears, wild dogs and wolves.

The provisions of this Act do not apply to:

- Zoos
- Circuses
- Licensed pet shops
- Premises authorised to
  be used for experiments (S 5)

Animals on Highways

S 155 HIGHWAYS ACT 1980

If any animal (or animals)

Horses, cattle, sheep, goats or swine

'Keeper' means the person in whose possession they are

are at at any time found straying or lying on or at the side of a highway their keeper is guilty of an offence

Does not apply to part of a highway passing over any common, waste or unenclosed ground

A person guilty of this offence is liable for the expenses incurred in the removal and impounding of the animal

Dogs to be kept on lead
Where a local authority has designated a road upon which dogs must be kept on a lead, a person who causes or permits a dog to be on the road in contravention of the order shall be guilty of an offence

Dogs fouling land
Where a local authority has designated land in that area, it is an offence for a person in charge of a dog to fail to remove faeces deposited by the dog forthwith.

Diseases of Animals

ANIMAL HEALTH ACT 1981

NOTIFICATION S 15(1)

Any person having possession or charge of a diseased animal shall keep it separate from unaffected animals and notify the police with all practicable speed.

'INFECTED AREAS'

If necessary, the veterinary inspector who is called to visit the infected place declares the premises and the area surrounding the premises to be an infected area.

MOVEMENT

Movement of animals from and to infected areas is then restricted to those authorised by licence. Various powers are then given to the minister and the local authority to make orders and regulations to control the situation.

POWER OF ARREST S 60

If a person is seen or found committing, or is reasonably suspected of being engaged in committing, an act which has been declared to be an offence against the Act or an order of the minister or a regulation of the local authority, a constable may stop and detain him and if his name and address are not given to the satisfaction of the constable, he **may be apprehended in accordance with** the provisions of the Police and Criminal Evidence Act 1984.

ANIMALS AND PROPERTY

Irrespective of the stopping or apprehension of the person the constable may stop, detain and examine any animal, vehicle, boat or thing to which the offence relates, and require the same to be returned to any place from which it was unlawfully removed, and he may execute and enforce that requisition.

OBSTRUCTION S 60

A person who obstructs or impedes or assists to obstruct or impede a constable or other officer in the execution of this Act or of orders or regulations made in consequence of it, may be arrested by the constable or officer.

POWERS OF ENTRY

In areas where constables are appointed as local authority inspectors, they also have power to enter land and buildings where they suspect that diseased animals are or have been kept or where provisions of the Act are not being complied with.

Diseases of Animals – continued

ANIMAL HEALTH ACT 1981

Meaning of 'Animals'

Animal means:

- cattle, sheep and goats,
- all other ruminating animals and swine,
- any mammals except whales, dolphins, porpoises, seals, dugongs, and manatees, and
- poultry (domestic fowls, turkeys, geese, ducks, guinea-fowls, pigeons, pheasants and partridges and all other birds).

'**Cattle**' means bulls, cows, steers, heifers and calves.

Meaning of 'Disease'

Disease means:

- african swine fever,
- anthrax,
- aujeszky's disease,
- bovine leukosis,
- brucellosis,
- brucellosis suis,
- cattle plague,
- equine viral arteritis,
- foot and mouth disease,
- infectious diseases of horses,
- pleuro-pneumonia,
- rabies,
- sheep pox,
- sheep scab,
- swine fever,
- swine vesicular disease,
- tuberculosis,
- tularaemia, and
- warble fly

and in relation to poultry means:

- fowl cholera,
- fowl paralysis,
- fowl pest,
- fowl plague,
- fowl pox,
- fowl typhoid,
- infectious bronchitis,
- infectious laryngotracheitis,
- Newcastle disease,
- paramyxovirus 1 in pigeons, and
- pullorum disease

Rabies

Ss 15, 61 & 62 ANIMAL HEALTH ACT 1981

The powers conferred by these sections are without prejudice to the diseases of animals powers given on the previous pages.

Offences specific to this disease involve landing or attempting to land or importing, or attempted importation through the channel tunnel, animals in contravention of the order introduced to prevent the introduction of rabies into GB; the failure by the person having charge or control of any vessel or boat to discharge any obligation imposed on him by such an order; and the unlawful movement of any animal into, within or out of an infected area or place.

Any person who knows or suspects that an animal is affected with rabies shall give notice of that fact to a constable (S 15).

POLICE POWERS

A constable may arrest without warrant any person whom he, with reasonable cause, suspects to be in the act of committing or to have committed an offence against this section.

For the purpose of arresting a person a constable may enter (if need be by force) and search any vessel, boat, hovercraft, aircraft or vehicle of any other description in which that person is or where the constable reasonably suspects him to be.

The above power of entry also applies in exercising the power to seize any animal.

Importation of Animals
ARTs. 4 & 4A RABIES (IMPORTATION OF DOGS, CATS AND OTHER MAMMALS) ORDER 1974

This order applies to a wide variety of mammals which can be found in Sched. 1 to the Order. It includes dogs, cats, lions, tigers, hedgehogs, shrews, moles, rabbits, kangaroos, monkeys, baboons, apes, rats and mice.

The landing in GB of an animal brought from a place outside GB is prohibited except:
1. An animal brought to GB from Northern Ireland, Republic of Ireland, Channel Islands or Isle of Man, provided that, if the animal was taken to one of those places from another country (other than GB), the prohibition **will** apply unless:
   - it was imported from another member state or Norway in accordance with Council Directive 92/65/EEC; or
   - in any other case it has been detained and quarantined for at least 6 months before coming to GB.
2. An animal brought to GB from Northern Ireland, Republic of Ireland, Channel Islands or Isle of Man, provided:
   - if it was admitted there under Regulation EC 998 2003; and
   - in the case of a dog, cat or ferret, it has been treated against Echinococcus Multilocularis and ticks between 24 and 48 hours before embarkation to that place.
3. An animal landing under the authority of a licence granted by the Minister.

Specified Ports listed below must be used for landing animals except:
- specifically authorised in the licence mentioned in para. 3 above;
- an animal to which para. 1 above applies;
- landing at Cheriton through the Channel Tunnel; or
- the vessel/aircraft has been diverted to another port/airport by an inspector in the interests of safety or other exceptional circumstances.

The ports are: Dover Eastern Docks; Harwich and Parkeston Quay; Hull; Portsmouth; and Southampton.

The airports are: Birmingham; Edinburgh; Gatwick; Glasgow; Heathrow; Leeds; Manchester; and Prestwick.

Animals taken from GB, Northern Ireland, Republic of Ireland, Channel Islands or Isle of Man, to a place outside those countries (whether or not landed at that place, or coming into contact with another animal), shall be deemed to be an animal brought from a place outside GB and therefore subject to the above rules.

Animals imported from a member State other than the Republic of Ireland are not subject to the prohibition on landing, nor the use of specified ports as above if imported in accordance with Council Directive 92/65/EEC or the Animal and Animal Products (Import and Export) Regulations 2004 (concerning the import, export or transport for intra community trade of certain animals and animal products).

Animals imported under the Non-Commercial Movement of Pet Animals Regulations 2004 or Regulation (EC) 998/2003 (which also deals with animal health requirements for the non-commercial movement of pet animals) are not subject to the provisions of this order. For provisions of the 2004 Regulations, see the following page.

Pet Travel Scheme

NON COMMERCIAL MOVEMENT OF PET ANIMALS (ENGLAND) REGULATIONS 2004

A pet animal may be brought into England without complying with the Rabies (Importation of Dogs, Cats and other Mammals) Order 1974 (quarantine, etc.) provided the Community Regulation (998/2003) and these Regulations are complied with. The regulations do not apply to Wales or Scotland, but where an animal has been brought into England in accordance with the regulations, it can then be taken to Wales or Scotland. (Reg. 4).

2004 Regulations

1. Pet dogs, cats and ferrets must be **identifiiable by microchi**. (Reg. 6).
2. A blood test must be carried out at least 6 months before arrival in England. (Reg.7).
3. Pet dogs, cats and ferrets must be brought into England by an **authorised carrier**. (Reg. 8).
4. Between 24 and 48 hours before embarkation to England, dogs, cats and ferrets must have been **treated by a vet** against Echinococcus Multilocularis and ticks. This is in addition to the Community Regulation requirement to be vaccinated against rabies, and lasts until 2009. (Reg. 9).
5. In addition to the **certifiicatio** required by the Community Regulation, the passport or health certificate shall also specify the manufacturer, product and date of administration of the treatment. (Reg. 9).

Exclusion. The above exemption from quarantine, etc. does not apply to the movement to England of:

1. more than 5 pet animals if they are travelling together and they come from a country other than Andorra, Iceland, Liechtenstein, Monaco, Norway, San Marino, Switzerland or The Vatican;
2. prairie dogs originating in or travelling from the U.S.A.;
3. cats travelling from Australia accompanied by an Australian Government Veterinary Certificate (but a cat in transit through Australia by air shall not be treated as travelling from Australia if it does not leave the airport). (Reg. 5).

Community Regulation 998/2003

Applies to the non commercial movement of pet animals which are dogs, cats, ferrets, invertebrates (except bees and crustaceans), ornamental tropical fish, amphibia, reptiles, birds (all species except poultry covered by other Council Directives), and mammals (rodents and domestic rabbits), between member states or from 3rd countries (Art. 2).

"Pet Animals" means those listed above which are accompanying their owners or other responsible person on their behalf and not intended to be sold or transferred to another person. (Art. 3).

Pet animals which are **dogs, cats or ferrets** being coming into the U.K. must be microchipped and have a passport issued by a vet. certifying valid antirabies vaccination (Art 5), and certifying a satisfactory blood test (Art. 6).

"Passport" means any document enabling it to be clearly identified and enabling the points relating to its status to be checked. (Art. 3).

Other pet animals which are: invertebrates (except bees and crustaceans), ornamental tropical fish, amphibia, reptiles, birds (all species except poultry covered by other Council Directives), and mammals (rodents and domestic rabbits) coming to the U.K. from a member state or from Andorra, Iceland, Liechtenstein, Monaco, Norway, San Marino, Switzerland or The Vatican, of shall not be subject to any requirements with regard to rabies. However, they may need a certificate and have their numbers limited. (Art. 7).

Game Licences

S 1 HARES ACT 1848, S 4 GAME LICENCES
ACT 1860, S 4 GROUND GAME ACT 1880

It is an offence, without having a
GAME LICENCE 1860 ACT

to take, kill or pursue by any means whatever, or to use any dog, gun, net or
other engine for the purpose of taking, killing or pursuing any

hare, pheasant, partridge, grouse, heath or moor game,
black game, woodcock, snipe, rabbit or deer
Except

A game licence is not required for
any of the following purposes:

- taking woodcock or snipe with
  nets or snares
- taking or destroying rabbits by
  the proprietor of a warren or
  grounds, or the tenant of land, or
  by his permission
- pursuing hares by coursing with
  greyhounds, or killing hares by
  hunting with beagles or other
  hounds
- taking, killing or destroying hares
  on enclosed land by the owner,
  occupier and person authorised
  by him in writing
- pursuing and killing of deer by
  hunting with hounds
- taking and killing of deer in
  enclosed lands by the owner or
  occupier of lands or by his
  permission

The following persons are exempt
from the requirement to hold a
licence:

- the royal family
- any person appointed as
  gamekeeper on behalf of Her
  Majesty
- a person aiding or assisting the
  holder of a licence
- a person authorised to kill hares
  under the Hares Act 1848
- the occupier of the land upon
  which the game is taken or killed,
  and persons authorised by him.

A police officer may demand production of the licence and, if not produced,
require the person's name and address. Failure to produce the licence or, in
default, to give the correct name and address, is an offence. S 31A

Game – Out of Season

GAME ACT 1831

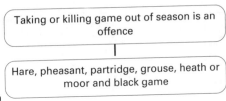

Taking or killing game out of season is an offence

Hare, pheasant, partridge, grouse, heath or moor and black game

Close Season
Sundays
Christmas Day

Partridge	1st February	to	1st September
Pheasant	1st February	to	1st October
Black Game*	10th December	to	20th August
Grouse	10th December	to	12th August
Bustard	1st March	to	1st September

(except in Somerset, Devon or the New Forest of Hampshire, where the close season is between 10th December and 1st September)

Eggs

S 24 GAME ACT 1831

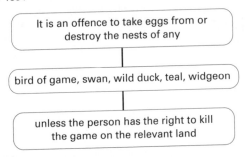

It is an offence to take eggs from or destroy the nests of any

bird of game, swan, wild duck, teal, widgeon

unless the person has the right to kill the game on the relevant land

Havings such eggs in one's possession or control is also an offence (see further restrictions under 'birds')

Poaching

Poaching (by Day)

Ss 30, 31, 32 & 35 GAME ACT 1831

It is an offence by day

'Day' begins 1 hour before sunrise until 1 hour after sunset

to trespass on any land in search or pursuit of

hares, pheasants, partridges, grouse, heath and moor game, black game, woodcocks, snipe or rabbits

An additional penalty is payable if 5 or more persons together are found on any land for the purpose of poaching

A further offence is committed if 5 or more together trespass to search for the above mentioned, any one of them being armed with a gun, and any of them, with intent to prevent an authorised person from exercising his powers under S 31 (see later), uses violence, intimidation or menace (S 32)

Exception The offence of trespassing in pursuit of game does not extend to hunting or coursing with hounds and being in fresh pursuit of any deer, hare or fox already started on other land (S 35).

Poaching (by Night)

S 1 NIGHT POACHING ACT 1828 AS AMENDED

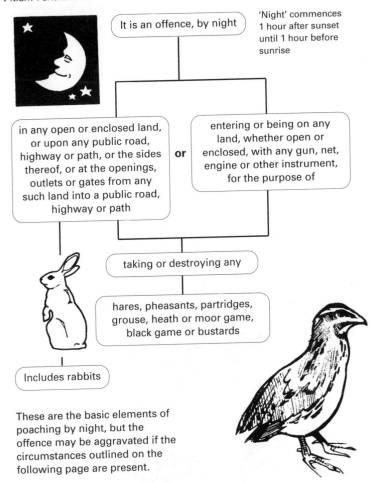

It is an offence, by night

'Night' commences 1 hour after sunset until 1 hour before sunrise

in any open or enclosed land, or upon any public road, highway or path, or the sides thereof, or at the openings, outlets or gates from any such land into a public road, highway or path

or

entering or being on any land, whether open or enclosed, with any gun, net, engine or other instrument, for the purpose of

taking or destroying any

hares, pheasants, partridges, grouse, heath or moor game, black game or bustards

Includes rabbits

These are the basic elements of poaching by night, but the offence may be aggravated if the circumstances outlined on the following page are present.

Poaching (by Night) – continued

Ss 2 & 9 NIGHT POACHING ACT 1828

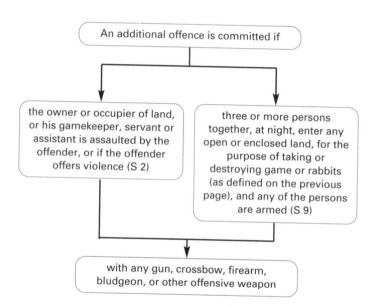

An additional offence is committed if

the owner or occupier of land, or his gamekeeper, servant or assistant is assaulted by the offender, or if the offender offers violence (S 2)

three or more persons together, at night, enter any open or enclosed land, for the purpose of taking or destroying game or rabbits (as defined on the previous page), and any of the persons are armed (S 9)

with any gun, crossbow, firearm, bludgeon, or other offensive weapon

Police Powers

On Land S 2 GAME LAWS (AMENDMENT) ACT 1960

A constable may enter land if he has reasonable grounds for suspecting that a person is trespassing on the land, by day or night, for the purpose of taking or destroying game or rabbits.

Night S 2 GAME LAWS (AMENDMENT) ACT 1960

Where a constable has reasonable grounds for suspecting that a person is committing an offence on any land under Ss 1 or 9 of the Night Poaching Act 1828, he may enter the land for the purpose of requiring him to quit and to give his name and address.

Daytime Ss 31 & 31A GAME ACT 1831

A constable may require any person he finds on any land in search or pursuit of game, woodcocks, snipe or rabbits, to quit the land and give his name and address. Any subsequent arrest must be in accordance with the Police and Criminal Evidence Act 1984. There is also power to enter the land for the above purpose under S 2 Game Laws (Amendment) Act, 1960. S 31 also applies to anyone having the right to kill game on the land, occupiers, persons authorised by the aforementioned, gamekeepers or servants, and wardens, rangers and others employed in a similar capacity in royal forests and parks, etc.

Street or Public Place

A constable may, in any public place, **search** any person whom he has good cause to **suspect** of coming from any land where he has been unlawfully in pursuit of game, and having in his possession any game, gun, ammunition, nets, snares, traps or other device for killing or taking game, and also to **stop** and **search** any cart or other conveyance which the constable has good cause to suspect is carrying any game or article mentioned above, and the constable may **seize** and detain any game or article found on the person or in the conveyance. Proceedings are then taken by **summons**. There is no power of arrest.

S 2 POACHING PREVENTION ACT 1862

A similar power to search and seize property and game is provided under S 4, Game Laws (Amendment) Act 1960, where the constable is arresting an offender under S 25, Police and Criminal Evidence Act 1984.

Deer

DEER ACT 1991

Poaching of Deer s 1

It is an offence

without the consent of the

OWNER
or
OCCUPIER
or
OTHER LAWFUL AUTHORITY

to ENTER any land in search or pursuit of any deer with the intention of TAKING, KILLING OR INJURING IT

it shall be a defence if the person believed that

- he would have the consent of the owner or occupier of the land if they knew of it, or

- he has other lawful authority to do it

- to intentionally take, kill or injure, or attempt to take, kill or injure any deer

- to search for or pursue any deer with the intention of taking, killing or injuring any deer, or

- to remove the carcass of any deer

  WHILST ON ANY LAND

Land includes buildings and other structures, land covered with water, and any interest, etc, over the land

If an offence is suspected by the owner or occupier or any person authorised by him or having the right to kill deer on the land, he may require the offender to give his name and address and to quit the land forthwith. Failure to comply is an offence.

Close Season

S 2 and sched 1

> It is an offence to intentionally take or kill, or attempt to take or kill, any deer in the close season:

RED DEER (Cervus elaphus)

Stags   1st May to 31st July inclusive
Hinds   1st March to 31st October inclusive

FALLOW DEER (Dama dama)

Buck   1st May to 31st July inclusive
Doe   1st March to 31st October inclusive

ROE DEER (Capreolus capreolus)

Buck   1st November to 31st March inclusive
Doe   1st March to 31st October inclusive

SIKA DEER (Cervus nippon)

Stags   1st May to 31st July inclusive
Hinds   1st March to 31st October inclusive

There is an exemption for businessmen keeping marked deer on enclosed land for meat, other foodstuffs, skin or other by-products, or breeding stock.

Night

It is an offence to take or intentionally kill any deer between the expiry of the first hour after sunset and the beginning of the last hour before sunrise (S 3).

Possession of prohibited weapons and articles

It is an offence to have in possession for the purpose of committing the above: any trap, snare, poisoned or stupefying bait; net, arrow, spear or similar missile; or any missile whether discharged from a firearm or otherwise carrying or containing any poison, stupefying drug or muscle relaxing agent; or any firearm or ammunition (S 5).

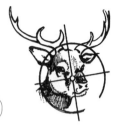

Use of Weapons etc S 4

It is an offence:

- To set any **traps, snare, or poisoned or stupefying bait** calculated to **cause bodily injury** to any deer.
- To use any **trap, snare, or poisoned or stupefying bait, or any net** for the purpose of **taking or killing** any deer.
- To use, for the purpose of **taking, killing or injuring** any deer:
  1. Any smooth-bore gun.
  2. Any rifle having a calibre of less than .240 inches or a muzzle energy of less than 2,305 joules (1,700 foot pounds).
  3. Any air gun, air rifle or air pistol.
  4. Any cartridge for use in a smooth-bore gun.
  5. Any bullet for use in a rifle other than a soft-nosed or hollow-nosed bullet.
  6. Any arrow, spear or similar missile.
  7. Any missile, whether discharged from a firearm or otherwise, carrying or containing any poison, stupefying drug or muscle-relaxing agent.
- To **discharge any firearm**, or project any missile, from any **mechanically propelled vehicle** at any deer.
- To use any **mechanically propelled vehicle** for the purpose of **driving deer**.
- To attempt to commit any of the above offences (S 5).

It shall be a defence to either of the last two offences if the act is done with the written authority of the occupier of any enclosed land in relation to deer usually kept on that land.

Other miscellaneous defences to this and previous sections are contained in Ss 6, 7 and 8 (eg to prevent suffering, causing damage to crops, and for nature conservancy).

Sale of Venison S 10

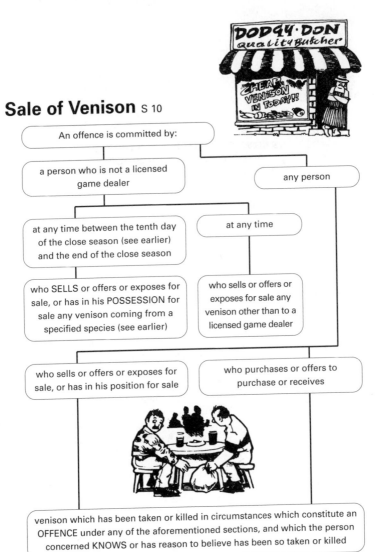

An offence is committed by:

a person who is not a licensed game dealer

any person

at any time between the tenth day of the close season (see earlier) and the end of the close season

at any time

who SELLS or offers or exposes for sale, or has in his POSSESSION for sale any venison coming from a specified species (see earlier)

who sells or offers or exposes for sale any venison other than to a licensed game dealer

who sells or offers or exposes for sale, or has in his position for sale

who purchases or offers to purchase or receives

venison which has been taken or killed in circumstances which constitute an OFFENCE under any of the aforementioned sections, and which the person concerned KNOWS or has reason to believe has been so taken or killed

Sale includes barter and exchange

Police Powers S 12

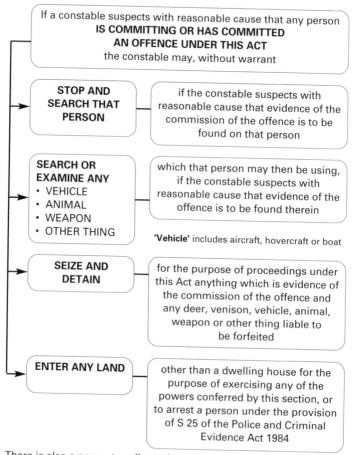

If a constable suspects with reasonable cause that any person
**IS COMMITTING OR HAS COMMITTED
AN OFFENCE UNDER THIS ACT**
the constable may, without warrant

STOP AND SEARCH THAT PERSON

if the constable suspects with reasonable cause that evidence of the commission of the offence is to be found on that person

SEARCH OR EXAMINE ANY
- VEHICLE
- ANIMAL
- WEAPON
- OTHER THING

which that person may then be using, if the constable suspects with reasonable cause that evidence of the offence is to be found therein

'Vehicle' includes aircraft, hovercraft or boat

SEIZE AND DETAIN

for the purpose of proceedings under this Act anything which is evidence of the commission of the offence and any deer, venison, vehicle, animal, weapon or other thing liable to be forfeited

ENTER ANY LAND

other than a dwelling house for the purpose of exercising any of the powers conferred by this section, or to arrest a person under the provision of S 25 of the Police and Criminal Evidence Act 1984

There is also a power to sell any deer or venison seized.

Badgers

PROTECTION OF BADGERS ACT 1992

Killing etc S 1(1)
It is an offence to wilfully kill, injure, take
or attempt to kill, injure or take a badger.
See next page for exceptions

Firearms S 2
It is an offence to use for killing a badger any firearm except: a smooth bore
weapon of not less than 20 bore, or a rifle using ammunition of muzzle
energy not less than 160ft/lbs and bullet weighing not less than 38 grains.
See next page for exceptions

Sale, possession, etc S 4
It is an offence to sell, offer for sale, or have in possession or under control,
any live badger.
See next page for exceptions

Possession, etc S 1(3)
It is an offence to have in possession or under control any dead
badger or any part of, or anything derived from a dead badger unless it was
not killed in contravention of this Act.
See next page for exceptions

Cruelty, etc
It is an offence to:
• Cruelly ill-treat a badger S 2
• Use any badger tongs in the course of taking or killing a badger S 2
• Dig for a badger S 2
• Mark or ring a badger, unless authorised by a licence S 5
• Interfere with a badger sett by:
  a) damaging a sett or part of it;
  b) destroying a sett;
  c) obstructing access to any entrance of a sett;
  d) causing a dog to enter a badger sett; or
  e) disturbing a badger when it is occupying a sett.
  Except: if necessary to prevent serious damage to crops, land or poultry
  (but licence must have been applied for); obstructing for fox hunting
  purposes (but only if done by hand); or incidental and unavoidable result of
  a lawful operation.

Exceptions

A person will not be guilty of the offences of killing, etc if:

- He is a 'licensed person' S 10, or
- A badger is found disabled and it is taken for the purpose of tending it S 6, or
- A badger is so seriously injured or in such a condition that to kill it would be an act of mercy S 6, or
- Where the killing or injuring was an unavoidable result of a lawful action S 6
- Authorised under the Animals (Scientific Procedures) Act 1986 (S 6)
- The act was necessary to prevent serious damage to land, crops or poultry (but if such damage foreseeable then a licence must have been applied for).

A person shall not be guilty of having a live badger in his possession under S 4 if:

- He has possession of it in the course of his business as a carrier
- He is a licensed person, or
- It is necessary to keep it in possession for the purpose of tending to its disability.

Police powers

Where a police constable has reasonable cause to suspect that an offence against the Act has been or is being committed he may:

stop and search that person and search any vehicle or article he may have with him. Order the person to quit the land and to give his name and address. Failure to do so is an offence.

seize and detain anything which may be evidence, any badger, whether dead or alive, and any weapon or article in that person's possession.

Birds

WILLIFE AND COUNTRYSIDE ACT 1981

The law relating to birds broadly covers restrictions on killing and taking wild birds; the prohibition of certain methods of killing or taking them; restrictions on the sale of birds and their eggs; and the prevention of disturbance to nesting birds. The various aspects are discussed in the following pages but for ease of reference the four categories into which birds are placed may be exemplified at this point.

Schedule 1
These are birds which are protected by special penalties
Part 1 At all times – eg barn owl, eagle, purple heron, osprey, stone curlew
Part 2 During the close season – eg goldeneye, greylag goose, pintail goose

Schedule 2
These are birds which may be taken or killed outside the close season – eg coot, mallard, woodcock.

Schedule 3
These are birds which may be sold
Part 1 Alive at all times if ringed and bred in captivity – eg blackbird, chaffinch, magpie, barn owl, starling
Part 2 Dead at all times – eg wood pigeon
Part 3 Dead from 1st Sept to 28th Feb – eg tufted duck, mallard, snipe, woodcock

Schedule 4
These are birds which must be registered and ringed if kept in captivity – eg falcon, hawks, osprey, crested tit, kestrel, woodlark.

Birds

WILDLIFE AND COUNTRYSIDE ACT 1981

'Wild bird' means of a species which is ordinarily resident in or is a visitor to the European Territory of any member state in a wild state but does not include poultry or game bird, nor does it include any bird which has been bred in captivity.

'Poultry' means domestic fowl, geese, ducks, guinea fowl, pigeons, quails and turkeys.

'Game bird' means pheasant, partridge, grouse (or moor) game, black (or heath) game or ptarmigan.

S 1

It is an offence for any person intentionally to

- kill, injure or take any wild bird

- have in possession or control any live or dead wild bird or part of one

- take or destroy an egg of a wild bird or have in his possession or control an egg or part of one

- take, damage or destroy the nest of a wild bird whilst in use or being built

- disturb any wild bird listed in Sched 1 while it is building a nest or is in, on or near a nest containing eggs or young; or disturb dependent young of such a bird (but if the bird is included in Part 2 of the Sched, the offence is only committed during the close season)

But see following page for exceptions.

198

Exceptions S 2

KILLING, etc

A person shall not be guilty of an offence under S 1 by reason of the killing or taking of a bird included in part 2 of Sched 2 (see earlier) or the taking, damaging or destruction of a nest of such a bird, or the taking or destruction of an egg of such a bird, when done in any case by an authorised person.

A person shall not be guilty of an offence under S 1 by reason of the killing, injuring or taking of a bird included in part 1 of Sched 2 (see earlier) outside the close season for that bird.

CLOSE SEASON

CAPERCAILLIE AND WOODCOCK (except Scotland)
1st February to 30th September

SNIPE 1st February to 11th August

WILD DUCK OR WILD GEESE (in any area below high water mark of ordinary spring tides) 21st February to 31st August

ANY OTHER CASE 1st February to 31st August

AUTHORISED PERSONS

An authorised person will not be guilty of an offence of killing or injuring a wild bird, other than a bird included in Sched 1, if he shows that it was necessary:

- For preserving public health or public or air safety;
- For preventing the spread of disease; or
- For preventing serious damage to livestock, foodstuffs for livestock, crops, vegetables, fruit, growing timber, fisheries or inland waters.

GENERAL

A person shall not be guilty of an offence by reason of:

- Taking a wild bird which has been disabled and which was taken to tend it and release when no longer disabled;
- Killing a wild bird so seriously disabled that it would not recover; or
- Any act which was the incidental result of a lawful operation and could not have been avoided. S 4

Prohibited Methods of Killing etc

S 5 WILDLIFE AND COUNTRYSIDE ACT 1981

Unless authorised by licence, it is an offence for any person to:

Set in position any article to cause bodily injury to any wild bird coming into contact with it, ie springe, trap, gin, snare, hook and line, any electrical device for killing, stunning or frightening, or any poisonous, poisoned or stupefying substance

Use for the purpose of taking or killing any wild bird any article as aforesaid, or any net, baited board, gas, bird-lime or other like substance

Use as a decoy, for the purpose of killing or taking a wild bird, any sound recording or any live bird or other animal which is tethered or similarly secured, or which is blind, maimed or injured

Use for the purpose of killing or taking any wild bird

- A bow or crossbow
- Explosive other than ammunition
- An automatic weapon
- Shotgun over 1 ¾" dia. barrel
- An illuminating or night sighting device
- A lighting or dazzling device
- Gas or smoke
- A chemical wetting agent

Use any mechanically propelled vehicle in immediate pursuit of a wild bird for the purpose of killing or taking it.

But it shall not be unlawful: a) for an authorised person to use a cage-trap or net to take a bird included in part 2 of Sched 2; b) to use nets for taking wild duck in a duck decoy which was in use immediately before the passing of the Protection of Birds Act 1954; or c) to use a cage-trap or net for taking any game bird for the purpose of breeding.

But it will not be lawful to use a net for taking birds in flight, or a net projected or propelled other than by hand for taking birds on the ground.

Restrictions on Sale

S 6 WILDLIFE AND COUNTRYSIDE ACT 1981

It is an offence to sell, offer or expose for sale, or have in possession or transport for the purpose of sale, or advertise the buying or selling of

live birds

other than a bird included in part 1 of Sched 3 (see earlier)

dead birds

other than a bird included in part 2 or 3 of Sched 3, or any part of, or anything derived from, such a wild bird

unless he is for the time being registered so to do

eggs

of a wild bird or any part of such an egg

It is an offence to show or cause or permit to be shown in a competition any live bird other than a bird included in part 1 of Sched 3; or a bird one of whose parents was such a wild bird.

Specific Offences
WILDLIFE AND COUNTRYSIDE ACT 1981

REGISTRATION OF CAPTIVE BIRDS (S 7)

It is an offence to keep or have in possession or have under control any bird included in Schedule 4, which has not been registered and ringed or marked in accordance with regulations. It is also an offence to have a Schedule 4 bird within 3 or 5 years (depending on the nature of the offence) of a conviction for certain offences relating to wild birds.

CONFINING (S 8)

It is an offence to keep or confine any bird in any cage or receptacle which does not allow sufficient room for the bird to stretch its wings freely.

But this offence does not apply to:

• Domestic fowl, ducks, geese, guinea fowl, pigeons and turkeys;

• Any bird whilst being conveyed, publicly exhibited (provided the time does not exceed 72 hours), or whilst undergoing veterinary treatment.

SHOOTING EVENTS (S 8)

It is an offence to be in any way involved in any event in which captive birds are liberated for the purpose of being shot immediately after their liberation.

Police Powers

S 19 WILDLIFE AND COUNTRYSIDE ACT 1981

In relation to any offence against the Act (this includes taking or killing birds or eggs; using illegal methods of taking or killing, etc; unlawful selling, etc; confining; and disturbing nesting birds) a constable may without warrant

STOP AND SEARCH

any person if the constable suspects that evidence of the commission of the offence is to be found on that person

and examine anything which that person may then be using or have in his possession if the constable suspects that evidence of the commission of the offence is to be found on that thing. The constable may, for the purpose of exercising these powers or arresting a person under S 25 Police and Criminal Evidence Act 1984, enter any land other than a dwelling house. A warrant to enter and search premises may be granted by a justice of the peace if the offence attracts a special penalty

and may SEIZE AND DETAIN

for the purpose of proceedings, any thing which may be evidence of the commission of the offence or may be liable to be forfeited under this Act

Fish

S 32 AND SCHED 1 THEFT ACT 1968

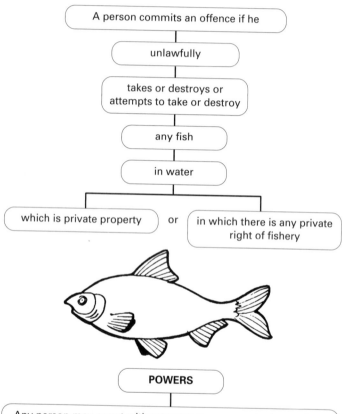

A person commits an offence if he

unlawfully

takes or destroys or attempts to take or destroy

any fish

in water

which is private property   or   in which there is any private right of fishery

POWERS

Any person may arrest without warrant anyone who is, or whom he, with reasonable cause, suspects to be committing this offence (except in the daytime (one hour before sunrise until one hour after sunset)) and may seize from any person who is, or whom he, with reasonable cause, suspects to be, committing the offence, anything which he has with him for use for taking or destroying fish

Offences

SALMON AND FRESHWATER FISHERIES ACT 1975

The following are offences connected with salmon, trout or freshwater fish:

Nets

To use nets with meshes smaller than 2″ between knots, or to use two nets of requisite mesh close together, or to work a draft net across more than ¾ of the width of any waters for salmon or migratory trout (S 3).

Poison, etc

To cause or knowingly permit any poisonous or injurious substances to flow in, or be put into, any waters containing fish (S 4).

Damage/Explosives

To use in or near any waters any explosive substance, any poison or other noxious substance, or any electrical device, with intent to take or destroy fish; or without lawful excuse destroy or damage any dam, flood-gate or sluice with intent to take or destroy fish (S 5).

Instruments

Using any firearm; an otter lath or jack, wire or snare; a crossline or setline; a spear, gaff, stroke-haul, snatch or other like instrument; or a light for the purpose of taking or killing salmon, trout or freshwater fish; or to have same in possession with intent to use for taking or killing such fish or to throw or discharge any stone or other missile for the purpose of taking or killing salmon, trout or freshwater fish (S 1).

Roe

To use fish roe for fishing, or to buy, sell or have salmon or trout roe for that purpose (S 2).

Young fish

To wilfully disturb any spawn or spawning fish.
To knowingly take, buy, sell or have in possession any unclean or immature fish (S 2).

Weirs

No fishing weir or mill dam may be used, which was not in use on 6.8.1861, for the purpose of taking salmon or migratory trout (S 7).

Fishing Licences

Ss 25, 27 & 35 SALMON AND FRESHWATER FISHERIES ACT 1975

Water authorities are required to control fishing for

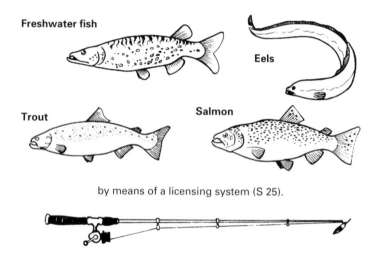

Freshwater fish

Eels

Trout

Salmon

by means of a licensing system (S 25).

It is an offence to fish for or take fish otherwise than by means of an instrument authorised in the licence, or to have in possession such an instrument with intent to use it (S 27)

Production

A constable, water bailiff, or person producing his authority may require any person found fishing or whom he reasonably suspects to be about to fish, or to have within the preceding half-hour fished, to produce his licence and give his name and address.

Failure to comply is an offence but if the person produces his licence within 7 days of the request at the water authority office he will not be convicted of the offence (S 35).

Close Season (Fish)

S 19 & SCHED 1 SALMON AND FRESHWATER FISHERIES ACT 1975

Unless there is a bylaw to the contrary, it is an offence to fish for, take, kill or attempt to take or kill at the following times:

Salmon

By rod and line	31st Oct - 1st Feb
By any other method	31st Aug - 1st Feb

The weekly close time is from
6am Saturday to 6am Monday

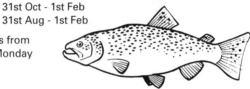

Trout

By rod and line	30th Sep - 1st March
By any other method	31st Aug - 1st March

The weekly close time is from
6am Saturday to 6am Monday

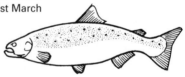

Freshwater fish

(other than salmon, trout, eels and migratory fish)
14th March - 16th June

Rainbow trout
The close season is
fixed by bylaws.

Seals
CONSERVATION OF SEALS ACT 1970

It is an offence to

use for the purpose of killing or taking any seal, any poisonous substance, or, use for the purpose of killing, injuring or taking any seal, any firearm other than a rifle using ammunition having a muzzle energy of not less than 600 foot pounds and a bullet not less than 45 grains.

attempt to commit any of these offences.

wilfully kill, injure or take a seal during the close season: **Grey Seals** – 1st September to 31st December; **Common Seals** – 1st June to 31st August.

wilfully kill, injure or take a seal in contravention of a prohibition order (for conservation) made by the Secretary of State. (Such an order has been made.)

Apprehension of Offenders
A constable may stop any person he suspects with reasonable cause of committing the above offence and may search any vehicle or boat which that person may be using at that time, and seize any seal, seal skin, firearm, ammunition or poisonous substance.

Defences (to offences other than using prohibited methods)
Disabled seal taken for tending and subsequent release.
Unavoidable killing resulting from a lawful act.
To prevent the seal causing damage to fishing nets, tackle, or fish in any net, provided the seal was in the vicinity of the net or tackle.

Defence (to all the above offences)
Killing any seal which was so seriously disabled that there was no reasonable chance of its recovering.

Hunting

HUNTING ACT 2004

A person commits an offence if he hunts a wild mammal with a dog unless his hunting is exempt. (S. 1).

The following is **"exempt hunting"**:

1. stalking or flushing out;
2. the use of dogs below ground to protect birds for shooting;
3. rats;
4. rabbits;
5. retrieval of hares;
6. falconry;
7. recapture of wild mammal;
8. rescue of wild mammal; and
9. research and observation.

These will now be explained in more depth.

1. Stalking a wild mammal or flushing it out of cover is exempt if the following conditions are met:

1. it is done for the purposes of:
   (a) preventing or reducing serious damage which the wild mammal would otherwise cause to livestock, game birds, wild birds, food for livestock, crops, growing timber, fisheries, other property, or the biological diversity of an area;
   (b) obtaining meat for human or animal consumption;
   (c) participation in a field trial (a competition, other than hare coursing, in which dogs are assessed as to their usefulness in flushing animals out of cover, or in retrieving an animal which has been shot);
2. it takes place on land: (a) which belongs to the person doing the stalking or flushing out, or (b) which he has been given permission to use for the purpose by the occupier or owner;
3. not more than 2 dogs are used;
4. it does not involve the use of a dog below ground otherwise than under the conditions outlined under "use of dogs below ground", in the next section;
5. as soon as possible after being found or flushed out, the wild mammal is shot dead by a competent person, and dogs are kept under sufficient control not to prevent that happening.

(CONTINUED ON NEXT PAGE)

Hunting – continued

HUNTING ACT 2004

2. The use of a dog below ground for stalking or flushing out of cover is exempt if the following conditions are met:

1. it is done for the purpose of reducing or preventing serious damage to game birds or wild birds being kept or preserved for the purpose of being shot;
2. the person doing the stalking or flushing out:(a) has with him written evidence that the land belongs to him, or that he has permission to use the land for that purpose, from the owner or occupier: and (b) he makes that evidence available for inspection by a constable;
3. it does not involve the use of more than one dog below ground at any one time;
4. reasonable steps are taken to ensure that (a) as soon as possible after being found the wild mammal is flushed out from below ground, (b) as soon as possible thereafter it is shot dead by a competent person, (c) the dog is kept under sufficient control so as not to obstruct or prevent that happening, (d) injury is prevented from being caused to the dog, and (e) the manner in which the dog is used complies with any code of practice issued by the secretary of State.

3. & 4. The hunting of rats or rabbits is exempt if it takes place on land which (a) belongs to the hunter, or (b) which he has been given permission to use for that purpose by the owner or occupier.

5. The hunting of a hare which has been shot is exempt if it takes place on land which (a) belongs to the hunter, or (b) which he has been given permission to use for that purpose by the owner or occupier.

6. Falconry is exempt if it consists of flushing a wild mammal from cover for the purpose of enabling a bird of prey to hunt the wild mammal, and it takes place on land which (a) belongs to the hunter, or (b) which he has been given permission to use for that purpose by the owner or occupier.

7. The hunting of a wild mammal which has escaped or been released from captivity or confinement is exempt if the following conditions are satisfied:

1. the hunting takes place on land which (a) belongs to the hunter, or (b) which he has been given permission to use for that purpose by the owner or occupier or (c) with the authority of a constable;

Hunting – continued

HUNTING ACT 2004

2. reasonable steps are taken to ensure that (a) as soon as possible after being found, it is either recaptured or shot dead by a competent person and (b) each dog used in the hunt is kept under sufficient control so as not to prevent or obstruct that happening;

3. the wild mammal was not released (or permitted to escape) for the purpose of being hunted.

8. The hunting of a wild mammal for the purpose of rescuing it is exempt if the following conditions are satisfied:

1. the hunter reasonably believes that the wild mammal is, or may be, injured;

2. the hunting is for the purpose of relieving the wild mammal's suffering;

3. it does not involve the use of more than 2 dogs;

4. it does not involve the use of a dog below ground;

5. the hunting takes place on land which (a) belongs to the hunter, or (b) which he has been given permission to use for that purpose by the owner or occupier or (c) with the authority of a constable;

6. reasonable steps are taken to ensure that (a) as soon as possible after being found, appropriate action is taken to relieve its suffering and (b) each dog used in the hunt is kept under sufficient control so as not to prevent or obstruct that happening;

7. the wild mammal was not harmed for the purpose of enabling it to be hunted in reliance on this exemption.

9. The hunting of a wild mammal for research and observation is exempt if the following conditions are satisfied:

1. hunting is for the purpose of or in connection with the observation or study of the wild animal;

2. it does not involve the use of more than 2 dogs;

3. it does not involve the use of a dog below ground;

4. the hunting takes place on land which (a) belongs to the hunter, or (b) which he has been given permission to use for that purpose by the owner or occupier;

5. each dog used in the hunt must be kept under sufficiently close control to ensure that it does not injure the wild animal.

Chapter 6
People

Children and Young Persons

S 107 CHILDREN AND YOUNG PERSONS ACT 1933

TERMS

Child

Under the age of 14 years

Young person

Attained the age of 14 years but under 17 years (changed to 18 years by the Criminal Justice Act 1991 – when in force)

Guardian

Any person who has, in the opinion of the court, for the time being the care of the child or young person

Street

Any highway and any public bridge, road, lane, footway, square, court, alley, or passage, whether a thoroughfare or not

Public place

Any public park, garden, sea, beach, railway station, and any ground to which the public have or are permitted to have access, whether on payment or otherwise

Cruelty

S 1 CHILDREN AND YOUNG PERSONS ACT 1933, AS AMENDED BY THE CHILDREN ACT 1989

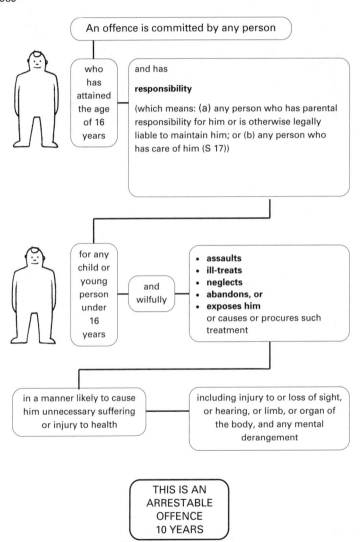

An offence is committed by any person

who has attained the age of 16 years

and has

responsibility

(which means: (a) any person who has parental responsibility for him or is otherwise legally liable to maintain him; or (b) any person who has care of him (S 17))

for any child or young person under 16 years

and wilfully

- **assaults**
- **ill-treats**
- **neglects**
- **abandons, or**
- **exposes him**
or causes or procures such treatment

in a manner likely to cause him unnecessary suffering or injury to health

including injury to or loss of sight, or hearing, or limb, or organ of the body, and any mental derangement

THIS IS AN ARRESTABLE OFFENCE
10 YEARS

Employment

S 18 CHILDREN AND YOUNG PERSONS ACT 1933 AS AMENDED BY THE CYP ACT 1963, THE CHILDREN ACT 1972 AND SI 1998/276.

Subject to any byelaws, it is an offence to employ a child of compulsory school age

who is under the age of 14 years; or

to do any work other than light work; or

Light work is work which is not likely to be harmful to the safety, health, development or education of the child.

if it is a day on which he is required to attend school, before the close of school hours or for more than 2 hours; or

for more than 2 hours on any Sunday; or

before 7am or after 7pm on any day; or

for more than 8 hours or, if he is under 15 years, for more than 5 hours in any day –
(a) on which he is not required to attend school and,
(b) which is not a Sunday, or

for more than 35 hours, or if under 15 years, 25 hours, in any week in which he is not required to attend school, or

for more than 12 hours in any week in which he is required to attend school, or

for more than 4 hours in any one day without a rest break of 1 hour or

at any time in a year unless he has at least 2 weeks without employment during the period when he is not at school

The offence is committed by the employer and any person (other than the person employed) to whose act or default this contravention is attributable

Tattoos

TATTOOING OF MINORS ACT 1969

It is an offence to tattoo a person under the age of 18 years except for medical reasons by a medical practitioner or by a person working under his direction. But it is a defence to show that there was reasonable cause to believe that the person was 18 or over and he did in fact so believe.

Tobacco

S 7 CHILDREN AND YOUNG PERSONS ACT 1933
CHILDREN AND YOUNG PERSONS (PROTECTION FROM TOBACCO) ACT 1991

It is an offence for a person to sell to a person under the age of 16 years any tobacco or cigarette papers, whether for his own use or not

It is an offence to sell loose (unpackaged) cigarettes to any person.

It is the duty of a constable in uniform to seize any tobacco or cigarette papers from persons apparently under 16 years found smoking in a street or public place

An order may be made by a court for the removal of any automatic cigarette machine which has been used by any person under 16 years

Alcohol S 5

It is an offence for any person to give or cause to be given to any child under the age of 5 years any intoxicating liquor (except under the order of a doctor or in a case of sickness or apprehended sickness, or other urgent case)

Truancy

S 16 CRIME AND DISORDER ACT 1998

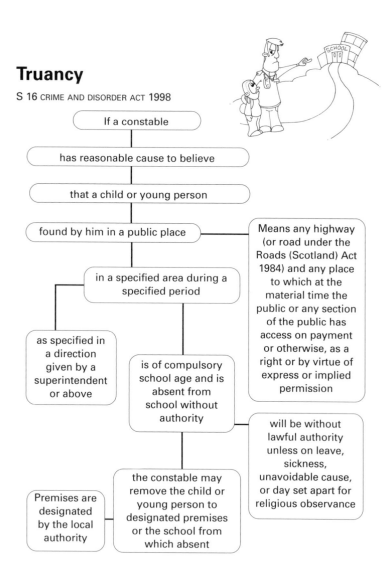

If a constable

has reasonable cause to believe

that a child or young person

found by him in a public place

Means any highway (or road under the Roads (Scotland) Act 1984) and any place to which at the material time the public or any section of the public has access on payment or otherwise, as a right or by virtue of express or implied permission

in a specified area during a specified period

as specified in a direction given by a superintendent or above

is of compulsory school age and is absent from school without authority

will be without lawful authority unless on leave, sickness, unavoidable cause, or day set apart for religious observance

Premises are designated by the local authority

the constable may remove the child or young person to designated premises or the school from which absent

Education

S 7 EDUCATION ACT 1966

The parent of every child of compulsory school age (5-16) shall cause him to receive efficient full-time education suitable to his age, ability, aptitude and subject to any special educational needs.

Begging

S 4 CHILDREN AND YOUNG PERSONS ACT 1933

It is an offence for any person to cause or procure any child or young person under 16 years, or having responsibility for such a child or young person, to allow him to be in any street, premises or place for the purpose of begging or receiving or inducing the giving of alms (whether or not there is any singing etc)

Burning

S 11 CHILDREN AND YOUNG PERSONS ACT 1933

If a person who has attained the age of 16 years, having responsibility for any child under the age of 12 years

allows the child to be in any room containing an open fire grate or any heating appliance liable to cause injury to any person

not sufficiently protected to guard against the risk of being burnt or scalded, without taking reasonable precautions against the risk

and by reason thereof the child is killed or suffers serious injury

then that person commits an offence

Brothels
S 3 CHILDREN AND YOUNG PERSONS ACT 1933

It is an offence for a person having the responsibility for a person

who has attained the age of 4 years and is under the age of 16 years

to allow that person to reside in or frequent a brothel

Police Protection

S 46 CHILDREN ACT 1989

Where a constable has reasonable cause to
believe that a **child** would otherwise be likely to

SUFFER SIGNIFICANT HARM
he may

remove the child to **suitable accommodation** and keep him there	or	take such steps as are reasonable to ensure that the child's removal from any hospital or other place in which he is then being accommodated is prevented

The child is then referred to
as having been taken into

POLICE PROTECTION ➤ No child may be kept in police protection
for more than 72 hours

As soon as reasonably practicable thereafter the constable shall:

- Inform the local authority of the reasons for the steps taken or to be taken and give details of the place where the child is being accommodated

- Inform the child (if he can understand) of the reasons for the steps taken or to be taken

- take steps to discover the wishes and feelings of the child

- secure that the case is enquired into by a designated officer

- where the place to which the child was taken was not provided by a local authority or an official refuge, secure that he is moved to such accommodation

- take such steps as are reasonably practicable to inform:
  - (a) the child's parents;
  - (b) every person who is not a parent of his but who has parental responsibility for him; and
  - (c) any other person with whom the child was living immediately before being taken into police protection.

Armed Forces

Absentees and Deserters

S 186 ARMY ACT 1955; S 186 AIR FORCE ACT 1955; S 105 NAVAL DISCIPLINE ACT 1957

A constable may arrest without warrant any person whom he has reasonable cause to suspect of being a member of the regular forces who has deserted or is absent without leave. This provision also applies to **visiting forces** but only where a request is made by the appropriate authority of the country to which he belongs (S 13 VISITING FORCES ACT 1952).

Uniforms

S 2 & S 3 UNIFORMS ACT 1894

It is an offence for any person not serving in Her Majesty's forces to wear without Her Majesty's permission the uniform of any of those forces, or any dress having the appearance, or bearing any of the regimental or other distinctive marks of any such uniform

but there is an exemption in the case of stage plays in properly authorised places for public performances, music halls, circus performances or any bona fide military representation

It is an offence for a person not serving in Her Majesty's Forces to wear any such uniform, etc in such a manner and under such circumstances as to bring contempt on that uniform, or to employ anyone so to do.

The unauthorised use of any official uniform to gain admission to a prohibited place is an offence under the Official Secrets Act 1920, S 1.

The impersonation of a member of a police force or a BTC constable is an offence under the Police Act 1996, S 90 and the British Transport Commission Act 1962, S 43.

The unauthorised wearing of a merchant navy uniform is an offence under the Merchant Shipping Act 1995, S 57.

Decorations and Badges etc
S 197 ARMY AND AIR FORCE ACTS 1955

An offence is committed by any person who:

Uses or wears any military decoration or badge, wound stripe or emblem supplied or authorised by the defence council; or any decoration, etc. so nearly resembling an official one as to be calculated to deceive; or falsely represents himself to be a person who is or has been entitled to wear any official decoration etc

but this does not prohibit the use or wearing of ordinary regimental badges or of brooches or ornaments representing them

and

A person shall be guilty of an offence if he

purchases, takes in pawn, solicits or procures any person to sell or pledge,

or

acts for any person in the sale or pledging of

any naval, military or air force decoration awarded to any member of Her Majesty's forces. But it shall be a defence to prove that at the time of the alleged offence the person to whom the decoration was awarded was dead or had ceased to be a member of those forces.

'Decoration' includes medals, medal ribbons, clasps and good conduct badges

Immigration

SS 1–3 IMMIGRATION ACT 1971

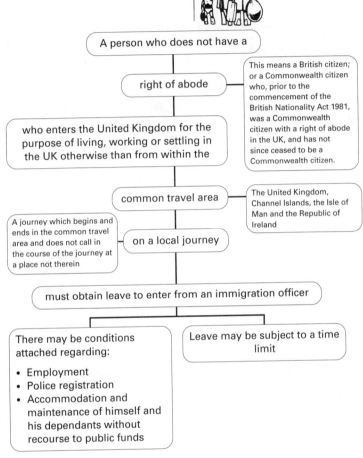

Arrivals foreign

A person who does not have a

right of abode

This means a British citizen; or a Commonwealth citizen who, prior to the commencement of the British Nationality Act 1981, was a Commonwealth citizen with a right of abode in the UK, and has not since ceased to be a Commonwealth citizen.

who enters the United Kingdom for the purpose of living, working or settling in the UK otherwise than from within the

common travel area

The United Kingdom, Channel Islands, the Isle of Man and the Republic of Ireland

A journey which begins and ends in the common travel area and does not call in the course of the journey at a place not therein

on a local journey

must obtain leave to enter from an immigration officer

There may be conditions attached regarding:

- Employment
- Police registration
- Accommodation and maintenance of himself and his dependants without recourse to public funds

Leave may be subject to a time limit

Except that persons exercising **European Community** rights and nationals of Member States (currently Austria, Belgium, Denmark, Finland, France, Germany, Greece, Ireland, Italy, Luxembourg, Netherlands, Portugal, Spain, Sweden and the UK) do not require leave to enter or remain.

Immigration Offences

IMMIGRATION ACT 1971

Illegal entry, etc (S 24)

A person who is not a British citizen, or a commonwealth citizen who has the right of abode in the UK, commits an offence if:

(a) he knowingly enters the UK in breach of a deportation order or without leave;

(b) having only a limited leave to enter the UK, he knowingly either remains beyond the time limit, or fails to observe a condition of the leave;

(c) having lawfully entered the UK as a member of the crew of a ship or aircraft, he fails to leave at the expiry of the time allowed;

(d) without reasonable cause he fails to comply with a requirement to report to a medical officer of health or to submit to a test or examination;

(e) without reasonable excuse he fails to observe any restriction imposed as to residence, employment or occupation, or as to reporting to the police or immigration officer;

(f) he disembarks in the UK from a ship or aircraft after being placed on board with a view to his removal from the UK; or

(g) he embarks in contravention of a restriction not to do so made by an Order in Council.

Deception (S 24A)

A person who is not a British citizen, or a commonwealth citizen who has the right of abode in the UK, commits an offence if, by means of deception:

(a) he obtains or seeks to obtain leave to enter or remain in the UK; or

(b) he secures or seeks to secure the avoidance, postponement or revocation of enforcement action against him.

'Enforcement action' means:

(a) directions for his removal from the UK under this Act or the Immigration and Asylum Act 1999;

(b) the making of a deportation order under this Act; or

(c) his removal from the UK in consequences of directions or a deportation order.

Assisting illegal entry, and harbouring (S 25)

An offence is committed by any person knowingly concerned in making or carrying out arrangements for securing or facilitating:

(a) entry into the UK of anyone he knows or has reasonable cause for believing to be an illegal entrant (whether the act was done in or outside the UK);

(b) entry into the UK of anyone he knows or has reasonable cause for believing to be an asylum claimant (whether the act was done in or outside the UK); or

(c) the obtaining by anyone of leave to remain in the UK by means which he knows or has reasonable cause for believing to include deception.

Subsection (b) above will not apply to anything done:

(a) to a person who has been detained or granted temporary admission under this Act;

(b) by a person otherwise than for gain; or

(c) by a person in the course of his employment by a bona fide organisation whose purpose is to assist such claimants.

An offence is committed by any person knowingly harbouring anyone whom he knows or has reasonable cause to believe to be an illegal entrant or to have committed an offence under S 24(1)(b) or (c) above.

Refugees

The UN Convention relating to the status of Refugees provides that illegal entrants should not be prosecuted for offences, eg forged travel documents, if they are coming directly from a territory where their life or freedom was threatened provided they present themselves without delay and show good cause for their illegal entry or presence. This was followed by the Divisional Court in *R v Uxbridge Magistrates' Court, ex p Adimi*.

Police Powers

S 25A & S 28A IMMIGRATION ACT 1971

Arrest

A constable or immigration officer may arrest without warrant a person:

(a) who has committed or attempted to commit an offence under S 24 (illegal entry, etc) or 24A (deception); or

(b) whom he has reasonable grounds for suspecting has committed that offence.

But the above will not apply to an offence under S 24(1)(d) (fail to report to a medical officer, etc)

Detention of Ships, Etc

A constable may detain a relevant ship, aircraft or vehicle where a person has been arrested under S 25(1)(a) or (b) (assisting illegal entry or assisting an asylum claimant).

Hotels etc

ARTS 3 & 4 IMMIGRATION (HOTEL RECORDS) ORDER 1972

When a person over 16 who has no right of abode in this country stays in an hotel or other premises where lodging or sleeping accommodation is provided for reward

then upon arrival at the premises he shall furnish the keeper with

before his departure he shall inform the keeper of his next destination and, if known, full address there

his full name and nationality and the number and place of issue of his passport or identity document

The keeper is required to obtain this information and keep the record of such for 12 months

The records shall be at all times open to inspection by any constable

Mental Health

S 136 MENTAL HEALTH ACT 1983

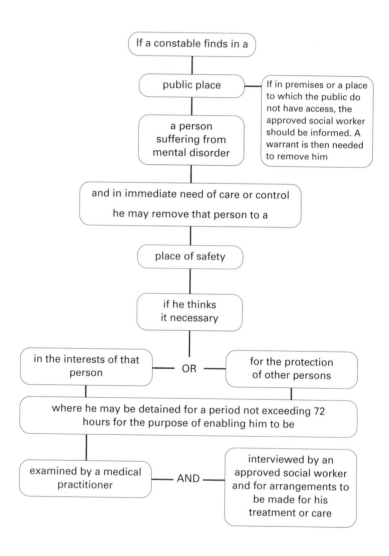

If a constable finds in a

public place

If in premises or a place to which the public do not have access, the approved social worker should be informed. A warrant is then needed to remove him

a person suffering from mental disorder

and in immediate need of care or control he may remove that person to a

place of safety

if he thinks it necessary

in the interests of that person — OR — for the protection of other persons

where he may be detained for a period not exceeding 72 hours for the purpose of enabling him to be

examined by a medical practitioner — AND — interviewed by an approved social worker and for arrangements to be made for his treatment or care

Pedlars

PEDLARS ACT 1871

A 'pedlar' is defined as:

any pedlar, hawker, petty chapman, tinker, caster of metals, mender of chairs, or other person who, without any horse or other beast bearing or drawing burden **travels and trades on foot** and goes from town to town or to other people's houses, carrying to sell, or exposing for sale any goods, wares or merchandise, or procuring orders for goods immediately to be delivered, or selling or offering for sale his skill in handicrafts (S 3).

The Act does not apply to commercial travellers or other persons selling or seeking orders for goods to or from dealers for resale; or to agents authorised by publishers selling or seeking orders for books; or sellers of vegetables, fish, fruit or victuals; or persons selling at any public market, etc (S 23).

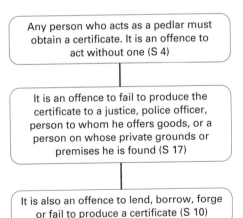

Any person who acts as a pedlar must obtain a certificate. It is an offence to act without one (S 4)

It is an offence to fail to produce the certificate to a justice, police officer, person to whom he offers goods, or a person on whose private grounds or premises he is found (S 17)

It is also an offence to lend, borrow, forge or fail to produce a certificate (S 10)

Scrap Metal Dealers

SCRAP METAL DEALERS ACT 1964

A scrap metal dealer is defined as:

a person who carries on a business of **buying** and **selling** scrap metal, whether the scrap metal is sold in the form in which it is bought or otherwise (S 9)

'Scrap metal' includes any old metal, manufactured articles made wholly or partly from metal and any metallic wastes.

S 2 At each scrap metal store, the dealer must keep a book in which he must enter particulars of:

1) All scrap metals received at that place

2) All scrap metal either processed at or despatched from that place

The particulars which must be recorded immediately after the processing or despatch are:

Received	Processed or Despatched
• Description and weight of the scrap metal	• Description and weight of the scrap metal
• Date and time of receipt	• Date of processing or despatch and, if applicable, the process applied
• Full name and address of person from whom received	• The full name and address of the person to whom it was sold or exchanged and the consideration given for it
• The price payable (if known)	
• Where price is not known, the value as estimated by the dealer	• If processed or despatched other than on sale or exchange, the value of the scrap metal immediately before despatch, as estimated by the dealer
• The registration mark of any vehicle used to deliver the metal	

A constable has a right at all reasonable times to enter a scrap metal dealer's business premises and inspect scrap metal, record books and receipts (S 6)

It is an offence to obstruct the exercise of the powers of entry and inspection conferred by these provisions (S 6)

These particulars may be kept in two separate books if preferred. In any case the books must be kept for 2 years from the date of completion

It is an offence for a person selling scrap metal to a scrap metal dealer to give him a false name and address (S 5)

It is an offence for a scrap metal dealer to acquire scrap metal from a person apparently under the age of 16 years (S 5)

Motor Salvage Operators

VEHICLE (CRIME) ACT 2001

A motor salvage operator is a person who carries on a business which consists:
1. wholly or partly in recovery for re-use or sale of salvageable parts from motor vehicles and the subsequent sale or other disposal for scrap of the remainder of the vehicles;
2. wholly or mainly in the purchase of written-off vehicles and their subsequent repair and resale;
3. wholly or mainly in the sale or purchase of motor vehicles which are to be the subject of any of the above activities;
4. wholly or mainly in activities which fall within 2 or 3 above.

A person who carries out the business of a motor salvage operator must **register** with the local authority. It is an offence to make false statements in an application for registration.

Entry and Inspection of Premises
A constable may at any reasonable time enter and inspect **registered** premises which are occupied by an operator as a motor salvage yard. (Force may not be used in executing any warrant to enter.)

Requirement to Keep Records
Records (electronic or manual) must be kept at the premises of details relating to the vehicle, the supplier or person receiving (including proof of identity), condition of vehicle, date of transaction and date details were entered on the record.

Inspection of Records
A constable may at any reasonable time:
1. require production of, and inspect, any motor vehicles or salvageable parts kept on **registered** premises; and
2. require production of, inspect and take copies of or extracts from any records which the operator is required to keep.

Warrant to Enter Premises
In order to secure compliance with regulations, or to ascertain whether provisions are being complied with, a Justice of the Peace may issue a warrant authorising a constable to enter and inspect specified premises. (Other than as mentioned above, reasonable force may be used to execute a warrant). If required by the owner or occupier of the premises, the constable shall produce evidence of his identity and his authority for entering, before doing so.

Giving False Particulars
A person who sells a motor vehicle to a motor salvage operator commits an offence if he gives him a false name or address.

Vagrancy

The following are offences under the VAGRANCY ACT 1824,
AMENDED BY THE VAGRANCY ACT 1935

LODGING IN OUTHOUSES

Every person who wanders abroad and lodges in any barn or
otherwise, or in any deserted or unoccupied building or in the open air,
or under a tent, or in any cart or wagon, and not giving a good account
of himself

AND

- he has been directed to a reasonably accessible place of free
  shelter and has failed to apply or has refused shelter there; or
- he persistently wanders abroad and there is a reasonably
  accessible place of free shelter; or
- he has caused damage to property, infection with vermin, or other
  offensive consequence, or lodges in such circumstances as to appear
  to be likely to do so (S 4).

POWER OF ARREST

S 25 POLICE AND CRIMINAL EVIDENCE ACT 1984

Vagrancy – continued
VAGRANCY ACT 1824

FOUND ON ENCLOSED PREMISES

Every person being found in or upon any dwelling house, warehouse, stable or outhouse, or in any enclosed yard, garden or area for any unlawful purpose (S 4)

EXPOSING WOUNDS

Every person who wanders abroad and endeavours by **exposing wounds or deformities** to obtain or gather alms (S 4)

POWER TO ARREST ONLY IN ACCORDANCE WITH THE POLICE AND CRIMINAL EVIDENCE ACT 1984

BEGGING

Every person who wanders abroad, or places himself in any public place, street, highway, court or passage, **to beg or gather alms** or causing, procuring or encouraging any child to do so (S 3)

FRAUDULENT COLLECTIONS

Any person who goes about as a gatherer or collector of alms, or endeavours to procure charitable contributions of any nature or kind, under any false or fraudulent pretence (S 4)

Police

S 90 POLICE ACT 1996

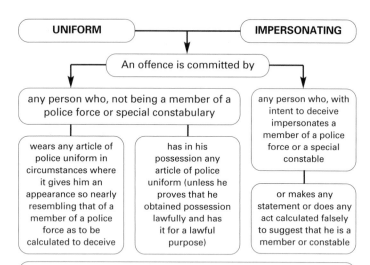

```
┌──────────────┐                    ┌──────────────────┐
│   UNIFORM    │                    │ IMPERSONATING    │
└──────────────┘                    └──────────────────┘
```

An offence is committed by

any person who, not being a member of a police force or special constabulary

wears any article of police uniform in circumstances where it gives him an appearance so nearly resembling that of a member of a police force as to be calculated to deceive

has in his possession any article of police uniform (unless he proves that he obtained possession lawfully and has it for a lawful purpose)

any person who, with intent to deceive impersonates a member of a police force or a special constable

or makes any statement or does any act calculated falsely to suggest that he is a member or constable

The unauthorised use of any uniform to gain admission to a 'prohibited place' is an offence under S 1 Official Secrets Act 1920

'Article of police uniform' means any article of uniform or any distinctive badge, mark or identification document (or any thing having the appearance of such article, etc)

ASSAULT, etc   S 89

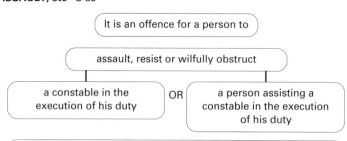

It is an offence for a person to

assault, resist or wilfully obstruct

a constable in the execution of his duty

OR

a person assisting a constable in the execution of his duty

It is a common law offence to refuse to aid and assist a constable in the execution of his duty when called upon to do so, if the person is physically capable of helping and has no lawful excuse for refusing

Chapter 7
Public Order

Litter

S 5 LITTER ACT 1983,
S 87 ENVIRONMENTAL
PROTECTION ACT 1990

It is an offence to ——— wilfully remove or otherwise interfere with any **LITTER BIN** or notice board provided or erected under S 5 of the Litter Act 1983 or S 185 of the Highways Act 1980

THROW DOWN ——— includes to drop or otherwise deposit

in, into or from

ANY PUBLIC OPEN PLACE OR ANY PLACE

which is:

a highway or road repairable at public expense; land in the open air which is open to the public and owned or controlled by the Crown, a designated undertaker, an education authority, a principal litter authority or within the litter control area of a local authority

AND LEAVE

anything whatsoever in such circumstances as to cause, contribute to, or tend to lead to

a 'public open place' is a place in the open air to which the public have access without payment; and any covered place open to the air on at least one side and available for public use.

DEFACEMENT BY LITTER

unless authorised by law or consent is obtained from the owner, occupier or person having control of that place

Abandoning Vehicles etc

S 2 REFUSE DISPOSAL (AMENITY) ACT 1978

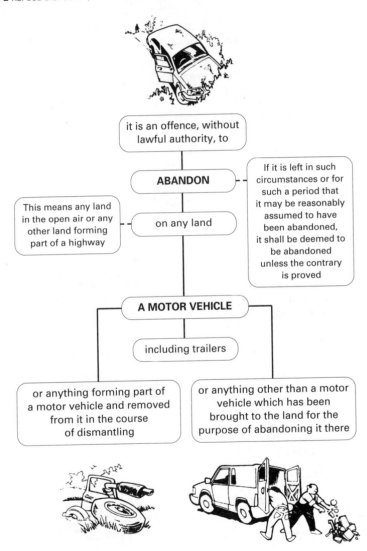

it is an offence, without lawful authority, to

ABANDON

If it is left in such circumstances or for such a period that it may be reasonably assumed to have been abandoned, it shall be deemed to be abandoned unless the contrary is proved

This means any land in the open air or any other land forming part of a highway

on any land

A MOTOR VEHICLE

including trailers

or anything forming part of a motor vehicle and removed from it in the course of dismantling

or anything other than a motor vehicle which has been brought to the land for the purpose of abandoning it there

Noise

S 62 CONTROL OF POLLUTION ACT 1974

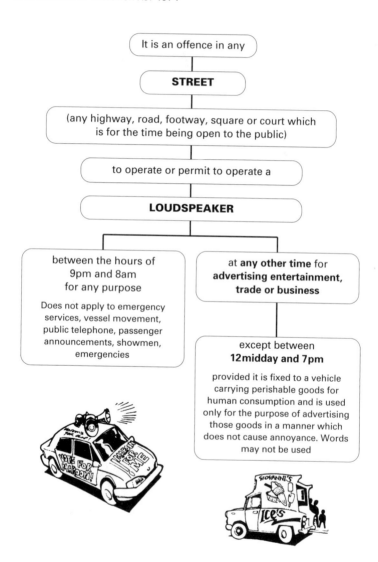

It is an offence in any

STREET

(any highway, road, footway, square or court which is for the time being open to the public)

to operate or permit to operate a

LOUDSPEAKER

between the hours of 9pm and 8am for any purpose

Does not apply to emergency services, vessel movement, public telephone, passenger announcements, showmen, emergencies

at **any other time** for **advertising entertainment, trade or business**

except between **12 midday and 7pm**

provided it is fixed to a vehicle carrying perishable goods for human consumption and is used only for the purpose of advertising those goods in a manner which does not cause annoyance. Words may not be used

Trade Disputes

S 241 TRADE UNION AND LABOUR RELATIONS (CONSOLIDATION) ACT 1992

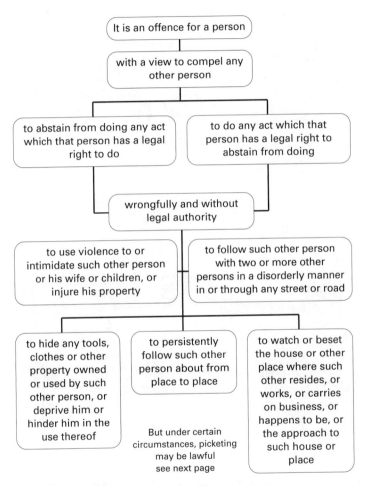

A constable may arrest without warrant anyone he reasonably suspects is committing one of the above offences

Peaceful Picketing

S 220 TRADE UNION AND LABOUR RELATIONS (CONSOLIDATION) ACT 1992

Fear or Provocation of Violence

S 4 PUBLIC ORDER ACT 1986

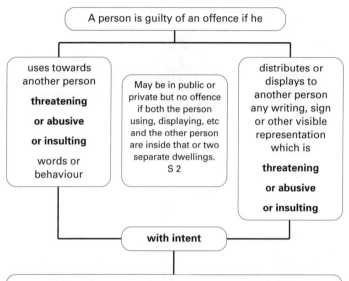

A person is guilty of an offence if he

uses towards another person

threatening

or abusive

or insulting

words or behaviour

May be in public or private but no offence if both the person using, displaying, etc and the other person are inside that or two separate dwellings.
S 2

distributes or displays to another person any writing, sign or other visible representation which is

threatening

or abusive

or insulting

with intent

- to cause that person to believe that immediate unlawful violence will be used against him or another by any person, or

- to provoke the immediate use of unlawful violence by that person or another, or

- whereby that person is likely to believe that such violence will be used or it is likely that such violence will be provoked

Violence includes conduct towards property. Need not cause, or be intended to cause, injury or damage (S 8)

A constable may arrest without warrant anyone he reasonably suspects is committing this offence (S 4(3))

Harassment, Alarm or Distress

S 5 PUBLIC ORDER ACT 1986

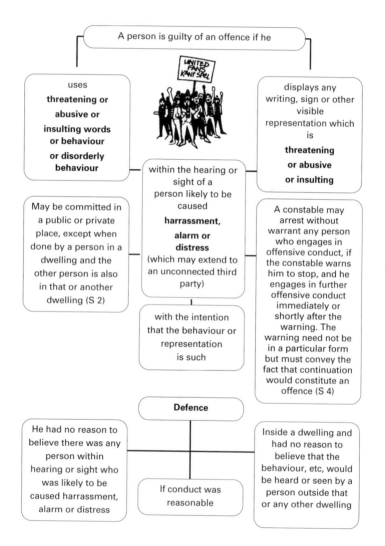

A person is guilty of an offence if he

uses

threatening or abusive or insulting words or behaviour

or disorderly behaviour

displays any writing, sign or other visible representation which is

threatening

or abusive

or insulting

within the hearing or sight of a person likely to be caused

harrassment, alarm or distress

(which may extend to an unconnected third party)

May be committed in a public or private place, except when done by a person in a dwelling and the other person is also in that or another dwelling (S 2)

A constable may arrest without warrant any person who engages in offensive conduct, if the constable warns him to stop, and he engages in further offensive conduct immediately or shortly after the warning. The warning need not be in a particular form but must convey the fact that continuation would constitute an offence (S 4)

with the intention that the behaviour or representation is such

Defence

He had no reason to believe there was any person within hearing or sight who was likely to be caused harrassment, alarm or distress

If conduct was reasonable

Inside a dwelling and had no reason to believe that the behaviour, etc, would be heard or seen by a person outside that or any other dwelling

Intentional Harassment, Alarm or Distress

S 4A PUBLIC ORDER ACT 1986 (INSERTED BY S 154 CRIMINAL JUSTICE AND PUBLIC ORDER ACT 1994)

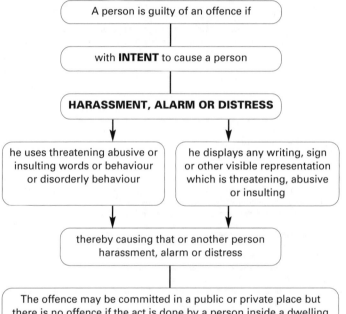

A person is guilty of an offence if

with **INTENT** to cause a person

HARASSMENT, ALARM OR DISTRESS

he uses threatening abusive or insulting words or behaviour or disorderly behaviour

he displays any writing, sign or other visible representation which is threatening, abusive or insulting

thereby causing that or another person harassment, alarm or distress

The offence may be committed in a public or private place but there is no offence if the act is done by a person inside a dwelling and seen only by a person also inside that or another dwelling

Defences: (i) he was inside the dwelling and had no reason to believe that the act would be seen or heard by someone outside the dwelling
(ii) the conduct was reasonable.

A constable may arrest without warrant anyone who he reasonably suspects is committing the offence.

Harassment Intended to Deter Lawful Activities

PROTECTION FROM HARASSMENT ACT 1997 (AS AMENDED BY THE SERIOUS ORGANISED CRIME AND POLICE ACT 2005)

PROHIBITION OF HARASSMENT

A person must not pursue a course of conduct-

(a) which amounts to harassment of another, and
(b) which he knows or ought to know amounts to harassment. (S 1(1))

A person must not pursue a course of conduct-

(a) which involves harassment of two or more persons, and
(b) which he knows or ought to know involves harassment of those persons, and
(c) by which he intends to persuade any person (whether or not those mentioned above)-
  (i) not to do something that he is required or entitled to do, or
  (ii) to do something that he is not under any obligation to do. (S 1(1A))

A person who pursues such a course of conduct will be guilty of an offence. An actual or apprehended breach of S 1 may be the subject of a claim in civil proceedings by the victim. This may result in damages or a restraining injunction, in relation to S 1(1), or a restraining injunction for S 1(1A).

PUTTING PEOPLE IN FEAR OF VIOLENCE

A person whose course of conduct causes another to fear, on at least two occasions, that violence will be used against him is guilty of an offence if he knows or ought to know that his course of conduct will cause the other so to fear on each of those occasions. (S 4). This is an arrestable offence (5 years).

INTERPRETATION

Presumption of knowledge of course of action
A person ought to know that a course of action amounts to or includes harassment (or, in the case of S 4, causes another to fear violence) if a reasonable person in possession of the same information would think it amounted to harassment (or fear of violence).

Defence
Conduct will not amount to harassment (or causing fear of violence) if it was for the purpose of preventing or detecting crime; if it was pursued under any enactment; or if it was reasonable in the circumstances.

'Harassing' includes alarming or causing distress.

'Course of conduct' must involve-

(a) if relating to a single person, conduct on at least 2 occasions in relation to that person, or
(b) if relating to 2 or more persons, conduct on at least one occasion in relation to each person.

'Conduct' includes speech.

Harassment in the Home – Prevention

S 42 CRIMINAL JUSTICE AND POLICE ACT 2001

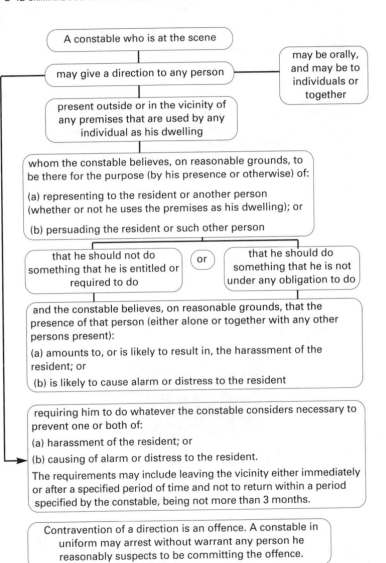

A constable who is at the scene

may give a direction to any person

may be orally, and may be to individuals or together

present outside or in the vicinity of any premises that are used by any individual as his dwelling

whom the constable believes, on reasonable grounds, to be there for the purpose (by his presence or otherwise) of:

(a) representing to the resident or another person (whether or not he uses the premises as his dwelling); or

(b) persuading the resident or such other person

that he should not do something that he is entitled or required to do

or

that he should do something that he is not under any obligation to do

and the constable believes, on reasonable grounds, that the presence of that person (either alone or together with any other persons present):

(a) amounts to, or is likely to result in, the harassment of the resident; or

(b) is likely to cause alarm or distress to the resident

requiring him to do whatever the constable considers necessary to prevent one or both of:

(a) harassment of the resident; or

(b) causing of alarm or distress to the resident.

The requirements may include leaving the vicinity either immediately or after a specified period of time and not to return within a period specified by the constable, being not more than 3 months.

Contravention of a direction is an offence. A constable in uniform may arrest without warrant any person he reasonably suspects to be committing the offence.

Harassment in the Home – Offence

S 42A CRIMINAL JUSTICE AND POLICE ACT 2001

A person commits an offence if-

(a) that person is present outside or in the vicinity of any premises that are used by an individual as his dwelling;

(b) that person is present there for the purpose (by his presence or otherwise) of representing to the resident or another individual (whether or not one who uses the premises as his dwelling), or of persuading the resident or such another individual-

  (i) that he should not do something that he is entitled or required to do; or

  (ii) that he should do something that he is not under any obligation to do;

(c) that person-

  (i) intends his presence (either alone or with any other person) to amount to the harassment of, or cause alarm or distress to, the resident, or

  (ii) knows or ought to know that his presence is likely to result in the harassment of, or to cause alarm or distress to, the resident, and

(d) the presence of that person-

  (i) amounts to the harassment of, or causes alarm or distress to, the resident, a person in the resident's dwelling, or a person in another dwelling in the vicinity of the resident's dwelling, or

  (ii) is likely to result in the harassment of, or to cause alarm or distress to, any such person.

PRESUMPTION OF KNOWLEDGE

A person ought to know that his presence is likely to result in the harassment of, or to cause alarm or distress to a resident if a reasonable person in possession of the same information would think that his presence would have that effect.

POWER OF ARREST

A constable in uniform may arrest without warrant any person he reasonably suspects is committing or has committed this offence.

Animal Research Organisations – Protection

S 145 SERIOUS ORGANISED CRIME AND POLICE ACT 2005

A person (A) commits an offence if, with the intention of harming an animal research organisation, he-

(a) does a relevant act, or

(b) threatens that he or someone else will do a relevant act,

in circumstances in which that act or threat is intended or likely to cause a second person (B)-

(a) not to perform any contractual obligation owed by B to a third person (C) (whether or not such non-performance amounts to a breach of contract);

(b) to terminate any contract B has with C;

(c) not to enter into a contract with C.

Relevant act means-

(a) an act amounting to a criminal offence, or
(b) a tortuous act causing B to suffer loss or damage of any description (except one which only induces another person to break a contract with B).

Contract includes any other arrangement.

Harm means-

(a) to cause the organisation to suffer loss or damage of any description, or

(b) to prevent or hinder the carrying out by the organisation of any of its activities.

Application. This section does not apply to any act done wholly or mainly in contemplation or furtherance of a trade dispute.

Police powers – this is an arrestable offence (5 years).

Animal research organisation. See following page.

Animal Research Organisations – Intimidation

S 146 SERIOUS ORGANISED CRIME AND POLICE ACT **2005**

A person (A) commits an offence if , with the intention of causing a second person (B) to abstain from doing something which B is entitled to do (or to do something which B is entitled to abstain from doing)-

(a) A threatens B that A or somebody else will do a relevant act, and

(b) A does so wholly or mainly because B is a person falling within the table below, **relating to an animal research organisation**:

(a)	an employee or officer
(b)	a student at an educational establishment
(c)	a lessor or licensor of premises
(d)	a person with financial interest in, or provides financial assistance to
(e)	a customer or supplier
(f)	a person contemplating becoming someone in (c), (d) or (e)
(g)	a person who is, or is contemplating becoming a customer or supplier of a person in (c), (d), (e) or (f)
(h)	an employee or officer of someone in (c), (d), (e), (f) or (g)
(i)	a person with financial interest in, or who provides financial assistance to, a person in (c), (d), (e), (f) or (g)
(j)	a spouse, civil partner, friend, or relative of, or a person who is personally known to, a person in (a) to (i)
(k)	a person who is, or is contemplating becoming, a customer or supplier of a person in (a), (b), (h), (i) or (j)
(l)	an employer of someone in (j)

Officer includes, where the organisation or person is-

(a) **a body corporate** - a director, manager or secretary,

(b) **a charity** – a charity trustee,

(c) **a partnership** – a partner.

Relevant act means-

(a) an act amounting to a criminal offence, or

(b) a tortuous act causing B or another person to suffer loss or damage of any description.

Application. This section does not apply to any act done wholly or mainly in contemplation or furtherance of a trade dispute.

Police powers – this is an arrestable offence (5 years).

Animal research organisation means any person who, or organisation which,-

1. is the owner, lessee or licensee of premises constituting or including-

(a) a place specified in a licence granted under the Animals (Scientific Procedures) Act 1986,

(b) a scientific procedure establishment designated under S 6 of that Act, or

(c) a breeding or supplying establishment designated under S 7 of that Act; or

2. employs, or engages under a contract for services, any of the following in his capacity as such-

(a) the holder of a personal licence granted under S 4 of that Act,

(b) the holder of a project licence granted under S 5 of that Act,

(c) a person specified under S 6(5) or 7(5) of that Act.

Dispersal of Groups

S30 ANTI-SOCIAL BEHAVIOUR ACT 2003

AUTHORISATION

Where a superintendent or above has reasonable grounds for believing:

(a) that any members of the public have been intimidated, harassed, alarmed or distressed as a result of the presence or behaviour of groups of 2 or more persons in public places; and

(b) that anti-social behaviour is a significant and persistent problem,

he may give an authorisation to a constable in uniform for a period not exceeding 6 months.

PROCESS

Any authorisation must be in writing, signed by the officer and must specify the relevant locality, the grounds and period the powers are exercisable. Consultation must take place with the relevant local authority and publicity must be given before the powers are exercisable.

CONSTABLE'S DIRECTION

Where an authorisation has been given, if the constable has reasonable grounds for believing that the presence or behaviour of such persons has resulted, or is likely to result in intimidation, harassment, alarm or distress, he may give a direction:

(a) requiring the group to disperse;

(b) requiring any person who does not live within that locality to leave the locality; and/or

(c) prohibiting persons who do not live in the locality from returning for up to 24 hours.

EXCEPTIONS

A direction may not be given to persons engaged in lawful trade union activities or lawful processions.

FAILURE TO COMPLY

Any person who fails to comply with a direction commits an offence and may be arrested without warrant by a constable in uniform.

UNSUPERVISED PERSONS UNDER 16

If a constable in uniform finds a person under 16 in a public place in the relevant locality between 9pm and 6am and not under the effective control of a parent or responsible person over 18, he may remove him to his home unless he believes he would be likely to suffer significant harm by taking him there.

DEFINITIONS

S 30 'Anti-social behaviour' means behaviour by a person which causes or is likely to cause harassment, alarm or distress to one or more other persons not of the same household as that person.

'Public place' means any highway and any place to which at the material time the public or any section of the public has access, on payment or otherwise, as of right or by virtue of express or implied permission.

Seizure of Vehicles Causing Annoyance etc

S 59 POLICE REFORM ACT 2002
POLICE (RETENTION AND DISPOSAL OF MOTOR VEHICLES) REGULATIONS 2002

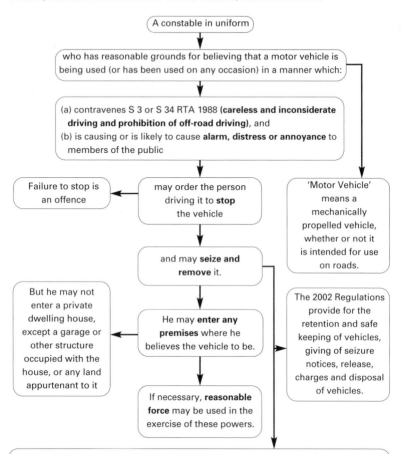

A constable in uniform

who has reasonable grounds for believing that a motor vehicle is being used (or has been used on any occasion) in a manner which:

(a) contravenes S 3 or S 34 RTA 1988 **(careless and inconsiderate driving and prohibition of off-road driving)**, and
(b) is causing or is likely to cause **alarm, distress or annoyance** to members of the public

may order the person driving it to **stop** the vehicle

Failure to stop is an offence

'Motor Vehicle' means a mechanically propelled vehicle, whether or not it is intended for use on roads.

and may **seize and remove** it.

He may **enter any premises** where he believes the vehicle to be.

But he may not enter a private dwelling house, except a garage or other structure occupied with the house, or any land appurtenant to it

The 2002 Regulations provide for the retention and safe keeping of vehicles, giving of seizure notices, release, charges and disposal of vehicles.

If necessary, **reasonable force** may be used in the exercise of these powers.

But he must first warn him that he will seize it if such use continues or is repeated; and the use has continued or been repeated after the warning. But a warning need not be given if: (a) it is impracticable for him to give the warning; (b) he has already given a warning on that occasion in respect of the use of that vehicle or another vehicle by that or another person; (c) he believes that such a warning has been given on that occasion by someone else; or (d) the person has already been warned by him or someone else within the previous 12 months whether or not it was in respect of the same vehicle or the same or similar use.

Football Offences

FOOTBALL (OFFENCES) ACT 1991

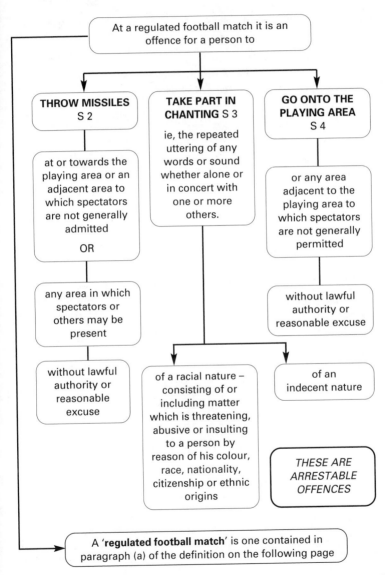

At a regulated football match it is an offence for a person to

THROW MISSILES S 2

at or towards the playing area or an adjacent area to which spectators are not generally admitted

OR

any area in which spectators or others may be present

without lawful authority or reasonable excuse

TAKE PART IN CHANTING S 3

ie, the repeated uttering of any words or sound whether alone or in concert with one or more others.

of a racial nature – consisting of or including matter which is threatening, abusive or insulting to a person by reason of his colour, race, nationality, citizenship or ethnic origins

GO ONTO THE PLAYING AREA S 4

or any area adjacent to the playing area to which spectators are not generally permitted

without lawful authority or reasonable excuse

of an indecent nature

THESE ARE ARRESTABLE OFFENCES

A '**regulated football match**' is one contained in paragraph (a) of the definition on the following page

Banning Orders

FOOTBALL SPECTATORS ACT 1989
FOOTBALL (DISORDER) ACT 2000
FOOTBALL SPECTATORS (PRESCRIPTION) ORDER 2004

The Chief Police Officer of the area in which a person resides may make an application for a **Banning Order**

if that person has at any time caused or contributed to any

VIOLENCE
(against persons or property, including threatening violence and doing anything which endangers life)

OR

DISORDER
Including:
(a) stirring up hatred against a group of persons defined by colour, race, nationality (including citizenship) or ethnic or national origins, or against an individual as a member of such a group;
(b) using threatening, abusive or insulting words or behaviour or disorderly behaviour;
(c) displaying any writing or other thing which is threatening, abusive or insulting.

A '**regulated football match**' is an association football match
(a) in **England and Wales**, involving one or both of the participating teams representing a club which is a full or associate member of the Football League, the Football Association Premier League, the Football Conference or the League of Wales, or representing a country or territory.
(b) **outside England and Wales**, involving (i) a national team appointed by the respective football assocation to represent England or Wales, or (ii) a team representing a club which is a full or associate member of the Football League, the Football Association Premier League, the Football Conference, or the League of Wales

not necessarily connected with football

The effect of a Banning Order in relation to **regulated football matches**

in England and Wales
prohibits the person entering any premises to attend such matches

outside England and Wales
requires the person to report at a police station and surrender his passport

Football Ticket Touts

S 166 CRIMINAL JUSTICE AND PUBLIC ORDER ACT 1994

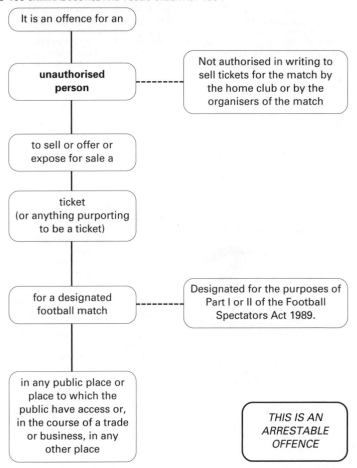

It is an offence for an

unauthorised person ---- Not authorised in writing to sell tickets for the match by the home club or by the organisers of the match

to sell or offer or expose for sale a

ticket (or anything purporting to be a ticket)

for a designated football match ---- Designated for the purposes of Part I or II of the Football Spectators Act 1989.

in any public place or place to which the public have access or, in the course of a trade or business, in any other place

THIS IS AN ARRESTABLE OFFENCE

Offensive Weapons

S 139 CRIMINAL JUSTICE ACT 1988

It is an offence to have an article which has a **blade** or which is **sharply pointed**

Folding pocket-knives are exempt provided the cutting edge of the blade is not longer than 3".

In a public place
(ie, any place to which at the material time the public have or are permitted access, whether on payment or otherwise)

It shall be a **defence** to show that he had good reason or lawful authority for having it, or that he had it with him for use at work, for religious reasons, or as part of a national costume.

School Premises
An additional offence was created by the Offensive Weapons Act 1996 to include possession of the above article (or offensive weapons as described below) whilst on **school premises** (S 139A Criminal Justice Act 1988).

A constable may **enter** (using reasonable force if necessary) and **search** school premises for weapons if he suspects this offence is being, or has been, committed and to **seize** such articles.

S 1 PREVENTION OF CRIME ACT 1953

It is an offence to have an **offensive weapon**

Offensive weapons will normally be one of two types:
- Any article **made or adapted** for causing injury
- Or other articles **intended to be used** for such purposes

whilst in a **public place** without lawful authority or reasonable excuse

Unless acting in the capacity of Crown servant, police, armed services, etc. (Public place means any highway and any other place to which at the material time the public have or are permitted access, whether on payment or otherwise.)

RESTRICTION OF OFFENSIVE WEAPONS ACTS 1959 & 1961

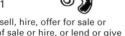

It is an offence for any person to manufacture, import, sell, hire, offer for sale or hire, or expose or have in possession for the purpose of sale or hire, or lend or give to any other person a **flick knife, flick gun or gravity knife**.

Offensive Weapons – Sale or Supply

S 141 CRIMINAL JUSTICE ACT 1988 AND CRIMINAL JUSTICE ACT 1988 (OFFENSIVE WEAPONS) ORDER 1988

> ### It is an offence to
> **import, manufacture, sell or hire, offer for sale or hire, expose or have in possession for the purpose of sale or hire or lend or give to any other person**
>
> ### ANY OF THE FOLLOWING WEAPONS
>
> not being antiques (manufactured more than 100 years before the date of the offence)

Balisong, or butterfly knife
being a blade enclosed by its handle, which is designed to split down the middle, without the operation of a spring or other mechanical means, to reveal the blade;

Knuckleduster
that is, a band of metal or other hard material worn on one or more fingers, and designed to cause injury, and any weapon incorporating a knuckleduster;

Telescopic truncheon
being a truncheon which extends automatically by hand pressure applied to a button, spring or other device in or attached to its handle;

Push dagger
being a knife the handle of which fits within a clenched fist and the blade of which protrudes from between two fingers;

Shuriken, shaken, or death star
being a hard non-flexible plate having three or more sharp radiating points and designed to be thrown;

Handclaw
being a band of metal or other hard material from which a number of sharp spikes protrude, and worn around the hand;

Footclaw
being a bar of metal or other hard material from which a number of sharp spikes protrude, and worn strapped to the foot;

(CONTINUED ON NEXT PAGE)

Offensive Weapons – continued

Manrikigusari, or kusari
being a length of rope, cord, wire or chain fastened at each end to a hard weight or hand grip;

Swordstick
that is, a hollow walking-stick or cane containing a blade which may be used as a sword;

Hollow kubotan
being a cylindrical container containing a number of sharp spikes;

Blowpipe, or blowgun
being a hollow tube out of which hard pellets or darts are shot by the use of breath;

Kusari gama
being a length of rope, cord, wire or chain fastened at one end to a sickle;

Kyoketsu shoge
being a length of rope, cord, wire or chain fastened at one end to a hooked knife;

Belt buckle knife
being a buckle which incorporates or conceals a knife;

Disguised knife
being any knife which has a concealed blade or concealed sharp point and is designed to appear to be an everyday object of a kind commonly carried on the person or in a handbag, briefcase, or other hand luggage (such as a comb, brush, writing instrument, cigarette lighter, key, lipstick or telephone);

Stealth knife
being a knife or spike, which has a blade, or sharp point, made from a material which is not readily detectable by apparatus used for detecting metal and which is not designed for domestic use or for use in the processing, preparation or consumption of food or as a toy;

Truncheon
being a straight, side handled or friction-lock truncheon (sometimes known as a baton).

Sale to Persons Under 16

S 141A CRIMINAL JUSTICE ACT 1988

Any person who sells to a person under the age of **16 years** any knife, knife blade, razor blade, axe, or any other article which has a blade or is sharply pointed, and made or adapted for causing injury to any person shall be guilty of an offence.

Marketing of Knives

KNIVES ACT 1997, S 60 CRIMINAL JUSTICE AND PUBLIC ORDER ACT 1994

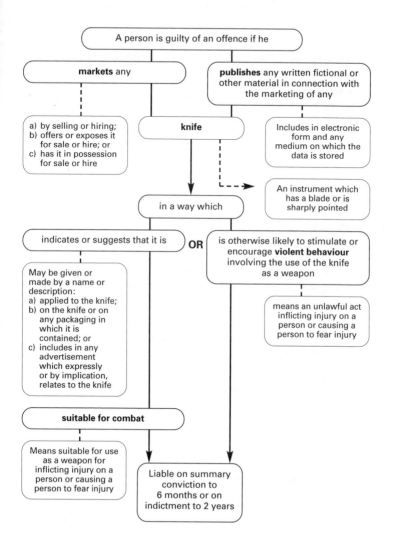

Marketing of Knives – continued

DEFENCES

The following defences are available to persons charged with an offence on the preceding page:

Exempt Trades:
a) It was marketed:
   i)   for use by the armed forces of any country;
   ii) as an antique or curio; or
   iii) as falling within such other category (if any) as may be prescribed;

b) It was reasonable for the knife to be marketed in that way; and

c) There were no grounds to suspect that it would be used for an unlawful purpose.

Other defences:
He did not know or suspect that the way in which the knife was marketed:
a) amounted to an indication or suggestion that the knife was suitable for combat; or

b) was likely to stimulate or encourage violent behaviour involving the use of the knife as a weapon.

General:
He took all reasonable precautions and exercised all due diligence to avoid committing the offence.

POLICE POWERS

A justices' warrant is required to search premises for knives and to seize them.

An Inspector or above may authorise stopping and searching in anticipation of violence (see following page).

Stop and Search for Knives or Offensive Weapons

S 60 CRIMINAL JUSTICE AND PUBLIC ORDER ACT 1994
AS AMENDED BY S 8 THE KNIVES ACT 1997

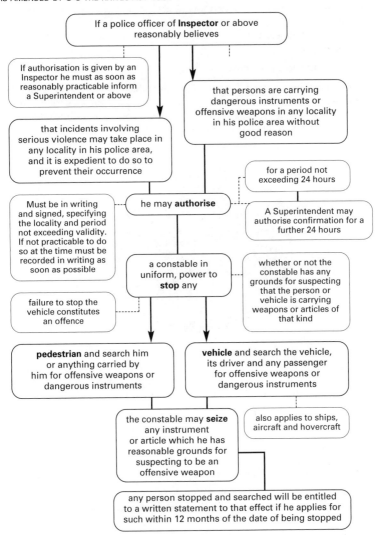

If a police officer of **Inspector** or above reasonably believes

If authorisation is given by an Inspector he must as soon as reasonably practicable inform a Superintendent or above

that persons are carrying dangerous instruments or offensive weapons in any locality in his police area without good reason

that incidents involving serious violence may take place in any locality in his police area, and it is expedient to do so to prevent their occurrence

for a period not exceeding 24 hours

he may **authorise**

A Superintendent may authorise confirmation for a further 24 hours

Must be in writing and signed, specifying the locality and period not exceeding validity. If not practicable to do so at the time must be recorded in writing as soon as possible

a constable in uniform, power to **stop** any

whether or not the constable has any grounds for suspecting that the person or vehicle is carrying weapons or articles of that kind

failure to stop the vehicle constitutes an offence

pedestrian and search him or anything carried by him for offensive weapons or dangerous instruments

vehicle and search the vehicle, its driver and any passenger for offensive weapons or dangerous instruments

the constable may **seize** any instrument or article which he has reasonable grounds for suspecting to be an offensive weapon

also applies to ships, aircraft and hovercraft

any person stopped and searched will be entitled to a written statement to that effect if he applies for such within 12 months of the date of being stopped

Removal of Disguises

S 60AA CRIMINAL JUSTICE AND PUBLIC ORDER ACT 1994

If a police officer of or above the rank of inspector reasonably believes:

(a) that activities may take place that are likely to involve the commission of offences, and
(b) that it is expedient to give an authorisation to prevent or control those activities,

he may authorise a constable in uniform:

(a) to require any person to remove any item which the constable reasonably believes is worn wholly or mainly to conceal that person's identity; and
(b) to seize any item which the constable reasonably believes any person intends to wear wholly or mainly for that purpose.

Any articles so seized may be retained in accordance with regulations.

The inspector's authority may be for a period not exceeding 24 hours, but a superintendent or above may authorise it to continue in force for a further 24 hours if he believes it is expedient to do so having regard to offences which have been, or are reasonably suspected to have been, committed.

An inspector who has given an authorisation must, as soon as it is practicable to do so, inform a superintendent or above.

Any authority given must be in writing and signed by the officer giving it, specifying the grounds on which it was given, the locality in which it is exercisable, and the period of validity.

A person will commit an offence if he fails to remove an item worn by him when required to do so by a constable exercising this power.

Crossbows

CROSSBOWS ACT 1987

OFFENCES

Sale   To sell or hire a crossbow or part of a crossbow to a person under the age of 17 years, unless he believes and has reasonable grounds to believe him to be 17 years.

Purchase For a person under 17 years to buy or hire a crossbow or part of a crossbow

Possession For a person under 17 years to have with him a crossbow (whether assembled to not) capable of discharging a missile unless under the supervision of a person of 21 years or older.

The Act does not apply to crossbows with a draw weight of less than 1.4 kg.

POLICE POWERS

Search   Where a PC suspects with reasonable cause, that a person is committing, or has committed an offence of unlawful possession, he may search that person or vehicle, and may detain the person or vehicle for that purpose.

Seizure A PC may seize and retain for the purpose of proceedings any crossbow or part of a crossbow discovered in the course of the search.

Entry   For the purpose of exercising the above powers a PC may enter any land **other than a dwelling house**.

Fireworks

FIREWORKS ACT 2003. FIREWORKS REGULATIONS 2004 (AS AMENDED)

Any person who contravenes a prohibition imposed by these Regulations commits an offence (S 11)

Possession under 18
No person under the age of 18 years shall possess an adult firework in a public place. (Reg. 4).

"Public Place" includes any place to which at the material time the public have or are permitted access, whether on payment or otherwise. (Reg. 4).

"Adult firework" means any firework (except for a cap, cracker snap, novelty match, party popper, serpent, sparkler or throwdown) which does not comply with BS 7114. (Reg. 3).

Possession of Category 4 firework
No person shall possess a category 4 firework. (Reg. 5). This does not apply to a person transporting fireworks in the course of employment in, or trade or business of, transporting fireworks. (Reg. 6).

"**Category 4 firework**" means classified as such by B.S. 7114.

Exceptions to Regs. 4 & 5
(a) Professional operator or organiser of firework displays;
(b) Manufacturer of fireworks or assemblies;
(c) Supplier of fireworks or assemblies;
(d) Local authority employee for a firework display, national public celebration or national commemorative event;
(e) Special effects in theatre, film or TV;
(f) A body having enforcement powers;
(g) Government department for firework display, national public celebration, national commemorative event, or research or investigation;
(h) Supplier of goods used for fireworks or assemblies, for testing purposes; or
(i) Navy, military or air force employees for firework display, national public celebration or national commemorative event. (Reg. 6).

Use of fireworks at night
No person shall use an adult firework during night hours (11pm to 7am) except:
(a) during a permitted fireworks night; or
(b) a person employed by a local authority putting on a firework display, national public celebration or national commemorative event. (Reg.7).

"**Permitted fireworks night**" means a period:
(a) beginning at 11pm on the first day of the Chinese New Year and ending at 1am the following day;
(b) beginning at 11pm and ending at midnight on 5th November;
(c) beginning at 11pm on the day of Diwali and ending at 1am the following day; or
(d) beginning at 11pm on 31st December and ending at 1am the following day.

Enforcement
The above offences concerning possession and use are enforced by the police. (Reg. 12). A power to stop, search and seize prohibited firearms was inserted into S1 PACE by the Serious Organised Crime and Police Act 2005 (see later).

Racially or Religiously Aggravated Offences

Ss 28-32 CRIME AND DISORDER ACT 1998

Where any of the following offences are committed and there exists 'racial or religious aggravation', the severity of the maximum liability is increased.

OFFENCE	LIABILITY ON INDICTMENT
Assaults S 20 Offences against the Person Act 1861 (malicious wounding or GBH)	7 years
S 47 of that Act (actual bodily harm)	7 years
Common Assault	2 years
Criminal Damage S 1(1) Criminal Damage Act 1971 (destroying or damaging property belonging to another)	14 years
Public Order Offences S 4 Public Order Act 1986 (fear or provocation of violence)	2 years ⎫ Constable may arrest without warrant if reasonably suspects to be committing
S 4A of that Act (intentional harassment, alarm or distress)	2 years ⎭
S 5 of that Act (harassment, alarm or distress)	Level 4 fine constable may arrest if warned to stop but conduct persists
Harassment etc S 2 Protection from Harassment Act 1997 (harassment)	2 years
S 4 of that Act (putting people in fear of violence)	7 years

Racially or religiously aggravated means

(a) at the time or immediately before or after doing so the offender demonstrates hostility based on the victim's racial or religious group; or

(b) the offence is wholly or partly motivated by hostility towards members of a racial or religious group.

Racial Hatred

Ss 17–23 PUBLIC ORDER ACT 1986

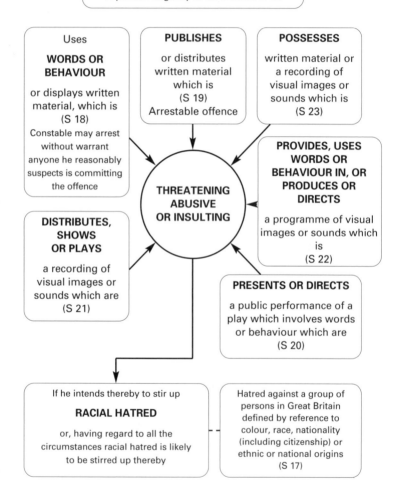

A person is guilty of an offence if he

Uses
WORDS OR BEHAVIOUR
or displays written material, which is
(S 18)
Constable may arrest without warrant anyone he reasonably suspects is committing the offence

PUBLISHES
or distributes written material which is
(S 19)
Arrestable offence

POSSESSES
written material or a recording of visual images or sounds which is
(S 23)

PROVIDES, USES WORDS OR BEHAVIOUR IN, OR PRODUCES OR DIRECTS
a programme of visual images or sounds which is
(S 22)

DISTRIBUTES, SHOWS OR PLAYS
a recording of visual images or sounds which are
(S 21)

THREATENING ABUSIVE OR INSULTING

PRESENTS OR DIRECTS
a public performance of a play which involves words or behaviour which are
(S 20)

If he intends thereby to stir up
RACIAL HATRED
or, having regard to all the circumstances racial hatred is likely to be stirred up thereby

Hatred against a group of persons in Great Britain defined by reference to colour, race, nationality (including citizenship) or ethnic or national origins
(S 17)

Trespassers on Land

Ss 61, 62, 62A, 62B & 62C CRIMINAL JUSTICE AND PUBLIC ORDER ACT 1994

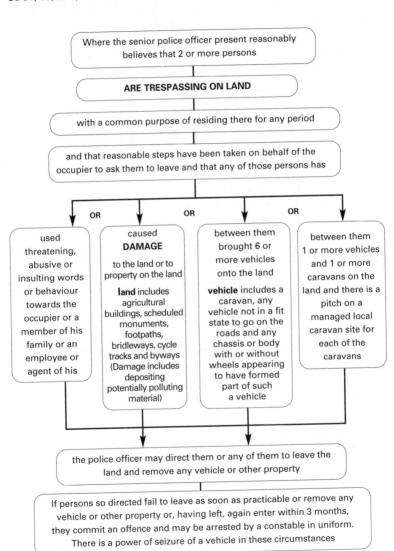

Where the senior police officer present reasonably believes that 2 or more persons

ARE TRESPASSING ON LAND

with a common purpose of residing there for any period

and that reasonable steps have been taken on behalf of the occupier to ask them to leave and that any of those persons has

OR used threatening, abusive or insulting words or behaviour towards the occupier or a member of his family or an employee or agent of his

OR caused **DAMAGE** to the land or to property on the land

land includes agricultural buildings, scheduled monuments, footpaths, bridleways, cycle tracks and byways (Damage includes depositing potentially polluting material)

OR between them brought 6 or more vehicles onto the land

vehicle includes a caravan, any vehicle not in a fit state to go on the roads and any chassis or body with or without wheels appearing to have formed part of such a vehicle

between them 1 or more vehicles and 1 or more caravans on the land and there is a pitch on a managed local caravan site for each of the caravans

the police officer may direct them or any of them to leave the land and remove any vehicle or other property

If persons so directed fail to leave as soon as practicable or remove any vehicle or other property or, having left, again enter within 3 months, they commit an offence and may be arrested by a constable in uniform. There is a power of seizure of a vehicle in these circumstances

Aggravated Trespass

S 68 CRIMINAL JUSTICE AND PUBLIC ORDER ACT 1994

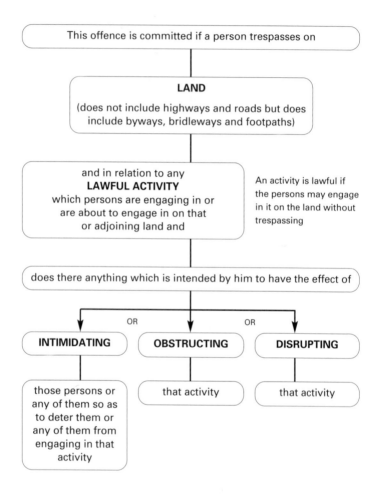

This offence is committed if a person trespasses on

LAND

(does not include highways and roads but does include byways, bridleways and footpaths)

and in relation to any
LAWFUL ACTIVITY
which persons are engaging in or are about to engage in on that or adjoining land and

An activity is lawful if the persons may engage in it on the land without trespassing

does there anything which is intended by him to have the effect of

OR   OR

INTIMIDATING   **OBSTRUCTING**   **DISRUPTING**

those persons or any of them so as to deter them or any of them from engaging in that activity

that activity

that activity

A constable in uniform who reasonably suspects that a person is committing this offence may arrest him without a warrant.

Aggravated Trespass – Removal of Persons

S 69 CRIMINAL JUSTICE AND PUBLIC ORDER ACT 1994

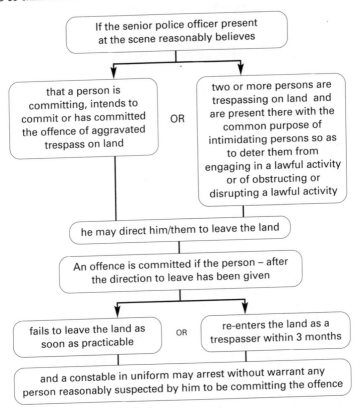

If the senior police officer present at the scene reasonably believes

that a person is committing, intends to commit or has committed the offence of aggravated trespass on land

OR

two or more persons are trespassing on land and are present there with the common purpose of intimidating persons so as to deter them from engaging in a lawful activity or of obstructing or disrupting a lawful activity

he may direct him/them to leave the land

An offence is committed if the person – after the direction to leave has been given

fails to leave the land as soon as practicable

OR

re-enters the land as a trespasser within 3 months

and a constable in uniform may arrest without warrant any person reasonably suspected by him to be committing the offence

The direction to leave may be communicated by a constable at the scene.

Defence

if a person shows he was not trespassing or that he had a reasonable excuse for not leaving or for re-entering.

Trespassory Assemblies

S 14A PUBLIC ORDER ACT 1986, INSERTED BY S 70 CRIMINAL JUSTICE AND PUBLIC ORDER ACT 1994

If the chief officer of police
(or the Commissioner of Police for the
City of London or Metropolis)
reasonably believes that an

**ASSEMBLY OF
2 OR MORE PERSONS**

is intended to be held in any district at a place on land
(in the open air) to which the public has no
(or limited) right of access and

it is likely to be held without the permission of the occupier of the
land or to conduct itself in such a way as to exceed the limits of
any permission or right of access

and may result:

(i) in a serious disruption to the life of the community, or

(ii) where the land or a building or monument on it is of historic,
architectural, archaeological or scientific importance, in
significant damage to the land, building or monument

he may apply to the council of the district for an order
prohibiting for a specified period the holding of such trespassory
assemblies in the specified district or part of it. In the City of
London and the Metropolitan area the relevant Commissioner
may, with the consent of the Home Secretary, make such an order

The order may only be made for a period not
exceeding 4 days and for an area not exceeding
5 miles radius from the specified centre

Trespassory Assemblies – Powers

Ss 14B & 14C PUBLIC ORDER ACT 1986,
INSERTED BY Ss 70-71 CRIMINAL JUSTICE AND PUBLIC ORDER ACT 1994

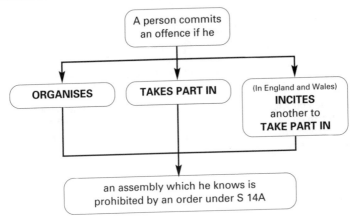

A person commits
an offence if he

ORGANISES | **TAKES PART IN** | (In England and Wales) **INCITES** another to **TAKE PART IN**

an assembly which he knows is
prohibited by an order under S 14A

STOPPING PERSONS FROM PROCEEDING TO TRESPASSORY ASSEMBLIES

If a constable in uniform reasonably believes that a person
is on his way to an assembly within the area to which
an order under S 14A applies, which the constable
reasonably believes to be an assembly prohibited by that order
he may **stop** that person and direct him not to proceed
towards the assembly (**but** the power may only be
exercised within the area to which the order applies)

Failure to comply is an offence

A constable in uniform may arrest without warrant any person he reasonably
suspects to be committing either of the above offences.

Trespassing, etc. on Designated Site

Ss 128 & 132 SERIOUS ORGANISED CRIME AND POLICE ACT 2005

The Secretary of State may designate a site for the purposes of introducing an order
making it illegal to trespass on the site. A constable in uniform may arrest without
warrant any person he reasonably suspects is committing or has committed this
offence. It is also an offence to organise, take part in, or carry on, an unauthorised
demonstration in a public place in a designated area in the vicinity of parliament. A
constable in uniform may arrest without warrant any person he reasonably suspects is
committing this offence (S 136).

Raves

S 63 CRIMINAL JUSTICE AND PUBLIC ORDER ACT 1994
(AS AMENDED BY THE ANTI-SOCIAL BEHAVIOUR ACT 2003)

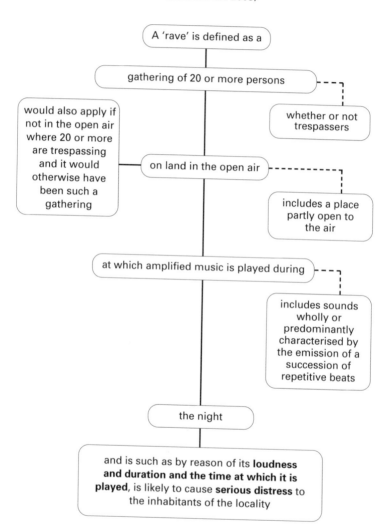

A 'rave' is defined as a

gathering of 20 or more persons

whether or not trespassers

would also apply if not in the open air where 20 or more are trespassing and it would otherwise have been such a gathering

on land in the open air

includes a place partly open to the air

at which amplified music is played during

includes sounds wholly or predominantly characterised by the emission of a succession of repetitive beats

the night

and is such as by reason of its **loudness and duration and the time at which it is played**, is likely to cause **serious distress** to the inhabitants of the locality

Raves – Powers

Ss 63 – 65 CRIMINAL JUSTICE AND PUBLIC ORDER ACT 1994

Removal of Persons S 63

A police officer of at least the rank of superintendent who reasonably believes that:

    (a) 2 or more persons are making preparations for a rave;

    (b) 10 or more persons are waiting for it to begin; or

    (c) 10 or more persons are attending a rave in progress;

may **direct** those persons and any other persons who arrive, to leave the land and remove any vehicles or other property that they have with them. The direction may be communicated by any constable at the scene. It will be treated as having been communicated if reasonable steps have been taken to bring it to their attention. Failure to leave or re-entry within 7 days is an offence arrestable by a constable in uniform who reasonably suspects a person to be committing the offence. A person also commits an offence if a direction has been given which he knows applies to him, and he makes preparations for or attends such a gathering within 24 hours of the direction being given.

Entry and Seizure S 64

A superintendent or above who believes the above direction would be justified in the circumstances, may authorise any constable to enter the land for the purposes of ascertaining whether such circumstances exist and to exercise any of the above powers and to seize and remove a vehicle or sound equipment which the person to whom a direction has been given has failed to remove and which appears to the constable to belong to him or to be in his possession or control. Also applies where a person has re-entered the land with a vehicle and/or sound equipment within 7 days.

Stopping Persons from Attending S 65

If a constable in uniform reasonably believes that a person is on his way to a gathering to which S 63 applies and in respect of which a direction is in force, he may stop that person and direct him not to proceed in the direction of that gathering. This power may be exercised within 5 miles of the boundary of the site of the gathering. Failure to comply is an offence and a constable in uniform who reasonably suspects that a person is committing the offence may arrest him without warrant.

Violent Entry to Premises

S 6 CRIMINAL LAW ACT 1977 AS AMENDED BY S 72 CRIMINAL JUSTICE AND
PUBLIC ORDER ACT 1994

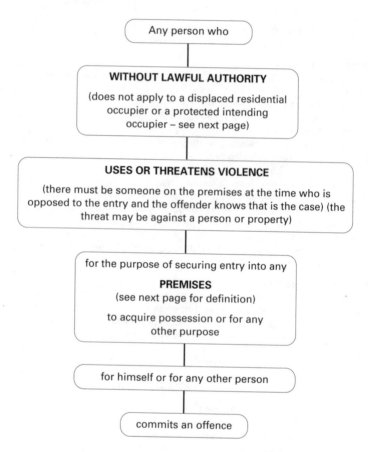

Any person who

WITHOUT LAWFUL AUTHORITY

(does not apply to a displaced residential
occupier or a protected intending
occupier – see next page)

USES OR THREATENS VIOLENCE

(there must be someone on the premises at the time who is
opposed to the entry and the offender knows that is the case) (the
threat may be against a person or property)

for the purpose of securing entry into any

PREMISES
(see next page for definition)

to acquire possession or for any
other purpose

for himself or for any other person

commits an offence

A constable in uniform may arrest without warrant anyone who is, or
whom he with reasonable cause suspects to be, guilty of this offence.

Squatters

S 7 CRIMINAL LAW ACT 1977, AS SUBSTITUTED BY S 73 CRIMINAL JUSTICE AND PUBLIC ORDER ACT 1994

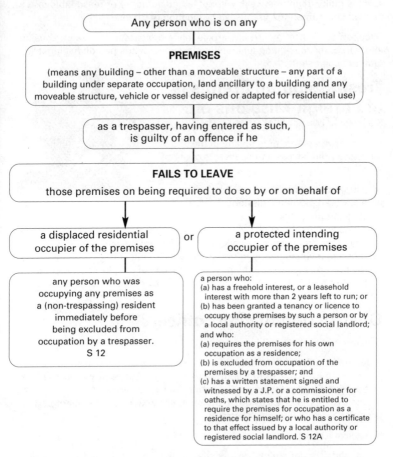

Any person who is on any

PREMISES

(means any building – other than a moveable structure – any part of a building under separate occupation, land ancillary to a building and any moveable structure, vehicle or vessel designed or adapted for residential use)

as a trespasser, having entered as such, is guilty of an offence if he

FAILS TO LEAVE

those premises on being required to do so by or on behalf of

a displaced residential occupier of the premises

or

a protected intending occupier of the premises

any person who was occupying any premises as a (non-trespassing) resident immediately before being excluded from occupation by a trespasser. S 12

a person who:
(a) has a freehold interest, or a leasehold interest with more than 2 years left to run; or
(b) has been granted a tenancy or licence to occupy those premises by such a person or by a local authority or registered social landlord; and who:
(a) requires the premises for his own occupation as a residence;
(b) is excluded from occupation of the premises by a trespasser; and
(c) has a written statement signed and witnessed by a J.P. or a commissioner for oaths, which states that he is entitled to require the premises for occupation as a residence for himself; or who has a certificate to that effect issued by a local authority or registered social landlord. S 12A

Defences: The premises were used mainly for non-residential purposes and offender was not on a residential part. Belief that person requiring him to leave was not a displaced residential occupier or protected intending occupier.

Power of arrest

A constable in uniform may arrest without warrant anyone who is, or whom he, with reasonable cause, suspects to be, guilty of this offence.

Trespassing With an Offensive Weapon

S 8 CRIMINAL LAW ACT 1977

A person who is on any premises as a trespasser, after having entered as such, is guilty of an offence if, without lawful authority or reasonable excuse, he has with him on the premises any weapon of offence.

'Weapon of offence' means any article made or adapted for use for causing injury to or incapacitating a person, or intended by the person having it with him for such use.

Trespassing on Premises of Foreign Missions etc

S 9 CRIMINAL LAW ACT 1977

A person who enters or is on any of the following premises as a trespasser is guilty of an offence:

(a) a diplomatic mission;
(b) a closed diplomatic mission;
(c) consular premises;
(d) a closed consular post;
(e) any other premises in respect of which any organisation or body is entitled to inviolability by or under any enactment; and
(f) any premises which are the private residence of a diplomatic agent or of any other person who is entitled to inviolability of residence by or under any enactment.

Obstruction of court officers

S 10 CRIMINAL LAW ACT 1977

A person is guilty of an offence if he resists or intentionally obstructs any person who is an officer of a court engaged in executing any process issued by the High Court or by any county court for the recovery of any premises or for the delivery of possession of any premises which have been entered or occupied without licence or consent.

'Officer of a court' means:

• any sheriff, under sheriff, deputy sheriff, bailiff or officer of a sheriff; and
• any bailiff or other person who is an officer of a county court

Power of Arrest
A constable in uniform may arrest without warrant anyone who is, or whom he, with reasonable cause, suspects to be, in the act of committing any of the above offences.

Affray

S 3 PUBLIC ORDER ACT 1986

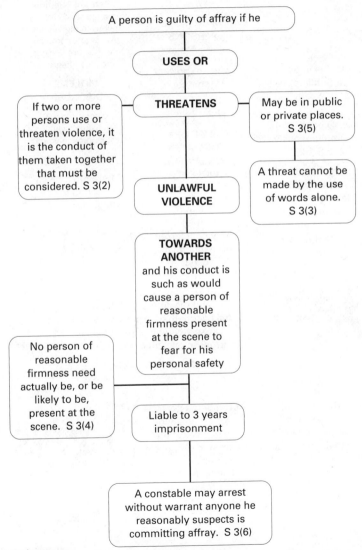

A person is guilty of affray if he

USES OR

THREATENS

If two or more persons use or threaten violence, it is the conduct of them taken together that must be considered. S 3(2)

May be in public or private places. S 3(5)

A threat cannot be made by the use of words alone. S 3(3)

UNLAWFUL VIOLENCE

TOWARDS ANOTHER and his conduct is such as would cause a person of reasonable firmness present at the scene to fear for his personal safety

No person of reasonable firmness need actually be, or be likely to be, present at the scene. S 3(4)

Liable to 3 years imprisonment

A constable may arrest without warrant anyone he reasonably suspects is committing affray. S 3(6)

Riot/Violent Disorder

S 1 & 2 PUBLIC ORDER ACT 1986

Where

12 OR MORE PERSONS

If there are 3 or more persons and all the following ingredients except the 'common purpose' are present, then the offence is

VIOLENT DISORDER

contrary to S 2 punishable with 5 years imprisonment

May be in private or public place. S 1(5)

who are present together

Need not be done simultaneously. S 1(2)

Includes conduct towards property. Need not cause or be intended to cause injury or damage. S 8

USE OR THREATEN UNLAWFUL VIOLENCE

There must be an intention to use violence or be aware that his conduct may be violent

for a common purpose. (may be inferred from conduct) S 1(3)

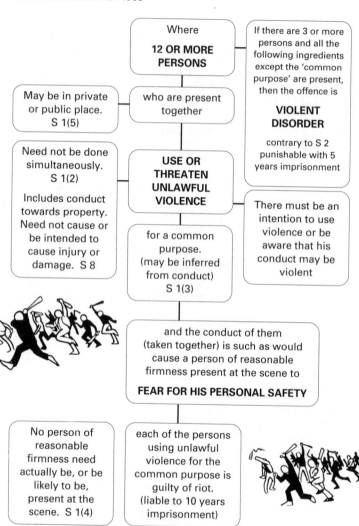

and the conduct of them (taken together) is such as would cause a person of reasonable firmness present at the scene to

FEAR FOR HIS PERSONAL SAFETY

No person of reasonable firmness need actually be, or be likely to be, present at the scene. S 1(4)

each of the persons using unlawful violence for the common purpose is guilty of riot. (liable to 10 years imprisonment)

Public Meetings

S 1 PUBLIC MEETING ACT 1908

Any person who at a lawful

PUBLIC MEETING

acts in a disorderly manner for the purpose of preventing the transaction of the business of the meeting shall be guilty of an offence

It is the duty of the police to prevent any action likely to result in a breach of the peace. Refusing to desist is an obstruction of the police in the execution of their duty

POWER OF ENTRY

The police have a right to enter premises at which the public have been invited to attend if they reasonably apprehend a **breach of the peace**

Any person who incites a person to commit such an offence shall be guilty of a like offence

If a constable reasonably suspects a person to be committing such an offence he may, if requested by the chairman of the meeting, request the offender to give his name and address. If he fails or refuses or gives a false name and address he shall be guilty of an offence

Uniforms

S 1 PUBLIC ORDER ACT 1936

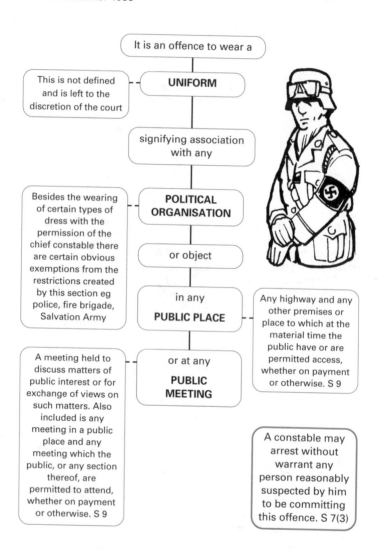

It is an offence to wear a

UNIFORM

This is not defined and is left to the discretion of the court

signifying association with any

POLITICAL ORGANISATION

Besides the wearing of certain types of dress with the permission of the chief constable there are certain obvious exemptions from the restrictions created by this section eg police, fire brigade, Salvation Army

or object

in any **PUBLIC PLACE**

Any highway and any other premises or place to which at the material time the public have or are permitted access, whether on payment or otherwise. S 9

or at any **PUBLIC MEETING**

A meeting held to discuss matters of public interest or for exchange of views on such matters. Also included is any meeting in a public place and any meeting which the public, or any section thereof, are permitted to attend, whether on payment or otherwise. S 9

A constable may arrest without warrant any person reasonably suspected by him to be committing this offence. S 7(3)

Organisations

S 2 PUBLIC ORDER ACT 1936

It is an offence to be involved in

CONTROLLING, MANAGING, ORGANISING, TRAINING OR EQUIPPING

any association of persons for the purpose of enabling them to be employed for

usurping the functions of the

POLICE OR ARMED FORCES

promoting any

POLITICAL OBJECT

by force, or arousing a fear that they are to be used for such a purpose

But this section does not prevent the employment of a reasonable number of stewards to assist in the preservation of order at any public meeting held on private premises, or giving them instruction in their duties, or giving them badges, etc

Chemical Weapons

CHEMICAL WEAPONS ACT **1996**

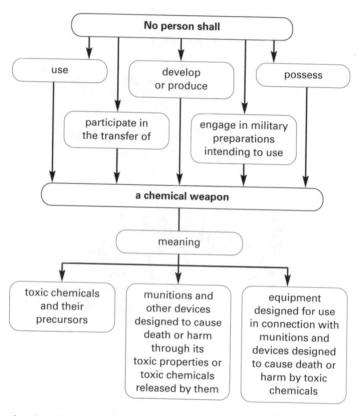

The Act describes various 'permitted purposes' i.e. peaceful purposes; purposes related to protection against toxic chemicals; legitimate military purposes; and purposes of enforcing the law.

> *THIS IS AN ARRESTABLE OFFENCE – LIFE IMPRISONMENT*

Biological Weapons

S 1 BIOLOGICAL WEAPONS ACT 1974

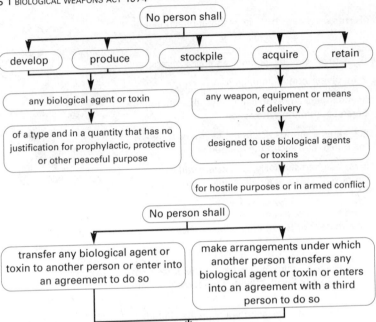

No person shall

- develop
- produce
- stockpile
- acquire
- retain

any biological agent or toxin

of a type and in a quantity that has no justification for prophylactic, protective or other peaceful purpose

any weapon, equipment or means of delivery

designed to use biological agents or toxins

for hostile purposes or in armed conflict

No person shall

transfer any biological agent or toxin to another person or enter into an agreement to do so

make arrangements under which another person transfers any biological agent or toxin or enters into an agreement with a third person to do so

if the biological agent or toxin is likely to be kept or used (whether by the transferee or any other person) otherwise than for prophylactic, protective or other peaceful purposes and he knows or has reason to believe that that is the case.

'biological agent' means any microbial or other biological agent.

'toxin' means any toxin, whatever its origin or method of production.

Extraterritorial application section 1
Section 1 applies to acts done outside the UK, but only if done by a UK national, a Scottish partnership or a body incorporated under a law of part of the UK.

THIS IS AN ARRESTABLE OFFENCE – LIFE IMPRISONMENT

Terrorism – Interpretation

S 1 TERRORISM ACT 2000

Terrorism means the use or threat of action which

1. involves serious violence against a person,

2. involves serious damage to property,

3. endangers a person's life, other than that of the person committing the action,

4. creates a serious risk to the health or safety of the public or a section of the public, or

5. is designed seriously to interfere with or seriously to disrupt an electronic system

and the use or threat is designed to influence the government or to intimidate the public, or a section of the public

But the use or threat of action which involves the use of firearms or explosives is 'terrorism' whether or not this part is satisfied

and the use or threat is made for the purpose of advancing a political, religious or ideological cause

'action' includes action outside the United Kingdom

the reference to any person or property means wherever situated

'public' includes the public of a country other than the United Kingdom

'government' means the government of the UK, or a part of the UK or of a country other than the UK

Terrorism – Offences

Ss 11 – 12 TERRORISM ACT 2000

Offences are committed in the following circumstances:

MEMBERSHIP (S 11): Belonging to or professing to belong to a proscribed organisation. *This is an arrestable offence.*

It is a **defence** to prove:
(a) that the organisation was not proscribed on the last occasion he became a member or began to profess to be a member, and
(b) that he has not taken part in the activities of the organisation at any time while it was proscribed.

SUPPORT (S 12(1)): Inviting support for a proscribed organisation, and the support is not, or is not restricted to, the provision of money or other property. *This is an arrestable offence.*

ARRANGING MEETINGS (S 12(2)): Arranging, managing or assisting in arranging or managing a meeting which he knows is:

(a) to support a proscribed organisation,
(b) to further the activities of a proscribed organisation, or
(c) to be addressed by a person who belongs or professes to belong to a proscribed organisation (but it would be a defence at a private meeting to prove that he had no reasonable cause to believe that the address would support a proscribed organisation or further its activities).

This is an arrestable offence.

ADDRESSING MEETINGS (S 12(3)):
Addressing a meeting and the purpose of the address is to encourage support for a proscribed organisation or to further its activities.

This is an arrestable offence.

'Meeting' means a meeting of 3 or more persons, whether or not the public are admitted. A meeting is *private* if the public are not admitted.

For list of organisations which are **'proscribed'** see later. *(CONTINUED ON NEXT PAGE)*

Terrorism – Offences – continued

Ss 13 & 15 Terrorism Act 2000

Offences are committed in the following circumstances:

UNIFORM (S 13)

In a public place if a person:

(a) wears an item of clothing, or
(b) wears, carries or displays an article,

in such a way or in such circumstances as to arouse reasonable suspicion that he is a member or supporter of a proscribed organisation.

A constable in Scotland may arrest a person if he has reasonable grounds to suspect the person to be guilty of this offence.

FUND-RAISING (S 15(1))

Inviting another to provide money or other property, intending that it should be used, or having reasonable cause to suspect that it may be used, for the purposes of terrorism.
This is an arrestable offence.

RECEIVING MONEY OR OTHER PROPERTY (S 15(2))

Receiving money or other property intending that it should be used, or having reasonable cause to suspect that it may be used, for the purposes of terrorism.

This is an arrestable offence.

PROVIDING MONEY OR OTHER PROPERTY (S 15(3))

Providing money or other property, knowing or having reasonable cause to suspect that it will or may be used for the purposes of terrorism.
This is an arrestable offence.

Provision of money or other property means being given, lent or otherwise made available, whether or not for consideration.
Purposes of terrorism includes for the benefit of a proscribed organisation (see later).

The offence will be committed even if the act is done outside the UK (S 63)

For list of organisations which are **'proscribed'** see later.

Terrorism – Offences – continued

Ss 16 – 18 & 21 TERRORISM ACT 2000

Offences are committed in the following circumstances:

USE AND POSSESSION (S 16)

(a) Using money or other property for the purposes of terrorism.
(b) Possessing money or other property, intending that it should be used, or having reasonable cause to suspect that it may be used, for the purposes of terrorism.

This is an arrestable offence.

The offence will be committed even if the act is done outside the UK (S 63)

FUNDING ARRANGEMENTS (S 17)

Entering into or becoming concerned in an arrangement as a result of which money or other property is made available or is to be made available to another, knowing or having reasonable cause to suspect that that it will or may be used for the purposes of terrorism.

This is an arrestable offence.

MONEY LAUNDERING (S 18)

Entering into or becoming concerned in an arrangement which facilitates the retention or control by or on behalf of another person of terrorist property:

(a) by concealment,
(b) by removal from the jurisdiction,
(c) by transfer to nominees, or
(d) in any other way.

It is a defence to prove that he did not know and had no reasonable cause to suspect that the arrangement related to terrorist property.

This is an arrestable offence.

'TERRORIST PROPERTY' MEANS:

(a) money or other property which is likely to be used for the purposes of terrorism (including any resources of a proscribed organisation),
(b) proceeds of the commission of acts of terrorism, and
(c) proceeds of the acts carried out for the purposes of terrorism (S 14).

CO-OPERATION WITH THE POLICE (S 21)

A person does not commit an offence under Ss 15 to 18 if he is acting with the express consent of a constable. Neither does he commit an offence under those sections by involvement in a transaction or arrangement relating to money or other property if he discloses to a constable:

(a) his suspicion or belief that the money or other property is terrorist property, and
(b) the information on which his suspicion or belief is based.

But the above only applies where he makes the disclosure
(a) after he becomes concerned in the transaction,
(b) on his own initiative, and
(c) as soon as reasonably practicable.

(CONTINUED ON NEXT PAGE)

Terrorism – Offences – continued

S 54 TERRORISM ACT 2000

Offences are committed in the following circumstances:

WEAPONS TRAINING (S 54)

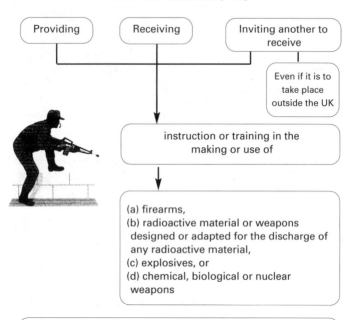

Providing	Receiving	Inviting another to receive

Even if it is to take place outside the UK

instruction or training in the making or use of

(a) firearms,
(b) radioactive material or weapons designed or adapted for the discharge of any radioactive material,
(c) explosives, or
(d) chemical, biological or nuclear weapons

'Providing instruction' and 'inviting' includes making it available either generally or to one or more specific persons.

It will be a defence to prove that his action or involvement was for a purpose other than terrorism.

THESE ARE ALL ARRESTABLE OFFENCES

Terrorism – Offences – continued

Ss 56 – 58 TERRORISM ACT 2000

Offences are committed in the following circumstances:

DIRECTING ORGANISATIONS (S 56)

Directing, at any level, the activities of a terrorist organisation.

This is an arrestable offence.

POSSESSION OF ARTICLES (S 57)

Possessing an article in circumstances which gave rise to a reasonable suspicion that it was connected with the commission, preparation or instigation of an act of terrorism.
It is a defence to prove that it was not for a terrorist purpose.
It will be assumed that the person *possessed* the article if it was:
(a) on any premises at the same time as that person, or
(b) on premises which the person occupied or habitually used other than as a member of the public,
unless he proves that he did not know of its presence or that he had no control over it.

This is an arrestable offence.

'Article' includes substance and any other thing (S 121)

COLLECTION OF INFORMATION (S 58)

Collecting or making a record of	Possessing a document or record containing

information likely to be useful to a person committing or preparing an act of terrorism

'record' includes a photographic or electronic record

It is a defence to prove that he had a reasonable excuse for his action or possession.

THIS IS AN ARRESTABLE OFFENCE

Terrorism – Offences – continued

Ss 59 – 63 TERRORISM ACT 2000

Offences are committed in the following circumstances:

INCITING TERRORISM OVERSEAS (S 59)

Inciting a person to commit an act of terrorism wholly or partly outside the UK, and the act would, if committed in England and Wales, constitute one of the following offences:

(a) murder,

(b) wounding with intent (S 18 Offences Against the Person Act 1861),

(c) poisoning (S 23 or 24 of the above Act),

(d) explosions (S 28 or 29 of the above Act), or

(e) endangering life by damaging property (S 1 Criminal Damage Act 1971).

It is immaterial whether or not the person incited is in the UK at the time of the incitement.

This is an arrestable offence.

ACTS OF TERRORISM OUTSIDE THE UK (S 62)

Doing anything outside the UK as an act of terrorism or for the purposes of terrorism, and the action would, if done in the UK, constitute one of the following offences:

(a) causing explosions, etc (S 2, 3 or 5 Explosive Substances Act 1883),

(b) biological weapons (S 1 Biological Weapons Act 1974)

(c) chemical weapons (S 2 Chemical Weapons Act 1996)

Terrorism – Disclosure of Information

TERRORISM ACT 2000, Ss 19 & 20

Where a person :

(a) believes or suspects that another person has committed an offence under sections 15 to 18 (see earlier), and

(b) bases his belief or suspicion on information which comes to his attention in the course of a trade, profession, business or employment

the person commits an offence if he does not disclose to a constable as soon as reasonably practicable:

(a) his belief or suspicion, and

(b) the information on which it is based.

This does not require disclosure by a professional legal adviser of

(a) information which he obtains in privileged circumstances, or

(b) a belief or suspicion based on information which he obtains in privileged circumstances.

This does not apply if the information came to the person in the course of a business in the regulated sector. (Sched 3A lists the types of business which are 'regulated'. These include national savings, credit unions, banking, building societies, investments, life insurance, etc) However, a similar offence of failure to disclose in the regulated sector is provided by section 21 A.

but it is a defence to prove that he had a reasonable excuse for not making the disclosure.

It is also a defence where:

(a) a person is in employment,

(b) his employer has established a procedure for the making of disclosures of such matters, and

(c) he is charged with such an offence,

to prove that he disclosed the matters in accordance with the procedure.

A person may make such disclosures to a constable notwithstanding any restriction on disclosing it imposed by statute or otherwise (S 20).

THIS IS AN ARRESTABLE OFFENCE – 5 YEARS

Terrorism – Investigations

Ss 33 – 39 TERRORISM ACT 2000

CORDONED AREAS (Ss 33 – 36)

If considered expedient for the purposes of a terrorist investigation, a Superintendent (or lower rank in the case of urgency) may designate an area to be cordoned.

A constable in uniform may:

(a) order a person in a cordoned area to leave it immediately;

(b) order a person immediately to leave premises which are wholly or partly in or adjacent to a cordoned area;

(c) order the driver or person in charge of a vehicle in a cordoned area to move it from the area immediately;

(d) arrange for the removal of a vehicle from a cordoned area;

(e) arrange for the movement of a vehicle within a cordoned area;

(f) prohibit or restrict access to a cordoned area by pedestrians or vehicles.

A person commits an offence if he fails to comply with an order, prohibition or restriction imposed as above. But it is a defence to prove that he had a reasonable excuse for his failure.

FAILURE TO DISCLOSE INFORMATION (S 38B)

Where a person has information which he knows or believes might be of material assistance:

(a) in preventing an act of terrorism, or

(b) in securing the apprehension, prosecution or conviction of another person in the UK, for an offence of terrorism,

he commits an offence if he does not disclose the information as soon as reasonably practicable to a constable or (in Northern Ireland) a member of HM Forces.

It is a defence to prove that he had a reasonable excuse for not making the disclosure.

This is an arrestable offence.

DISCLOSURE OF INFORMATION (S 39)

Where a person knows or has reasonable cause to suspect that a constable is conducting or proposes to conduct a terrorist investigation, he commits an offence if he:

(a) discloses to another anything which is likely to prejudice an investigation, or

(b) interferes with material which is likely to be relevant to the investigation.

He would also commit an offence by a similar disclosure or interference where a disclosure had been or was to be made under the aforementioned sections 19, 21 or 38B.

It would be a defence to prove that:

(a) he did not know and had no reasonable cause to suspect that the disclosure or interference was likely to affect a terrorist investigation, or

(b) that he had a reasonable excuse for the disclosure or interference.

An offence would not be committed in the case of a professional legal adviser.

This is an arrestable offence.

Terrorism – Police Powers

Ss 40 – 43 TERRORISM ACT 2000

ARREST WITHOUT WARRANT (S 41)

A constable may arrest without warrant anyone he reasonably suspects to be a terrorist.

'Terrorist' is defined as a person who:

(a) has committed any offence under any of sections 11 (membership), 12 (support), 15 (fund raising), 16 (use and possession), 17 (funding), 18 (money laundering), 54 (weapon training), 56 (directing organisations), 57 (possession of articles), 58 (collection of information), 59 (inciting overseas), 60 (Northern Ireland), 61 (Scotland), 62 (bombing outside UK) or 63 (finance outside UK), or

(b) is or has been concerned in the commission, preparation or instigation of acts of terrorism.

SEARCH OF PREMISES (S 42)

A justice of the peace may issue a warrant for a constable to search specified premises if he is satisfied that there are reasonable grounds to suspect that a person to whom para (b) in the above definition applies is to be found there.

SEARCH OF PERSONS (S 43)

A constable may stop and search a person whom he reasonably suspects to be a terrorist (see above definition) or a person arrested under S 41 above to discover whether he has in his possession anything which may constitute evidence that he is a terrorist.

The search must be carried out by a person of the same sex.

A constable may seize and retain anything discovered in the course of the search which he reasonably suspects may constitute evidence that the person is a terrorist.

GENERAL (S 114)

Any power conferred by this Act is additional to any other powers at common law or other enactment, and will not affect those powers. A constable may use reasonable force if necessary in exercising the powers under this Act.

Terrorism – Stop and Search

Ss 44 - 45 TERRORISM ACT 2000

A constable in uniform may be authorised to **stop**

a vehicle
and to *search*-
(a) the vehicle;
(b) the driver of the vehicle;
(c) a passenger in the vehicle;
(d) anything in or on the vehicle or carried by the driver or a passenger.

a pedestrian
and to *search*-
(a) the pedestrian;
(b) anything carried by him.

Authorisation may be given:
by an ACC, a commander in London or the metropolitan area, or an ACC in Northern Ireland.
Authorisation may be given by an ACC of the BTP or MOD police but only in relation to BTP or MOD premises respectively.

if he considers it expedient for the prevention of acts of terrorism.

Exercise of Power
The power may be exercised only for the purpose of searching for articles of a kind which could be used in connection with terrorism, whether or not the constable has grounds for suspecting the presence of such articles.

Seizure
Articles which are discovered and which are reasonably suspected to be intended to be used in connection with terrorism may be seized and retained.

Removal of Clothing
A constable may not require a person to remove any clothing in public except headgear, footwear, an outer coat, a jacket or gloves.

Detention
A constable may detain the person or vehicle for such time as is reasonably required to permit the search to be carried out.

Offences
A person will be guilty of an offence if he fails to stop, or if he fails to stop the vehicle, when required to do so, or if he wilfully obstructs the constable.

Terrorism – Restrictions on Parking

Ss 48 - 52 TERRORISM ACT 2000

A constable in uniform may be authorised to prohibit or restrict the parking of vehicles on a road specified in the authorisation.

Authorisation may be given

by an ACC, a commander in London or the metropolitan area, or an ACC in Northern Ireland, if he considers it expedient for the prevention of acts of terrorism.

Exercise of Power

The power is exercised by placing a traffic sign on the road concerned. A constable may suspend a parking place and this will be treated as a restriction for the purposes of removal of vehicles illegally parked or for the purposes of committing offences (see below).

Duration of Authorisation

The period of authorisation shall not exceed 28 days but it may be renewed.

Offences

A person commits an offence if:

(a) he parks a vehicle in contravention of a prohibition or restriction.

(b) he is the driver or other person in charge of the vehicle which has been permitted to remain at rest in contravention of a prohibition or restriction and he fails to remove the vehicle when ordered to do so by a constable in uniform.

It will be a defence to prove that he had a reasonable excuse for the act or omission. Possession of a disabled person's badge shall not itself constitute a reasonable excuse.

No Parking

Terrorism – Proscribed Organisations

S 3 & SCHED 2 TERRORISM ACT 2000

An organisation is **'proscribed'** if it is mentioned in the list below or operates under the same name as an organisation so mentioned:

The Irish Republican Army
Cumann na mBan
Fianna na hEireann
The Red Hand Commando
Saor Eire
The Ulster Freedom Fighters
The Ulster Volunteer Force
The Irish National Liberation Army
The Irish People's Liberation Organisation
The Ulster Defence Association
The Loyalist Volunteer Force
The Continuity Army Council
The Orange Volunteers
The Red Hand Defenders
Al-Qaeda
Egyptian Islamic Jihad
Al-Gama'at al-Islamiya
Armed Islamic Group (GIA)
Salafist Group for Call and Combat (GSPC)
Babbar Khalsa
International Sikh Youth Federation
Harakat Mujahideen
Jaish e Mohammed
Lashkar e Tayyaba
Liberation Tigers of Tamil Eelam (LTTE)
Hizballah External Security Organisation
Hamas-Izz al-Din al-Qassem Brigades
Palestinian Islamic Jihad – Shaqaqi
Abu Nidal Organisation
Islamic Army of Aden
Mujaheddin e Khalq
Kurdistan Worker's Party (PKK)
Revolutionary People's Liberation Party – Front (DHKP-C)
Basque Homeland and Liberty (ETA)
17 November Revolutionary Organisation (N17)
Abu Sayyaf Group
Asbat Al-Ansar
Islamic Movement of Uzbekistan
Jemaah Islamiyah

Terrorism – Nuclear Weapons

S 47 ANTI-TERRORISM, CRIME AND SECURITY ACT 2001

A person commits an offence if he:

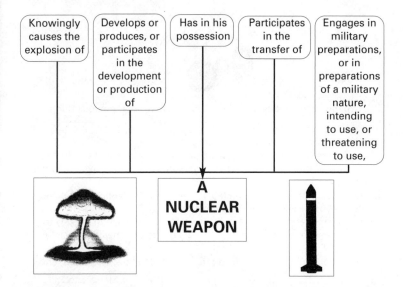

| Knowingly causes the explosion of | Develops or produces, or participates in the development or production of | Has in his possession | Participates in the transfer of | Engages in military preparations, or in preparations of a military nature, intending to use, or threatening to use, |

A NUCLEAR WEAPON

'Participates in the development or production' means doing any act which:
(a) facilitates the development by another of the capability to produce or use, a nuclear weapon; or
(b) facilitates the making by another of a nuclear weapon
knowing or having reason to believe that his act has (or will have) that effect.

'Participates in the transfer' means:
(a) buying or otherwise acquiring it or agreeing with another to do so;
(b) selling or otherwise disposing of it or agreeing with another to do so; or
(c) making arrangements under which another person either acquires or disposes of it or agrees with a third person to do so.

THIS IS AN ARRESTABLE OFFENCE

Terrorism – Use of Noxious Substances

S 113 ANTI-TERRORISM, CRIME AND SECURITY ACT 2001

A person commits an offence if he takes any action which:

involves the use of a noxious substance or other noxious thing;

which has or is likely to have the effect of:
(a) causing serious violence against a person anywhere in the world;
(b) causing serious damage to real or personal property anywhere in the world;
(c) endangers human life or creates a serious risk to the health or safety of the public or a section of the public; or
(d) induces in members of the public the fear that the action is likely to endanger their lives or create a serious risk to their health or safety;

but any effect on the person taking the action is to be disregarded; and

is designed to influence a government or to intimidate the public or a section of the public

An offence will also be committed if a person:
(a) makes a threat that he or another will take any action which constitutes the above offence; and
(b) intends thereby to induce in a person anywhere in the world the fear that the threat is likely to be carried out.

'**substance**' includes any biological agent and any other natural or artificial substance (whatever its form, origin or method of production).
'**government**' means the government of the UK, of a part of the UK or of a country other than the UK.
'**public**' includes the public of a country other than the UK.

*THESE ARE
ARRESTABLE
OFFENCES.*

Terrorism – Hoaxes Involving Noxious Substances

S 114 ANTI-TERRORISM, CRIME AND SECURITY ACT 2001

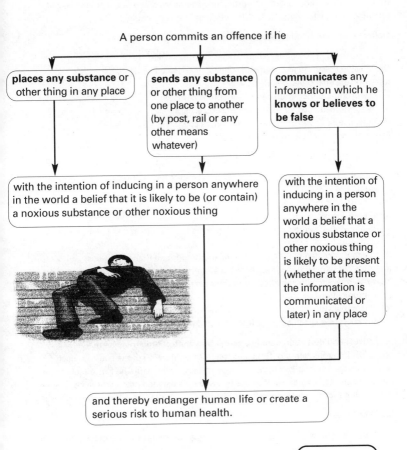

A person commits an offence if he

places any substance or other thing in any place

sends any substance or other thing from one place to another (by post, rail or any other means whatever)

communicates any information which he **knows or believes to be false**

with the intention of inducing in a person anywhere in the world a belief that it is likely to be (or contain) a noxious substance or other noxious thing

with the intention of inducing in a person anywhere in the world a belief that a noxious substance or other noxious thing is likely to be present (whether at the time the information is communicated or later) in any place

and thereby endanger human life or create a serious risk to human health.

For meaning of **'substance'** see previous page.

THESE ARE ARRESTABLE OFFENCES.

Terrorism – Control Orders

PREVENTION OF TERRORISM ACT 2005

S 1. A **Control Order** means an order against an individual that imposes **obligations** on him for purposes connected with protecting members of the public from a risk of terrorism. It may be made by the Secretary of State or a court.

Obligations may include a **prohibition or restriction** on-

(a) possession or use of specified articles or substances;
(b) specified services or specified facilities, or specified activities;
(c) work, occupation or business;
(d) association or communication with other persons;
(e) place of residence, or to whom he gives access;
(f) presence at specified places, areas, times and days;
(g) movement to, from or within the U.K.;

or the following **requirements**-

(h) to comply with restrictions on other movements for a period not exceeding 24 hours;
(i) to surrender his passport or anything specified in the order;
(j) to give access to specified persons to his residence or other place;
(k) to allow specified persons to search premises to ascertain contravention of obligations;
(l) to allow specified persons to remove anything found in the premises;
(m) to allow himself to be photographed;
(n) to co-operate with specified arrangements to allow his movements, communications or other activities to be monitored by electronic or other means;
(o) to comply with a demand to provide information to a specified person;
(p) to report to a specified person at specified times and places.

S 5. **Arrest and detention pending derogating control order** may be made by a constable if the Secretary of State has made an application to the court for such an order, and the constable believes arrest is necessary to ensure he is available to be given notice of the order. He must be taken to a designated place, where he may be held for not more than 48 hours (extendable by a court for a further 48 hours)

S 9. **Offences-**

(a) contravention of an obligation imposed by a control order (arrestable offence (5 years));
(b) failing to report to a specified person on his re-entry to the U.K. after an order has expired (arrestable offence (5 years));
(c) obstructing a person carrying out a search of premises for a person on whom a notice of a control order is to be served (arrestable offence (Sched. 1A PACE)).

Fraudulent Use Of Telecommunications System

Ss 42 TELECOMMUNICATIONS ACT 1984

A person who dishonestly obtains a licensed telecommunications service with intent to avoid payment of any charge shall be guilty of an offence.

> *THIS IS AN ARRESTABLE OFFENCE*

Possession of Equipment for Fraudulent Use

S 42A

Where a person has in his custody or under his control anything which may be used to obtain a licensed telecommunications service, he commits an offence if he intends:

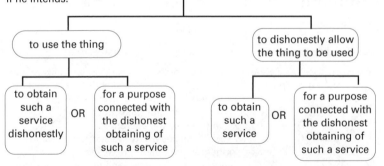

to use the thing	to dishonestly allow the thing to be used
to obtain such a service dishonestly **OR** for a purpose connected with the dishonest obtaining of such a service	to obtain such a service **OR** for a purpose connected with the dishonest obtaining of such a service

An offence is also committed if a person supplies or offers to supply anything which may be used for the above purposes if he knows or believes the person to whom it is supplied or offered intends to use it for such a purpose.

> *THIS IS AN ARRESTABLE OFFENCE*

Postal Offences

POSTAL SERVICES ACT 2000

Prohibition of Advertisements
(S 86)

A person commits an offence if, without due authority:

- he affixes any advertisement, document, board or thing in or on any universal postal service post office, letter box or other property belonging to, or used by, a universal postal service provider, or
- he paints or in any way disfigures any such office, box or property.

Prohibition on sending certain articles by post (S 85)

A person commits an offence if he sends by post a postal packet:

- which encloses any creature, article or thing of any kind which is likely to injure other postal packets in course of their transmission by post or any person engaged in the business of a postal operator (does not apply to things allowed by the operator);
- which encloses any indecent or obscene print, painting, photograph, lithograph, engraving, cinematograph film or other record of a picture or pictures, book, card or written communication, or any other indecent or obscene article; or
- which has on the packet, or on the cover of the packet, any words, marks or designs which are of an indecent or obscene character.

Malicious Communications

S 1 MALICIOUS COMMUNICATIONS ACT 1988 (AS AMENDED BY THE CRIMINAL JUSTICE AND POLICE ACT 2001)

A person is guilty of an offence if he sends to another person

a letter, electronic communication or article of any description which conveys:
(a) a message which is indecent or grossly offensive;
(b) a threat; or
(c) information which is false and known or believed to be false by the sender

any article or electronic communication which is, in whole or part, of an indecent or grossly offensive nature

if his purpose in sending it is that it should cause distress or anxiety to the recipient or to any other person to whom he intends that it should be communicated.

But, in relation to (b) he will not be guilty if he shows:

(a) that the threat was used to reinforce a demand made by him on reasonable grounds; and
(b) that he believed, on reasonable grounds, that the use of the threat was a proper means of reinforcing the demand.

'Electronic communication' includes:

(a) any oral or other communication by means of a telecommunication system; and
(b) any communication (however sent) that is in electronic form.

'Sends' includes delivering or transmitting and causing to be sent, delivered or transmitted.

Improper Use of Public Telecommunication System

S 43 TELECOMMUNICATIONS ACT 1984

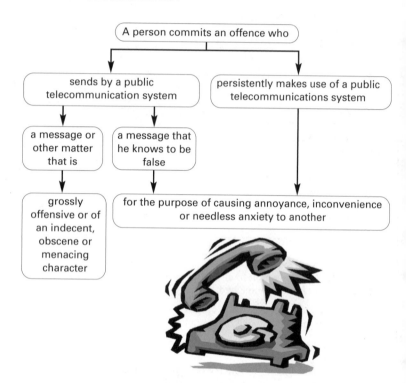

A person commits an offence who

sends by a public telecommunication system

a message or other matter that is

a message that he knows to be false

grossly offensive or of an indecent, obscene or menacing character

for the purpose of causing annoyance, inconvenience or needless anxiety to another

persistently makes use of a public telecommunications system

'Telecommunications system' means a system for the conveyance, through the agency of electric, magnetic, electromagnetic, electrochemical or electromechanical energy, of:

(a) speech, music and other sounds;
(b) visual images;
(c) signals serving for the impartation of any matter otherwise than in the form of sounds or visual images; or
(d) signals serving for the actuation or control of machinery or apparatus.

Bomb Hoaxes

S 51 CRIMINAL LAW ACT 1977

It is an offence to

PLACE

any article in any place whatever

COMMUNICATE

any information which he knows or believes to be false to another person that a bomb or other thing **liable to explode or ignite** is present in any place or location whatever

DISPATCH

any article by post, rail or any other means

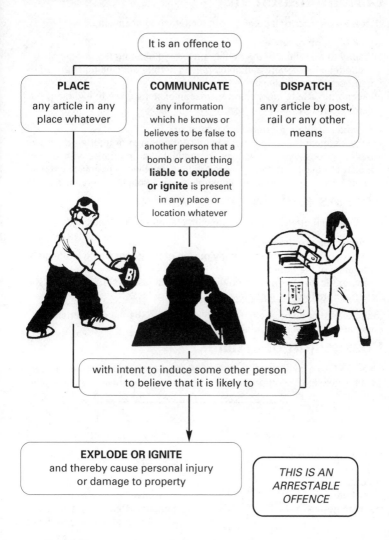

with intent to induce some other person to believe that it is likely to

EXPLODE OR IGNITE
and thereby cause personal injury or damage to property

THIS IS AN ARRESTABLE OFFENCE

Contamination of Goods

S 38 PUBLIC ORDER ACT 1986

Contamination etc

(1) It is an offence for a person, with the intention of causing:

(a) public alarm or anxiety;
(b) injury to members of the public consuming or using the goods;
(c) economic loss to any person by reason of the goods being shunned by members of the public; or
(d) economic loss to any person by reason of steps taken to avoid any such alarm or anxiety, injury or loss,

- to contaminate or interfere with goods, or
- make it appear that goods have been contaminated or interfered with, or
- to place goods which have been contaminated or interfered with, or which appear to have been contaminated or interfered with, in a place where goods of that description are consumed, used, sold or otherwise supplied.

Threats and claims

(2) It is also an offence for a person with the intention of causing:

(a) public alarm or anxiety;
(b) economic loss to any person by reason of the goods being shunned by members of the public; or
(c) economic loss to any person by reason of steps taken to avoid any such alarm or anxiety, injury or loss,

to threaten that he or another will do, or to claim that he or another has done, any of the acts mentioned above.

Possession of articles

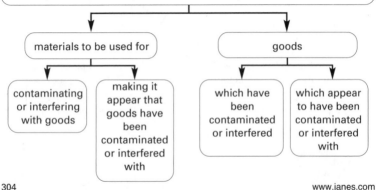

It is an offence for a person to be in possession of any of the following articles with a view to the commission of an offence under subsection (1) above:

materials to be used for

goods

contaminating or interfering with goods

making it appear that goods have been contaminated or interfered with

which have been contaminated or interfered

which appear to have been contaminated or interfered with

Taxi Touts

S 167 CRIMINAL JUSTICE AND PUBLIC ORDER ACT 1994

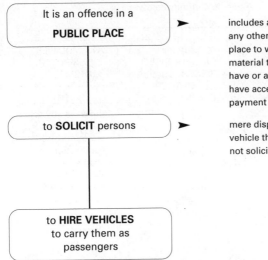

It is an offence in a **PUBLIC PLACE** ▶ includes any highway and any other premises or place to which at the material time the public have or are permitted to have access, whether on payment or otherwise

to **SOLICIT** persons ▶ mere display of a sign on a vehicle that it is for hire is not soliciting

to **HIRE VEHICLES** to carry them as passengers

No offence is committed where sharing of taxis is permitted under S 10 of the Transport Act 1985 (schemes for sharing taxis).

It is a defence if soliciting for passengers to be carried at separate fares by public service vehicles on behalf of, and with the authority of, the holder of a PSV operator's licence.

THIS IS AN ARRESTABLE OFFENCE

Computer Misuse

COMPUTER MISUSE ACT 1990

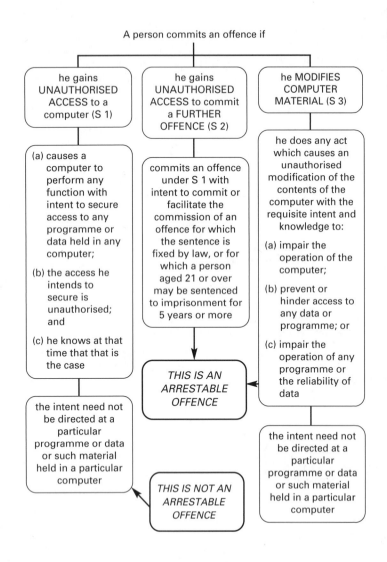

A person commits an offence if

he gains UNAUTHORISED ACCESS to a computer (S 1)

he gains UNAUTHORISED ACCESS to commit a FURTHER OFFENCE (S 2)

he MODIFIES COMPUTER MATERIAL (S 3)

(a) causes a computer to perform any function with intent to secure access to any programme or data held in any computer;

(b) the access he intends to secure is unauthorised; and

(c) he knows at that time that that is the case

commits an offence under S 1 with intent to commit or facilitate the commission of an offence for which the sentence is fixed by law, or for which a person aged 21 or over may be sentenced to imprisonment for 5 years or more

he does any act which causes an unauthorised modification of the contents of the computer with the requisite intent and knowledge to:

(a) impair the operation of the computer;

(b) prevent or hinder access to any data or programme; or

(c) impair the operation of any programme or the reliability of data

the intent need not be directed at a particular programme or data or such material held in a particular computer

THIS IS AN ARRESTABLE OFFENCE

THIS IS NOT AN ARRESTABLE OFFENCE

the intent need not be directed at a particular programme or data or such material held in a particular computer

Intimidation of Witnesses, Jurors and Others

S 51 CRIMINAL JUSTICE AND PUBLIC ORDER ACT 1994

Ss 39 & 40 CRIMINAL JUSTICE AND POLICE ACT 2001

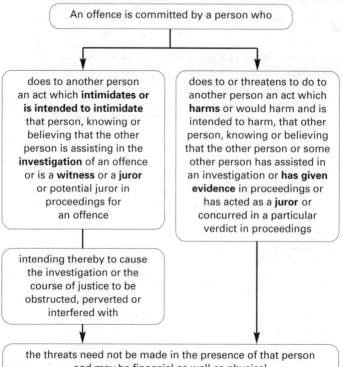

An offence is committed by a person who

does to another person an act which **intimidates or is intended to intimidate** that person, knowing or believing that the other person is assisting in the **investigation** of an offence or is a **witness** or a **juror** or potential juror in proceedings for an offence

does to or threatens to do to another person an act which **harms** or would harm and is intended to harm, that other person, knowing or believing that the other person or some other person has assisted in an investigation or **has given evidence** in proceedings or has acted as a **juror** or concurred in a particular verdict in proceedings

intending thereby to cause the investigation or the course of justice to be obstructed, perverted or interfered with

the threats need not be made in the presence of that person and may be financial as well as physical (to the person or property and intimidation need not be the predominating intention or motive)

The above offences relate to criminal proceedings. The Criminal Justice and Police Act 2001, extending the provisions to proceedings which are not for an offence, introduced 2 similar offences.

THESE ARE ARRESTABLE OFFENCES

Exclusion Zones

SERIOUS ORGANISED CRIME AND POLICE ACT 2005

A constable may **direct a person to leave** a place if he believes, on reasonable grounds, that the person is in the place at a time when he would be prohibited from entering it by virtue of–

(a) an order which was made following his conviction for an offence; or
(b) a condition imposed by virtue of an enactment as a condition of his release from prison

which, in either case, prohibits him from entering the place or from doing so during a period specified in the order.

Such a direction may be given orally. A person who contravenes such a direction commits an offence. **A constable in uniform may arrest without warrant any person he reasonably suspects is committing or has committed this offence**.

Chapter 8
Procedure

Cautions

CODE OF PRACTICE, CODE C

When a caution must be given

1. **Suspected of an offence.** Where there are grounds to suspect a person of an offence, he must be cautioned before any questions about an offence, or further questions if the answers provide the grounds for suspicion, are put to him. This applies if the person's answers or silence may be given in evidence. But no caution is necessary if questions are for other purposes, eg to establish identity or ownership of a vehicle. At the same time as the caution the person must be told that he is not under arrest and is free to leave.

2. **Arrest.** A person who is arrested, or further arrested, must be informed at the time, or as soon as practicable thereafter, that he is under arrest and the grounds for his arrest. He must also be cautioned unless:
   (a) it is impracticable to do so by reason of his condition or behaviour at the time; or
   (b) he has already been cautioned immediately prior to arrest when being questioned.

Terms of the caution

The caution must be in the following terms:

> **"You do not have to say anything. But it may harm your defence if you do not mention when questioned something which you later rely on in Court. Anything you do say may be given in evidence."**

Where the restriction on drawing adverse inferences from silence applies (eg because he has not been allowed legal advice), the caution will be:

> **"You do not have to say anything, but anything you do say may be given in evidence."**

Minor deviations from the words of any caution do not constitute a breach provided the sense of the caution is preserved.

After any break in questioning under caution, the person must be made aware they remain under caution.

A person who, after being cautioned, fails to co-operate or answer questions which may affect his immediate treatment, must be informed of any relevant consequences, eg failure to give name and address when charged may make him liable to detention.

Juveniles and persons who are mentally disordered or mentally vulnerable. If such persons are cautioned in the absence of the appropriate adult, the caution must be repeated in the adult's presence.

Documentation. When a caution is given a record shall be made, either in the interviewer's pocket book or in the interview record.

Adverse Inferences

Ss 34, 36 & 37 CRIMINAL JUSTICE AND PUBLIC ORDER ACT 1994

Circumstances under which inferences may be drawn (S 34)

If at any time:

(a) before being charged with an offence, on being questioned under caution by a constable investigating the offence; or

(b) on being charged with an offence or informed that he might be prosecuted for it,

the person failed to mention any fact which he could reasonably have been expected to mention, and later relied on it in his defence in any court proceedings, the court may draw such inferences from the failure as appear proper.

Failure to account for objects, substances or marks (S 36)

Where:

(a) a person is arrested by a constable and there is on his person, clothing, footwear, or in his possession, or in any place where he was when arrested, an object, substance or mark, or there is a mark on any object; and

(b) the constable believes that it may be attributable to the person being involved in an offence; and

(c) the constable asks the person to account for the presence of it; and

(d) the person fails or refuses to do so,

the court may draw such inferences from the failure or refusal as appear proper.

Failure to account for presence at a particular place (S 37)

Where:

(a) a person arrested by a constable was found at a place at or about the time of the commission of the offence for which arrested; and

(b) the constable believes that the person's presence at that place and time may be attributable to him being involved in the offence; and

(c) the constable asks him to account for that presence; and

(d) the person fails or refuses to do so,

the court may draw such inferences from the failure or refusal as appear proper.

But where the accused was at an authorised place of detention at the time of the failure under Ss 34, 36 or 37 above inferences may not be drawn if he had not been allowed to consult a solicitor prior to being questioned or the request being made.

Adverse Inferences – continued

CODES OF PRACTICE, CODE C

Drawing adverse inferences (CODE C)
For an inference to be drawn when a suspect fails to answer a question, he must first be told in ordinary language:

(a) what offence is being investigated;
(b) what fact they are being asked to account for;
(c) this fact may be due to them taking part in the commission of the offence;
(d) a court may draw an inference if they fail to account for this fact; and
(e) the interview is being recorded and it may be given in evidence.

Restrictions on drawing adverse inferences (CODE C)
The restriction applies:

(a) to a detainee at a police station who, **before being interviewed, charged or informed he may be prosecuted**, has asked for legal advice, has not been allowed to consult a solicitor, and has not changed his mind about wanting legal advice; or
(b) to any person **charged** with, or informed he may be prosecuted for an offence who:
  (i) has had brought to his notice a written statement made by another person or the content of an interview with such person, which relates to that offence;
  (ii) is interviewed about the offence; or
  (iii) makes a written statement about the offence.

Terms of the caution when the restriction applies
If a restriction on drawing adverse inferences from silence applies, the caution shall be:

> **"You do not have to say anything, but anything you do say may be given in evidence."**

Where a restriction either begins to apply, or ceases to apply, the person should be told that the caution he was given previously no longer applies, and the reason. The relevant caution should then be given.

Interviews – General

CODES OF PRACTICE, CODE C

Action

Interviews must be carried out under caution. The person must be informed of the nature of the offence.

If arrested, the interview must take place at a police station or other authorised place of detention, unless the consequent delay would be likely to:

(a) lead to interference with or harm to evidence or people, or serious loss of, or damage to, property;

(b) lead to alerting other people suspected of committing an offence but not yet arrested for it; or

(c) hinder the recovery of property obtained by the commission of an offence.

Interviewing in these circumstances must cease once the risk has been averted, or the necessary questions have been put to attempt to avert it.

Before any interview at a police station or other authorised place of detention, the suspect should be reminded of his entitlement to free legal advice, and that the interview can be delayed to obtain it.

At the beginning of the interview, the suspect shall be asked whether he confirms or denies any significant statement or silence which occurred before the start of the interview.

Answers and statements may not be obtained by oppression. The interviewer may not volunteer information on what action will be taken as a result of the suspect answering questions, making a statement or refusing to do either.

Where a person has not been charged, or has not been told they may be prosecuted, the interview must cease when all relevant questions have been put, account has been taken of any other evidence, and there is sufficient evidence for a conviction.

Interview records

Must be kept for every interview stating the place, time it began and ended, breaks, and the names of persons present. It must be made and completed during the interview unless not practicable or would interfere with the conduct of the interview, in which case it must be made as soon as practicable afterwards and the reason recorded. It must be a verbatim record of what has been said or an account which adequately and accurately summarises it. The record must be timed and signed by the maker. Unless impracticable, the suspect (and the appropriate adult or solicitor) should be allowed to read it and sign it as correct. If a person cannot read or refuses to read it the interviewer should read it to the suspect and record what has occurred. Any refusal to sign must be recorded.

(CONTINUED ON NEXT PAGE)

Interviews – General – continued

CODES OF PRACTICE, CODE C

Juveniles and mentally disordered or mentally vulnerable people
Such persons should not be interviewed or asked to read or sign statements
or records in the absence of the appropriate adult. Juveniles may only be
interviewed at school in exceptional circumstances, in which case the parent,
person responsible or appropriate adult should be notified and allowed to be
present. Unless unavoidable they should not be arrested at school.

Vulnerable suspects
The following persons may not be interviewed unless a superintendent or
above considers delay would lead to one of the consequences above, and
the interview would not harm the person's physical or mental state:

(a) of a juvenile or mentally disordered or mentally vulnerable person, if the
    appropriate adult is not present;
(b) of any other person who appears to be unable to appreciate the
    significance of the questions and answers, or understand what is
    happening because of drink, drugs or any illness, ailment or condition; or
(c) of a person who has difficulty understanding English or has a hearing
    disability, if an interpreter is not present.

'Appropriate adult' means, in the case of a **juvenile**:
(a) the parent, guardian, or, if in care, the representative of the authority or
    organisation;
(b) social worker of the local authority social services; or
(c) failing these, a responsible adult over 18 who is not a police officer or
police employee;

and in the case of a **mentally disordered or mentally vulnerable** person:

(a) a relative, guardian or other person responsible for his care or custody;
(b) someone experienced in dealing with such persons but not a police
    officer or police employee; or
(c) failing these, a responsible adult over 18 who is not a police officer or
    police employee.

Interviews at Police Stations

CODES OF PRACTICE, CODE C

(1) Action

Delivery into interviewer's custody. The custody officer is responsible for deciding whether a detainee may be delivered into an officer's custody to be interviewed.

Period of rest. In any period of 24 hours a detainee must be allowed a continuous period of at least 8 hours for rest, free from questioning, travel, or any interruption in connection with the investigation. This period should normally be at night. If a detainee is arrested at a police station after voluntarily attending, the 24 hours starts at the time of arrest. The period of rest may not be interrupted or delayed except:

(a) where not delaying or interrupting would involve (i) a risk of harm to people or serious loss of, or damage to, property; (ii) delaying the person's release from custody; or (iii) otherwise prejudicing the outcome of the investigation;

(b) at the request of the detainee, the appropriate adult or legal representative; or

(c) where it is necessary to (i) comply with the legal obligations and duties regarding reviews of detention, or (ii) take action relating to the detainee's care and treatment or in accordance with medical advice.

If interrupted under (a) above, a fresh period must be allowed.

Fitness to be interviewed. Before interview, the custody officer must assess whether the detainee is fit enough to be interviewed.

Heating, lighting and ventilation. As far as practicable interview rooms should be adequately heated, lit and ventilated.

Refusal of interview. If a detainee takes steps to prevent himself being interviewed, eg by refusing to leave his cell, he should be advised that his consent for interview is not required, cautioned and informed the interview may take place in the cell, and that fact may be given in evidence. He should then be invited to go to the interview room.

Standing. People being questioned or making statements shall not be required to stand.

Introductions. Before an interview begins, the interviewer shall identify himself and any other persons present (except enquiries linked to terrorism or if such identification might put them in danger, in which case they shall use their warrant or other identification numbers).

Breaks. Breaks from interviewing should be made at recognised meal times, or taking account of when the detainee last had a meal. Short breaks shall be provided at 2-hour intervals unless the interviewer believes it would:

(a) involve a risk of harm to people, or serious loss of, or damage to, property;

(b) delay the detainee's release; or

(c) otherwise prejudice the outcome of the investigation.

Complaints. If during the interview a complaint is made concerning the provisions of this Code, the interviewer should record it on the interview record and inform the custody officer.

(2) Documentation

A record shall be made of the:

(a) time the detainee is not in the custody of the custody officer;

(b) reason for refusal to deliver the detainee out of that custody;

(c) reasons for not using an interview room;

(d) action taken as a result of the detainee's refusal to be interviewed; and

(e) reasons for delaying a break in an interview.

All written statements made at police stations under caution shall be on the forms provided and the interviewee shall be reminded of his right to legal advice.

Written Statements under Caution

CODES OF PRACTICE, CODE C, ANNEX D

1. Written by a person under caution

A person shall always be invited to write down what they say.

Whether or not a person has been charged with, or informed that he may be prosecuted for, an offence to which the statement relates, he shall:

(a) unless a restriction on drawing adverse inferences from silence applies, be asked to write out and sign the following before writing what he wants to say:

> "I make this statement of my own free will. I understand that I do not have to say anything but that it may harm my defence if I do not mention when questioned something which I later rely on in court. This statement may be given in evidence."

(b) if a restriction on drawing adverse inferences from silence applies, be asked to write out and sign the following before writing what he wants to say:

> "I make this statement of my own free will. I understand that I do not have to say anything. This statement may be given in evidence."

Where the person has already been charged with, or informed they may be prosecuted for any offence, asks to make a statement relating to the offence and wants to write it he shall be asked to write out and sign the following before writing what he says:

> "I make this statement of my own free will. I understand that I do not have to say anything. This statement may be given in evidence."

Any person writing his own statement shall be allowed to do so without any prompting except an indication as to which matters are material, or to question any ambiguity in the statement.

Written Statements under Caution – continued

CODES OF PRACTICE, CODE C, ANNEX D

2. Written by a police officer or civilian interviewer

If a person says he would like someone to write the statement for him, a police officer or civilian interviewer shall write the statement.

Whether or not a person has been charged with, or informed that he may be prosecuted for, an offence to which the statement relates, he shall, before starting:

(a) unless a restriction on drawing adverse inferences from silence applies, be asked to sign, or make his mark, to the following:

> **"I, ..., wish to make a statement. I want someone to write down what I say. I understand that I do not have to say anything but that it may harm my defence if I do not mention when questioned something which I later rely on in court. This statement may be given in evidence."**

(b) if a restriction on drawing adverse inferences from silence applies, be asked to sign, or make his mark, to the following:

> **"I, ..., wish to make a statement. I want someone to write down what I say. This statement may be given in evidence. I understand that I do not have to say anything".**

Where the person has already been charged with, or informed he may be prosecuted for any offence, asks to make a statement relating to the offence he shall, before starting, be asked to sign, or make his mark, to the following:

> **"I,..................., wish to make a statement. I want someone to write down what I say. This statement may be given in evidence. I understand that I do not have to say anything."**

The person writing the statement must take down the exact words without editing or paraphrasing. Any questions necessary, eg to make it more intelligible must be recorded, together with the answers given, on the statement form.

When the statement is finished the person making it shall be asked to read it and to make any corrections, alterations or additions he wants, then asked to write and sign or make his mark on the following:

> **"I have read the above statement, and I have been able to correct, alter or add anything I wish. This statement is true. I have made it of my own free will.".**

If the person cannot read, or refuses to read it, or to write the certificate at the end or to sign it, the person taking it shall read it to him and ask him if he would like to correct, alter or add anything and put his signature or mark at the end. The person taking it shall certify on the statement what has occurred.

Interpreters

CODES OF PRACTICE, CODE C

General

Arrangements must be in place for the provision of suitably qualified interpreters for people who are deaf, or do not understand English. Wherever possible, interpreters should be drawn from the National Register of Public Service Interpreters.

Foreign languages

A person must not be interviewed in the absence of a person capable of interpreting if:

(a) he has difficulty understanding English;
(b) the interviewer cannot speak the person's own language; and
(c) the person wants an interpreter present.

The interpreter must make a note of the questions and answers in the interview at the time, in the person's own language, and certify its accuracy. The person should be allowed to read the record or have it read to him and sign it as correct.

Where the person makes a written statement other than in English, the interpreter records the statement in the language it is made, the person is invited to sign it, and an official English translation is made.

Deaf people and people with speech difficulties

If a person appears to be deaf or there is doubt about his hearing or speaking ability, he must not be interviewed in the absence of an interpreter unless he agrees in writing to be interviewed without one. The same applies if the parent or appropriate person has such a disability where a juvenile is to be interviewed.

Circumstances where an interpreter will not be required

An interpreter will not be required if one of the following applies:

(1) the consequent delay would be likely to:
  (a) lead to interference with or harm to evidence or people, or serious loss of, or damage to, property;
  (b) lead to alerting other people suspected of committing an offence but not yet arrested for it; or
  (c) hinder the recovery of property obtained by the commission of an offence; or

Interpreters – continued

CODES OF PRACTICE, CODE C

(2) a superintendent or above considers delay would lead to one of the consequences above, and the interview would not harm the person's physical or mental state:
   (a) in the case of a juvenile or mentally disordered or mentally vulnerable person, if the appropriate adult is not present;
   (b) in the case of any other person who appears to be unable to appreciate the significance of the questions and answers, or understand what is happening because of drink, drugs or any illness, ailment or condition; or
   (c) in the case of a person who has difficulty understanding English or has a hearing disability, if an interpreter is not present.

Interviewing in these circumstances must cease once the risk has been averted, or the necessary questions have been put to attempt to avert it.

Additional rules

All reasonable attempts should be made to make the detainee understand that interpreters will be provided at public expense.

If the detainee cannot communicate with his solicitor, an interpreter must be called. The interpreter may not be a police officer or civilian support staff in this case. In other cases a police officer or civilian support staff may act as interpreter if the detainee and the appropriate adult agree in writing or if the interview is tape-recorded or visually recorded.

Where a custody officer cannot establish effective communication with a detainee, arrangements must be made as soon as possible to have an interpreter explain the offence and any other information.

Powers of Arrest – Arrestable Offences

S 24 POLICE AND CRIMINAL EVIDENCE ACT 1984

Any person may arrest without warrant

anyone who is in the act of committing an arrestable offence

where an arrestable offence has been committed:

- anyone who is guilty of the offence
- anyone whom he has reasonable grounds for suspecting to be guilty of it

anyone whom he has reasonable grounds for suspecting to be committing an arrestable offence

A constable may arrest without warrant

(where he has reasonable grounds for suspecting an arrestable offence has been committed) anyone whom he has reasonable grounds for suspecting to be guilty of the offence

anyone who is about to commit an arrestable offence or whom he has reasonable grounds for suspecting to be about to commit an arrestable offence

Arrestable Offences

S 24 POLICE AND CRIMINAL EVIDENCE ACT 1984

'Arrestable offence' means:
1. an offence for which the sentence is fixed by law;
2. an offence for which a person aged 21 years or over (not previously convicted) may be sentenced to imprisonment for 5 years; and
3. any of the following offences:

OFFENCE	ENACTMENT
Customs and Excise Offences	S 1(1) Customs and Excise Management Act 1979
Official secrets	Official Secrets Act 1920 and 1989 (except S 8(1), (4) or (5))
Exposure	S 66 Sexual Offences Act 2003
Voyeurism	S 67 Sexual Offences Act 2003
Intercourse with an animal	S 69 Sexual Offences Act 2003
Sexual penetration with a corpse	S 70 Sexual Offences Act 2003
Sexual activity in public lavatory	S 71 Sexual Offences Act 2003
Placing advertisements relating to prostitution	S 6 Criminal Justice and Police Act 2001
Taking motor vehicle or other conveyance without authority	S 12(1) Theft Act 1968
Going equipped for stealing	S 25(1) Theft Act 1968
Making off without payment	S 3 Theft Act 1978
Football Offences	Football Offences Act 1991
Publication of obscene matter	S 2 Obscene Publications Act 1959
Indecent photographs of children	S 1 Protection of Children Act 1978
Kerb-crawling	S 1 Sexual Offences Act 1985
Failing to stop and report an accident causing personal injury	S 170(4) Road Traffic Act 1988
Driving whilst disqualified	S 103(1)(b) Road Traffic Act 1988
Sale of football match tickets by unauthorised persons	S 166 Criminal Justice and Public Order Act 1994
Publishing material likely to stir up racial hatred	S 19 Public Order Act 1986
Touting for hire car services	S 167 Criminal Justice and Public Order Act 1994
Carrying offensive weapons	S 1(1) Prevention of Crime Act 1953
Having article with blade or point in public place	S 139(1) Criminal Justice Act 1988
Having article with blade or point on school premises	S 139A Criminal Justice Act 1988
Assaulting a police officer or person assisting	S 89(1) Police Act 1996
Harassment	S 2 Protection from Harassment Act 1997
Failing to remove disguise	S 60AA(7) Criminal Justice and Public Order Act 1994
Racial or religious harassment	S 32(1)(a) Crime and Disorder Act 1988
Failing to comply with football banning order	S 14J or 21C Football Spectators Act 1989
Alcohol consumption in public place	S 12(4) Criminal Justice and Police Act 2001
Taking, etc wild birds included in Sched 1	S 1(1) or (2) or 6 Wildlife and Countryside Act 1981
Disturbance of wild birds	S 1(5) Wildlife and Countryside Act 1981
Taking, etc wild animals or plants	S 9 or 13(1)(a) or (2) " "
Introduction of new species, etc	S 14 " "
Unauthorised presence in zone or aircraft	S 21C(1) or 21D(1) Aviation Security Act 1982
Trespass on aerodrome	S 39(1) Civil Aviation Act 1982
Firearm or imitation carried in public place in respect of an air weapon or imitation firearm	S 19 Firearms Act 1968
Making an untrue statement to procure a passport	S36 Criminal Justice Act 1925
Possession of cannabis or cannabis resin	S 5(2) Misuse of Drugs Act 1971
Making a false statement or withholding material information to obtain, etc., a licence	S 174 Road Traffic Act 1988
Obstructing a person searching premises to serve a control order notice	S 9(3) Prevention of Terrorism Act 2005

Conspiring to commit any of the above offences; inciting, aiding, abetting, counselling or procuring the commission of any of the above offences; and attempting to commit any of the above offences other than summary offences.

Repealed and Preserved Powers of Arrest

S 26 & SCHED 2 POLICE AND CRIMINAL EVIDENCE ACT 1984

Repealed powers of arrest

Apart from the powers listed below, those parts of any Act (including a local Act) passed before this Act which enable a constable to:

1. arrest a person for an offence without warrant; or

2. arrest a person otherwise than for an offence without warrant or order of a court,

shall cease to have effect.

Preserved powers of arrest

The powers of arrest under the following enactments are preserved:

ENACTMENT	PRESERVED POWER OF ARREST
Military Lands Act 1892, S 17(2)	
Protection of Animals Act 1911, S 12(1)	Cruelty to animals
Emergency Powers Act 1920, S 2	Contravention of regulations
Public Order Act 1936, S 7(3)	Wearing political uniforms
Prison Act 1952, S 49	Unlawfully at large
Visiting Forces Act 1952, S 13	Deserters and absentees without leave
Army Act 1955, S 186 & 190B	Deserters, absentees without leave and persons unlawfully at large
Air Force Act 1955, S 186 & 190B	Deserters, absentees without leave and persons unlawfully at large
Naval Discipline Act 1957, S 104 & 105	Deserters, absentees without leave and persons unlawfully at large
Street Offences Act 1959, S 1(3)	Loitering or soliciting for prostitution
Children and Young Persons Act 1969, S 32	Absentee from remand home, etc.
Immigration Act 1971,Sched 2 (paras 17, 24 & 33), Sched 3 (para 7)	Persons liable to examination or removal, breaking bail, or contravening restrictions imposed by a court
Bail Act 1976, S 7	Absconding or breaking conditions of bail
Criminal Law Act 1977, S 6(6), 7(6), 8(4), 9(7) & 10(5)	Violence for securing entry to premises, adverse occupation of residential premises, trespassing on premises with an offensive weapon, trespassing on foreign missions, etc, and obstruction of court officers executing process against unauthorised occupiers
Animal Health Act 1981, S 60(5) & 61(1)	Obstructing an officer other than a constable, or committing a rabies offence
Representation of the People Act 1983, Sched 1, rule 36	
Mental Health Act 1983, S 18, 35(10), 36(8), 38(7), 136(1) and 138	Absence from hospital detention, absconding from hospital to which remanded or detained by interim order, mentally disordered person found in public place, or escaping from custody whilst being conveyed
Repatriation of Prisoners Act 1984, S 5(5)	

Serious Arrestable Offences

S 116 & SCHED 5 POLICE AND CRIMINAL EVIDENCE ACT 1984

The following table lists arrestable offences which are always serious:

OFFENCE	ENACTMENT
Treason	Common Law
Murder	Common Law
Manslaughter	S 5 Offences Against the Person Act 1861
Kidnapping	Common Law
Rape	S 1 Sexual Offences Act 2003
Assault by penetration	S 2 Sexual Offences Act 2003
Causing sexual activity involving penetration without consent	S 4 Sexual Offences Act 2003
Rape of child under 13	S 5 Sexual Offences Act 2003
Assault of child under 13 by penetration	S 6 Sexual Offences Act 2003
Causing or inciting a child under 13 to engage in sexual activity involving penetration	S 8 Sexual Offences Act 2003
Sexual activity involving penetration with a person with a mental disorder impeding choice	S 30 Sexual Offences Act 2003
Causing or inciting a person with a mental disorder impeding choice to engage in sexual activity involving penetration	S 31 Sexual Offences Act 2003
Importing indecent or obscene articles	S 170 Customs and Excise Management Act 1979
Causing explosion likely to endanger life or property	S 2 Explosive Substances Act 1883
Possessing firearm with intent to injure	S 16 Firearms Act 1968
Use of firearm or imitation to resist arrest	S 17(1) Firearms Act 1968
Carrying firearm with criminal intent	S 18 Firearms Act 1968
Hostage-taking	S 1 Taking of Hostages Act 1982
Hi-jacking	S 1 Aviation Security Act 1982
Torture	S 134 Criminal Justice Act 1988
Causing death by dangerous driving	S 1 Road Traffic Act 1988
Causing death by careless driving when under the influence of drink or drugs	S 3A Road Traffic Act 1988
Endangering safety at aerodromes	S 1 Aviation and Maritime Security Act 1990
Hi-jacking of ships	S 9 Aviation and Maritime Security Act 1990
Seizing or exercising control of fixed platforms	S 10 Aviation and Maritime Security Act 1990
Indecent photographs or pseudo-photographs of children	S 1 Protection of Children Act 1978
Causing death of child or vulnerable adult	S 5 Domestic Violence, Crime and Victims Act 2004
Publication of obscene matter	S 2 Obscene Publications Act 1959
Production, supply and possession for supply of drugs	S 4(2), (3) or 5(3) Misuse of Drugs Act 1971
Assisting in or inducing a drugs offence outside the UK	S 20 Misuse of Drugs Act 1971
Improper importation of drugs	S 50(2) or (3) Customs and Excise Management Act 1979
Exportation of drugs	S 68(2) Customs and Excise Management Act 1979
Fraudulent evasion in connection with drugs	S 170 Customs and Excise Management Act 1979
Manufacture or supply of substances listed in Sched 2 (drugs)	S 12 Criminal Justice (International Co-operation) Act 1990
Using ship for illicit traffic in controlled drugs	S 19 Criminal Justice (International Co-operation) Act 1990
Concealing or transferring proceeds of drug trafficking	S 49 Drug Trafficking Act 1994
Assisting another to retain the benefit of drug trafficking	S 50 Drug Trafficking Act 1994
Acquisition, possession or use of proceeds of drug trafficking	S 51 Drug Trafficking Act 1994

(CONTINUED ON NEXT PAGE)

Serious Arrestable Offences – continued

S 116 & SCHED 5 POLICE AND CRIMINAL EVIDENCE ACT 1984

Any other offence is serious only if:

- its commission has led to, or is intended to lead to, or is likely to lead to, or
- it consists of making a threat which would be likely to lead to:
  (a) serious harm to the security of the State or to public order;
  (b) serious interference with the administration of justice or with the investigation of offences or a particular offence;
  (c) the death of any person;
  (d) serious injury to any person;
  (e) substantial financial gain to any person; or
  (f) serious financial loss to any person.

Powers of Arrest – Not an Arrestable Offence

S 25 POLICE AND CRIMINAL EVIDENCE ACT 1984

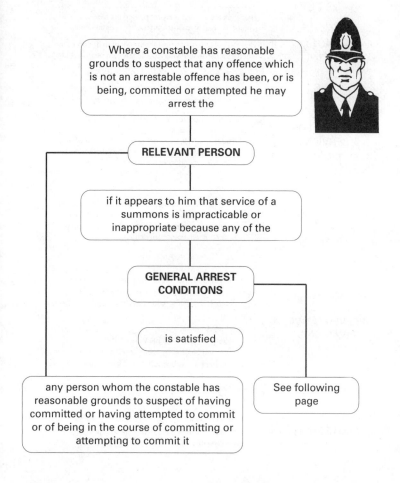

Where a constable has reasonable grounds to suspect that any offence which is not an arrestable offence has been, or is being, committed or attempted he may arrest the

RELEVANT PERSON

if it appears to him that service of a summons is impracticable or inappropriate because any of the

GENERAL ARREST CONDITIONS

is satisfied

any person whom the constable has reasonable grounds to suspect of having committed or having attempted to commit or of being in the course of committing or attempting to commit it

See following page

General Arrest Conditions

S 25 Police and Criminal Evidence Act 1984

IDENTITY

That the name of the relevant person is unknown to, and cannot be readily ascertained by, the constable; or

That the constable has reasonable grounds for doubting whether a name furnished by the relevant person is his real name

ADDRESS FOR SERVICE

That:
- The relevant person has failed to furnish a satisfactory address for service; or
- The constable has reasonable grounds for doubting whether an address furnished by the relevant person is a satisfactory address for service

'Satisfactory for service' means that the relevant person will be at that address sufficiently long to serve a summons; or that some other specified person will accept service for him

PREVENTATIVE MEASURES

That the constable has reasonable grounds for believing that arrest is necessary to prevent the relevant person
- Causing physical injury to himself or any other person
- Suffering physical injury
- Causing loss of or damage to property
- Committing an offence against public decency where members of the public could not be expected to avoid him
- Causing an unlawful obstruction of the highway

PROTECTION

That the constable has reasonable grounds for believing that arrest is necessary to protect a child or other vulnerable person from the relevant person

Powers of Arrest – Cross-border

S 137 CRIMINAL JUSTICE AND PUBLIC ORDER ACT 1994

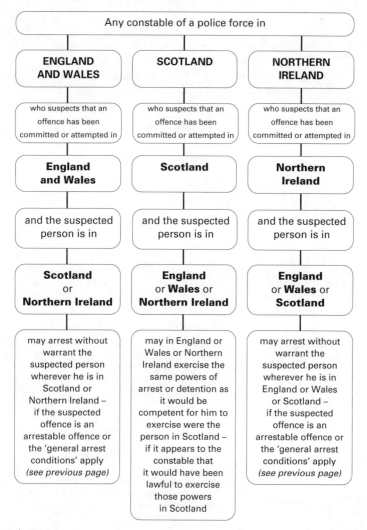

Any constable of a police force in		
ENGLAND AND WALES	**SCOTLAND**	**NORTHERN IRELAND**
who suspects that an offence has been committed or attempted in	who suspects that an offence has been committed or attempted in	who suspects that an offence has been committed or attempted in
England and Wales	**Scotland**	**Northern Ireland**
and the suspected person is in	and the suspected person is in	and the suspected person is in
Scotland or **Northern Ireland**	**England** or **Wales** or **Northern Ireland**	**England** or **Wales** or **Scotland**
may arrest without warrant the suspected person wherever he is in Scotland or Northern Ireland – if the suspected offence is an arrestable offence or the 'general arrest conditions' apply *(see previous page)*	may in England or Wales or Northern Ireland exercise the same powers of arrest or detention as it would be competent for him to exercise were the person in Scotland – if it appears to the constable that it would have been lawful to exercise those powers in Scotland	may arrest without warrant the suspected person wherever he is in England or Wales or Scotland – if the suspected offence is an arrestable offence or the 'general arrest conditions' apply *(see previous page)*

Mode of Arrest

Ss 28 AND 30 POLICE AND CRIMINAL EVIDENCE ACT 1984

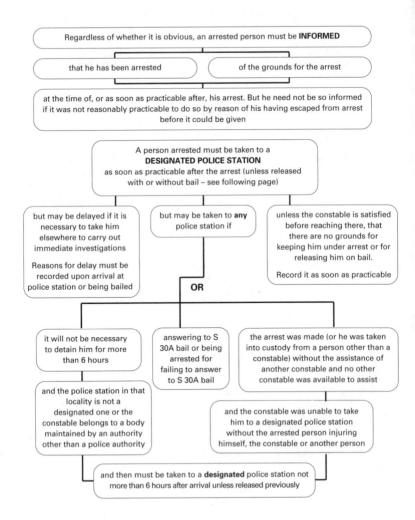

Regardless of whether it is obvious, an arrested person must be **INFORMED**

that he has been arrested | of the grounds for the arrest

at the time of, or as soon as practicable after, his arrest. But he need not be so informed if it was not reasonably practicable to do so by reason of his having escaped from arrest before it could be given

A person arrested must be taken to a **DESIGNATED POLICE STATION** as soon as practicable after the arrest (unless released with or without bail – see following page)

but may be delayed if it is necessary to take him elsewhere to carry out immediate investigations

Reasons for delay must be recorded upon arrival at police station or being bailed

but may be taken to **any** police station if

unless the constable is satisfied before reaching there, that there are no grounds for keeping him under arrest or for releasing him on bail.

Record it as soon as practicable

OR

it will not be necessary to detain him for more than 6 hours

and the police station in that locality is not a designated one or the constable belongs to a body maintained by an authority other than a police authority

answering to S 30A bail or being arrested for failing to answer to S 30A bail

the arrest was made (or he was taken into custody from a person other than a constable) without the assistance of another constable and no other constable was available to assist

and the constable was unable to take him to a designated police station without the arrested person injuring himself, the constable or another person

and then must be taken to a **designated** police station not more than 6 hours after arrival unless released previously

Bail Elsewhere than at a Police Station

Ss 30A, 30B, 30C & 30D POLICE AND CRIMINAL EVIDENCE ACT 1984

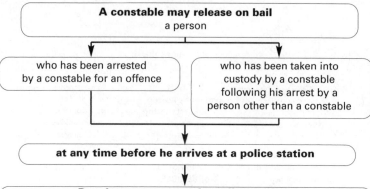

A constable may release on bail
a person

| who has been arrested by a constable for an offence | who has been taken into custody by a constable following his arrest by a person other than a constable |

at any time before he arrives at a police station

Requirement to attend a police station.
The person must be required to attend any police station (but if not a designated police station, he must be either released or taken to a designated police station within 6 hours of answering bail). No other conditions may be attached to the bail.

Service of notice.
The constable must serve the person with a notice before he is released stating the offence and grounds for arrest.
The notice may contain the name of the police station to which bailed and the time and date to attend, but if it does not, a separate notice must be served on the person giving that information. The name of the police station and time and date may be changed by serving a written notice of the change, but only one such notice may be served. A notice may also be served to say that attendance is no longer required.

Re-arrest
A person may be re-arrested if new evidence comes to light after his release.

Failure to answer bail.
A person failing to answer bail may be arrested by a constable and taken to a police station.

Conduct of a Search

S 2 Police and Criminal Evidence Act 1984

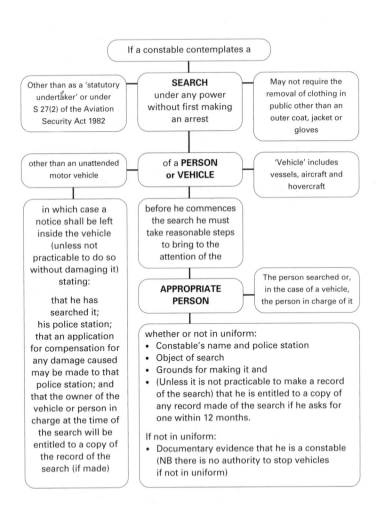

If a constable contemplates a

SEARCH
under any power
without first making
an arrest

Other than as a 'statutory
undertaker' or under
S 27(2) of the Aviation
Security Act 1982

May not require the
removal of clothing in
public other than an
outer coat, jacket or
gloves

of a **PERSON
or VEHICLE**

other than an unattended
motor vehicle

'Vehicle' includes
vessels, aircraft and
hovercraft

in which case a
notice shall be left
inside the vehicle
(unless not
practicable to do so
without damaging it)
stating:

before he commences
the search he must
take reasonable steps
to bring to the
attention of the

that he has
searched it;
his police station;
that an application
for compensation for
any damage caused
may be made to that
police station; and
that the owner of the
vehicle or person in
charge at the time of
the search will be
entitled to a copy of
the record of the
search (if made)

**APPROPRIATE
PERSON**

The person searched or,
in the case of a vehicle,
the person in charge of it

whether or not in uniform:
• Constable's name and police station
• Object of search
• Grounds for making it and
• (Unless it is not practicable to make a record
  of the search) that he is entitled to a copy of
  any record made of the search if he asks for
  one within 12 months.

If not in uniform:
• Documentary evidence that he is a constable
  (NB there is no authority to stop vehicles
  if not in uniform)

Conduct of a Search – continued

CODE OF PRACTICE, CODE A

Principles

Powers to stop and search must be used fairly, responsibly, with respect, and without unlawful discrimination (on the grounds of race, colour, ethnic origin, nationality or national origins). However, there may be circumstances, eg in response to a specific terrorist threat, where it would be appropriate to take account of a person's ethnic origin.

Detention for the purposes of a search must be brief, and at or near the location of the stop.

A search must not be carried out, even with the person's consent, where no power to search is applicable. The only exception is in relation to persons entering sports grounds or other premises carried out with their consent given as a condition of entry.

Reasonable suspicion

There must be an objective basis for the suspicion based on facts, information and/or intelligence.

It may not be based on personal factors alone, eg race, age, appearance or previous convictions.

Nor can it be based on generalisations or stereotypes of certain groups or categories of people as more likely to be involved in criminal activity. However, where there is reliable information or intelligence that members of a group or gang habitually carry weapons or drugs, and wear distinctive clothing or other means of identification to indicate their membership of that group, that means of identification may provide reasonable grounds to stop and search.

An officer who has reasonable suspicion may stop and question a suspect, but reasonable grounds for suspicion may not be retrospectively formed after he stopped and questioned the person. However, where an officer has an encounter with a member of the public otherwise than in the course of stopping for purposes of a search, reasonable grounds for suspicion may be formed during such an encounter, justifying a search even there were no grounds to justify a search before the encounter began.

Conduct of a Search – continued

CODE OF PRACTICE, CODE A

Minimising embarrassment
All stops and searches must be carried out with courtesy, consideration and respect for the person concerned. Embarrassment to the person being searched must be kept to a minimum.

Co-operation.
The co-operation of the person searched must be sought in every case, even if the person initially objects.

Use of force
A forcible search may only be made if the person is unwilling or resists. Reasonable force may be used as a last resort to search a person or to detain a person or vehicle for the purposes of a search.

Duration
The length of time a person is detained must be kept to a minimum.

Extent
The extent of the search will depend on the nature of the thing being searched for, eg where an article is seen to be placed into a pocket, the search will be limited to that pocket. If, however, it is a small article which could be concealed anywhere on the person, the search may have to be more extensive.

Where reasonable suspicion not required.
In the case of searches:
- under S 60 Criminal Justice and Public Order Act 1994 (anticipation of serious violence or carrying offensive weapons);
- under S 44 Terrorism Act 2000 (prevention of acts of terrorism); or
- of a person in the exercise of powers to search premises,

which do not require reasonable grounds of suspicion, a search may still be carried out for items for which the power exists.

Removal of outer clothing
There is no power to require a person to remove any clothing in public other than an outer coat, jacket or gloves (except under the Terrorism Act 2000 where the removal of headgear and footwear may be required, or the Criminal Justice and Public Order Act 1994 where items worn to conceal identity may be removed). The search in public of clothing which has not been removed must be restricted to superficial examination of outer garments. This, however, does not prevent searching inside pockets, feeling inside collars, socks or shoes or searching hair.

Removal of other clothing
More thorough searches involving the removal of other clothing must be done out of public view. Any search involving the removal of clothing other than an outer coat, jacket, gloves, headgear or footwear, or any other item concealing identity, may only be done by persons of the same sex as the person being searched, and may not be in the presence of any person of the opposite sex unless the person being searched specifically requests it.

Intimate searches
Searches involving exposure of intimate parts of the body must not be a routine extension of a less thorough search, simply because nothing was found in the initial search. Such searches may only be carried out at a nearby police station or other place (not a police vehicle) out of public view and in accordance with procedures (see later under intimate searches).

Conduct of a Search – continued

CODE OF PRACTICE, CODE A

Steps to be taken prior to a search

Provision of information

Before any search of a person or attended vehicle the officer must give to the person to be searched the following information:

(a) that they are being detained for the purposes of a search;

(b) the officer's name (except in the case of terrorism or where the officer believes that by giving his name might put him in danger – in which case a warrant or other identification number may be given) and the police station to which he is attached;

(c) the legal search power which is being exercised; and

(d) a clear explanation of:

  (i) the purpose of the search in terms of the articles for which there is a power of search; and

  (ii) in the case of powers requiring reasonable suspicion, the grounds for that suspicion; or

  (iii) in the case of powers which do not require reasonable suspicion, the nature of the power and of any necessary authorisation and the fact that it has been given.

Warrant cards

Officers not in uniform must show their warrant cards.

Requirement to be in uniform

Stops and searches under S 60 Criminal Justice and Public Order Act 1994, or S 44 Terrorism Act 2000, may only be carried out by an officer in uniform.

Copy of search record

The officer must inform the person (or the owner or person in charge of a vehicle which is to be searched) of his or her entitlement to:

• a copy of the record of the search; or

• if it was not practicable to make a record at the time, a copy of the record if an application is made within 12 months.

Where the copy was not made at the time, the person must be told how he may obtain a copy.

Individual's rights

The person should be given information about police powers to stop and search and the individual's rights.

If the person does not appear to understand what is being said, or there is any doubt about his ability to understand English, reasonable steps must be taken to bring to his attention information about his rights and any relevant provisions of the Code of Practice.

If the person is deaf or cannot understand English and is accompanied by someone, the officer must try to establish whether that person can interpret or otherwise help the officer to give the information.

Records of Searches

S 3 POLICE AND CRIMINAL EVIDENCE ACT 1984

Where a constable has carried out a

SEARCH under any power

Other than as a 'statutory undertaker' or under S 27(2) of the Aviation Security Act 1982

he shall make a **RECORD** of it in writing unless it is **NOT PRACTICABLE** to do so

If it could be made, but not practicable to make it on the spot, he shall make it as soon as practicable afterwards

The person who was searched, and the owner or person in charge of a vehicle at the time it was searched, are entitled to a **COPY** of any record made if they ask for one within 12 months

- Stating the name of the person searched (but he may not be detained to find out his name)

- Including (if name not known by constable) a description of the person

- Including a description of any vehicle searched

- Stating
  - object of the search
  - grounds for making it
  - date and time made
  - place made
  - whether anything found, and if so, what
  - any injury to a person or damage to property which appears to the constable to have resulted from the search
  - identity of constable

'Vehicle' includes vessels, aircraft and hovercraft

Recording of Encounters not Governed by Statutory Powers

CODES OF PRACTICE, CODE A

When a record must be made
Where an officer (includes a Community Support Officer) requests a person in a public place to account for themselves, i.e. their actions, behaviour, presence in an area or possession of anything, a record of the encounter must be completed at the time and a copy given to the person who has been questioned.

Identification of the officer
The record must identify the name of the officer who has made the stop and conducted the encounter (unless linked to the investigation of terrorism or otherwise where there is reasonable belief that by recording the name the officer might be endangered, in which case the officer's identification number and station should be recorded).

When a record need not be made
The requirements do not apply:

1. if there are exceptional circumstances which would make it wholly impracticable;
2. to general conversations such as giving directions or seeking witnesses;
3. when seeking general information or questioning people to establish background to incidents which have required officers to intervene to keep the peace or resolve a dispute;
4. when stopping a person in a vehicle where a HORT/1, VDRS or endorsable fixed penalty is issued; or
5. when requiring a specimen of breath under Section 6 of the Road Traffic Act 1988.

Entitlement to a copy
Officers must inform the person of their entitlement to a copy of a record of the encounter.

Information to be included in the record
(a) date, time and place of the encounter;
(b) registration number of vehicle (if applicable);
(c) reason why the officer questioned that person;
(d) the person's self-defined ethnic background; and
(e) the outcome of the encounter.

Requirement to give information
There is no power to require the person to give personal details. If the person refuses to give their self-defined ethnic background, a form must still be completed, including a description of the person's ethnic background.

Requests for records to be made
A record of an encounter must always be made when a person requests it, regardless of whether the officer considers it necessary (in which case this should be recorded on the form).

Summary of Main Stop and Search Powers

CODES OF PRACTICE, CODE A

POWER	OBJECT	EXTENT	WHERE
Public Stores Act 1875, S 6	HM stores	Persons, vehicles, vessels	Anywhere
Firearms Act 1968, S 47	Firearms	Persons & vehicles	Anywhere
Misuse of Drugs Act 1971	Drugs	Persons & vehicles	Anywhere
Customs & Excise Management Act 1979, S 163	Duty not paid; import/export; liable to forfeiture	Vehicles & vessels	Anywhere
Aviation Security Act 1982, S 27(1)	Stolen/unlawfully obtained goods	Airport employees & vehicles, aircraft	Designated airport
Police & Criminal Evidence Act 1984, S 1	Stolen goods, goods used in theft, offensive weapons; criminal damage, articles made, intended or adapted for use in destroying or damaging property	Persons & vehicles	Public Access
Police & Criminal Evidence Act 1984, S 6(3)	HM stores (UKAEA)	Persons, vehicles, vessels	Anywhere
Sporting Events (Control of Alcohol etc) Act 1985, S 7	Intoxicating Liquor	Persons, coaches, trains	Designated sports grounds & transport travelling to/from
Crossbows Act 1987, S 4	Crossbows or parts	Persons & vehicles	Anywhere except dwellings
Criminal Justice Act 1988, S 139B	Offensive weapons	Persons	School premises
Poaching Prevention Act 1862, S 2	Game or equipment	Persons & vehicles	Public Place
Deer Act 1991, S 12	Evidence	Persons & vehicles	Anywhere except dwellings
Conservation of Seals Act 1970, S 4	Seals or equipment	Vehicles	Anywhere
Badgers Act 1992, S 11	Evidence	Persons & vehicles	Anywhere
Wildlife & Countryside Act 1981, S 19	Evidence	Persons & vehicles	Anywhere except dwellings
Terrorism Act 2000, S 43	Evidence to arrest under S 14	Persons	Anywhere
Terrorism Act 2000, S 44(1)	Articles for terrorism	Vehicles, drivers & passengers	Anywhere in authorised area
Terrorism Act 2000, S 44(2)	Articles for terrorism	Pedestrians	Anywhere in authorised area
Terrorism Act 2000, sched 7	Anything relevant	Persons, vehicles, vessels, etc.	Ports & airports
Criminal Justice & Public Order Act 1994, S 60	Offensive weapons, dangerous instruments	Persons & vehicles	Anywhere in authorised area

Selector

The subject of searching, etc is rather involved and the reader may be assisted by selecting the appropriate circumstances below and referring to the relevant section in the following pages. In addition, specific powers relating to Firearms, Drugs, Crossbows, Game and Offensive Weapons may be found in the relevant pages of this book.

HAS AN ARREST BEEN MADE?	REASON FOR SEARCH?	TYPE OF SEARCH		
		PERSON	PREMISES	VEHICLE
YES	Material valuable to the investigation and relevant evidence		Ⓕ	
	Evidence on premises occupied or controlled by arrested person		Ⓒ	Ⓒ
	Offender, potential offender or witness to serious arrestable offence, or person unlawfully at large			Ⓖ
YES, OTHER THAN AT A POLICE STATION	Anything which might cause injury	Ⓔ		
	Evidence of offence for which arrested		Ⓔ	
NO	Arresting a person, saving life or preventing damage		Ⓑ	Ⓑ
	Stolen or prohibited articles	Ⓐ		Ⓐ
	Securing evidence or seizing anything obtained in commission of an offence		Ⓓ	Ⓓ
	Material valuable to the investigation and relevant evidence		Ⓕ	
	Offender, potential offender or witness to serious arrestable offence, or person unlawfully at large			Ⓖ
	Prevention of serious violence/offensive weapons	Ⓗ		Ⓗ

For conduct and recording of a search see section 'A'

Stop and Search (General)

S 1 POLICE AND CRIMINAL EVIDENCE ACT 1984

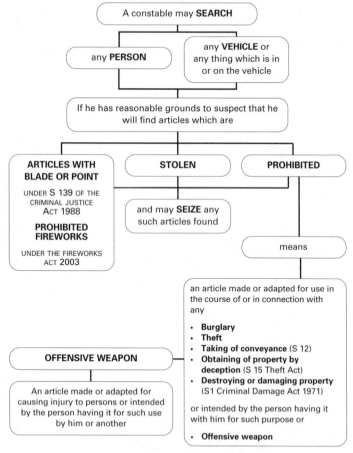

A constable may **SEARCH**

any **PERSON**

any **VEHICLE** or any thing which is in or on the vehicle

If he has reasonable grounds to suspect that he will find articles which are

ARTICLES WITH BLADE OR POINT

UNDER S 139 OF THE CRIMINAL JUSTICE ACT 1988

PROHIBITED FIREWORKS

UNDER THE FIREWORKS ACT 2003

STOLEN

PROHIBITED

and may **SEIZE** any such articles found

means

an article made or adapted for use in the course of or in connection with any

- **Burglary**
- **Theft**
- **Taking of conveyance** (S 12)
- **Obtaining of property by deception** (S 15 Theft Act)
- **Destroying or damaging property** (S1 Criminal Damage Act 1971)

or intended by the person having it with him for such purpose or

- **Offensive weapon**

OFFENSIVE WEAPON

An article made or adapted for causing injury to persons or intended by the person having it for such use by him or another

A constable may detain a person or vehicle for the purposes of such a search and may use reasonable force if necessary.

Stop and Search – continued

S 1 POLICE AND CRIMINAL EVIDENCE ACT 1984

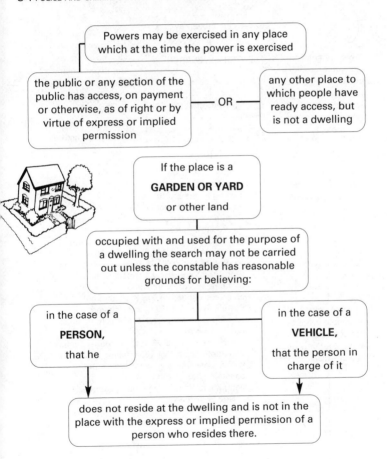

Powers may be exercised in any place which at the time the power is exercised

the public or any section of the public has access, on payment or otherwise, as of right or by virtue of express or implied permission

— OR —

any other place to which people have ready access, but is not a dwelling

If the place is a **GARDEN OR YARD** or other land

occupied with and used for the purpose of a dwelling the search may not be carried out unless the constable has reasonable grounds for believing:

in the case of a **PERSON,** that he

in the case of a **VEHICLE,** that the person in charge of it

does not reside at the dwelling and is not in the place with the express or implied permission of a person who resides there.

Entry and Search of Premises

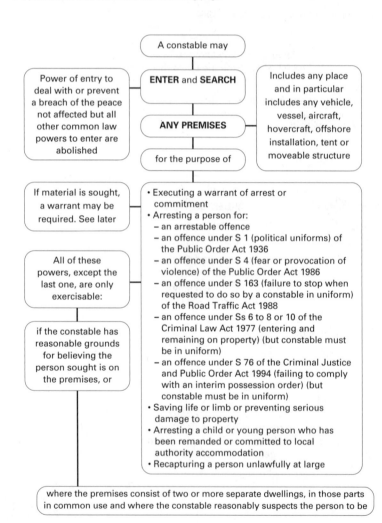

S 17 POLICE AND CRIMINAL EVIDENCE ACT 1984
If a person has been arrested, see following page

A constable may

ENTER and SEARCH

Power of entry to deal with or prevent a breach of the peace not affected but all other common law powers to enter are abolished

ANY PREMISES

Includes any place and in particular includes any vehicle, vessel, aircraft, hovercraft, offshore installation, tent or moveable structure

for the purpose of

If material is sought, a warrant may be required. See later

All of these powers, except the last one, are only exercisable:

if the constable has reasonable grounds for believing the person sought is on the premises, or

- Executing a warrant of arrest or commitment
- Arresting a person for:
  - an arrestable offence
  - an offence under S 1 (political uniforms) of the Public Order Act 1936
  - an offence under S 4 (fear or provocation of violence) of the Public Order Act 1986
  - an offence under S 163 (failure to stop when requested to do so by a constable in uniform) of the Road Traffic Act 1988
  - an offence under Ss 6 to 8 or 10 of the Criminal Law Act 1977 (entering and remaining on property) (but constable must be in uniform)
  - an offence under S 76 of the Criminal Justice and Public Order Act 1994 (failing to comply with an interim possession order) (but constable must be in uniform)
- Saving life or limb or preventing serious damage to property
- Arresting a child or young person who has been remanded or committed to local authority accommodation
- Recapturing a person unlawfully at large

where the premises consist of two or more separate dwellings, in those parts in common use and where the constable reasonably suspects the person to be

Entry and Search of Premises (Occupier Arrested)

Ⓒ

S 18 POLICE AND CRIMINAL EVIDENCE ACT 1984
See also S 32 relating to search of arrested person and premises upon arrest

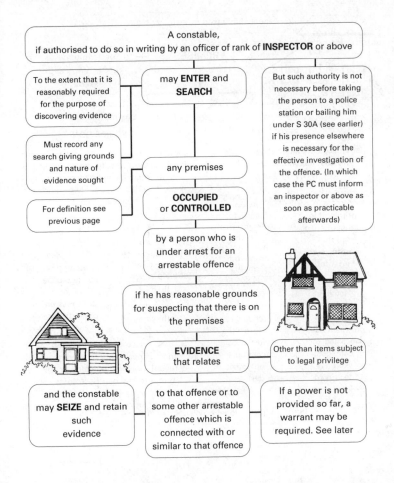

A constable,
if authorised to do so in writing by an officer of rank of **INSPECTOR** or above

To the extent that it is reasonably required for the purpose of discovering evidence

may **ENTER** and **SEARCH**

But such authority is not necessary before taking the person to a police station or bailing him under S 30A (see earlier) if his presence elsewhere is necessary for the effective investigation of the offence. (In which case the PC must inform an inspector or above as soon as practicable afterwards)

Must record any search giving grounds and nature of evidence sought

any premises

OCCUPIED or **CONTROLLED**

For definition see previous page

by a person who is under arrest for an arrestable offence

if he has reasonable grounds for suspecting that there is on the premises

EVIDENCE that relates

Other than items subject to legal privilege

and the constable may **SEIZE** and retain such evidence

to that offence or to some other arrestable offence which is connected with or similar to that offence

If a power is not provided so far, a warrant may be required. See later

Seizure to Prevent Loss etc

S 19 POLICE AND CRIMINAL EVIDENCE ACT 1984

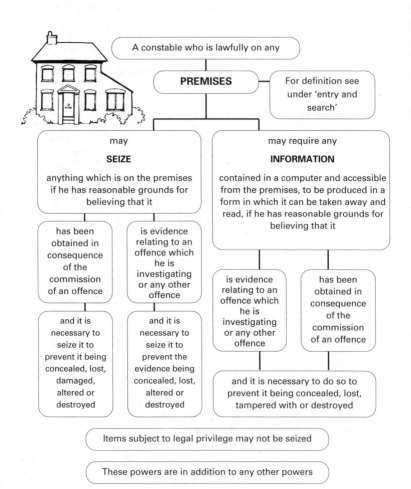

A constable who is lawfully on any

PREMISES

For definition see under 'entry and search'

may

SEIZE

anything which is on the premises if he has reasonable grounds for believing that it

has been obtained in consequence of the commission of an offence

is evidence relating to an offence which he is investigating or any other offence

and it is necessary to seize it to prevent it being concealed, lost, damaged, altered or destroyed

and it is necessary to seize it to prevent the evidence being concealed, lost, altered or destroyed

may require any

INFORMATION

contained in a computer and accessible from the premises, to be produced in a form in which it can be taken away and read, if he has reasonable grounds for believing that it

is evidence relating to an offence which he is investigating or any other offence

has been obtained in consequence of the commission of an offence

and it is necessary to do so to prevent it being concealed, lost, tampered with or destroyed

Items subject to legal privilege may not be seized

These powers are in addition to any other powers

Additional Powers of Seizure from Premises or Person

S 50 & S 51 CRIMINAL JUSTICE AND POLICE ACT 2001

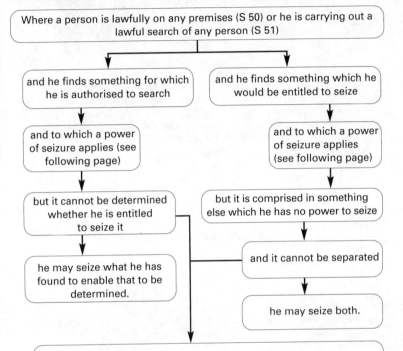

Where a person is lawfully on any premises (S 50) or he is carrying out a lawful search of any person (S 51)

and he finds something for which he is authorised to search

and he finds something which he would be entitled to seize

and to which a power of seizure applies (see following page)

and to which a power of seizure applies (see following page)

but it cannot be determined whether he is entitled to seize it

but it is comprised in something else which he has no power to seize

he may seize what he has found to enable that to be determined.

and it cannot be separated

he may seize both.

The factors to be taken into account in determining whether he is entitled to seize it, or whether it can be separated, are confined to the following:

(a) how long it would take;
(b) the number of persons that would be required to carry it out within a reasonable time;
(c) whether it would involve damage to property;
(d) the apparatus or equipment needed; and
(e) in the case of separation, whether it would be likely to prejudice the use of the seized property.

Powers to Which S 50 Applies

CRIMINAL JUSTICE AND POLICE ACT 2001, SCHED 1

The Schedule contains a long list of powers of seizure to which this section applies. The following are the ones most likely to affect operational police work.

SEIZURE FROM PREMISES

DESCRIPTION	ENACTMENT
Betting, gaming and lotteries	Betting, Gaming and Lotteries Act 1963, S 51(1)
Biological weapons	Biological Weapons Act 1974, S 4(1)(b), (c) & (d)
Chemical weapons	Chemical Weapons Act 1996, S 29(2)(c), (d) & (e)
Club documents	Licensing Act 1964, S 54
Drug trafficking	Drug Trafficking Act 1994, S 56(5)
Drugs	Misuse of Drugs Act 1971, S 23(2) & (3)
Firearms	Firearms Act 1968, S 46
Gaming	Gaming Act 1968, S 43(5)
General entry, search and seizure	P.A.C.E. Act 1984, Parts 2 & 3
Harmful publications	C. & Y. P. (Harmful Publications Act 1955, 3(1)
Immigration	Immigration Act 1971, S 28D(3), 28E(5) & 28F(6)
Indecent photographs	Protection of Children Act 1978, S 4(2)
Knives publications	Knives Act 1997, S 5(2)
Lotteries and Amusements	Lotteries and Amusements Act 1976, S 19
Obscene publications	Obscene Publications Act 1959, S 3(1) & (2)
Official secrets	Official Secrets Act 1911, S 9(1)
Stolen goods	Theft Act 1968, S 26(3)
Terrorist investigations	Terrorism Act 2000 Sched 5

SEIZURE FROM THE PERSON

Arrest	P.A.C.E. Act 1984, Part 3
Firearms	Firearms Act 1968, S 46
Drugs	Misuse of Drugs Act 1971, S 23(2) & (3)
Immigration	Immigration Act 1971, S 28G(7)
Biological weapons	Biological Weapons Act 1974, S 4(1)(b), (c) & (d)
Arrest under cross border powers	Criminal Justice and Public Order Act 1994, S 139
Terrorist investigations	Terrorism Act 2000 Sched. 5
Terrorist arrest	Terrorism Act 2000, S 43(4)

Notice of Seizure
S 52 CRIMINAL JUSTICE AND POLICE ACT 2001

Where a person exercises a power of seizure from premises under S 50 (or seizure from the person (S 51), he must give to the occupier of the premises (or person from whom the seizure is made) a written notice specifying:
(a) what has been seized;
(b) the grounds for the seizure;
(c) his remedies and safeguards;
(d) to whom he may apply for return of the property; and
(e) to whom he may apply to attend the initial examination of the property.
If the occupier of the premises is not there but some other person in charge of the premises is present, the notice is to be served on that other person. If no one is present, he shall, before leaving the premises, attach the notice in a prominent place on the premises.

Examination and Return of Seized Property
S 53 CRIMINAL JUSTICE AND POLICE ACT 2001

The person in charge of property seized under Ss 50 or 51 must ensure that:
(a) an initial examination is carried out as soon as reasonably practicable after the seizure;
(b) that examination is confined to whatever is necessary to determine how much of the property:
  (i) is property for which there was a power to search (but is not subject to legal privilege);
  (ii) is property which it is necessary to retain to prevent it being concealed, lost, altered, damaged or destroyed, it having been obtained by the commission of an offence, or is evidence relating to an offence; or
  (iii) cannot be separated from property falling within (i) or (ii) above;
(c) anything which is found not to fall within (b) above is returned as soon as reasonably practicable; and
(d) the seized property is kept separate from anything seized under any other power.

Legally Privileged Property
S 50(4) and 51(4) of this Act state that S 19(6) of the Police and Criminal Evidence Act 1984 (power to seize not to include a power to seize anything which is legally privileged) will not apply to the power of seizure in circumstances where it is comprised in something else which cannot be seized, but the two cannot be separated.
'Legally privileged' means communications between a professional legal adviser and his client in connection with legal advice or legal proceedings, and items enclosed with or referred to in such communications. Items held with the intention of furthering a criminal purpose are not legally privileged. (P.A.C.E. Act 1984, S 10).

Search Upon Arrest

S 32 POLICE AND CRIMINAL EVIDENCE ACT 1984

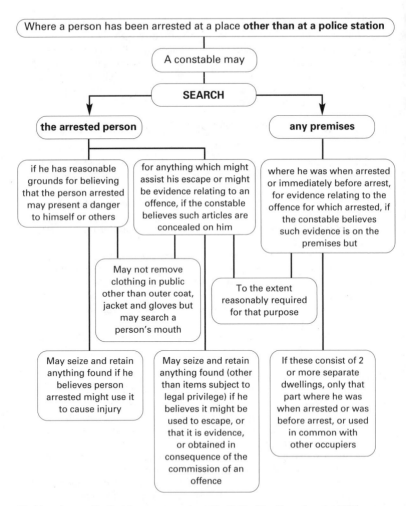

Where a person has been arrested at a place **other than at a police station**

A constable may

SEARCH

the arrested person

any premises

if he has reasonable grounds for believing that the person arrested may present a danger to himself or others

for anything which might assist his escape or might be evidence relating to an offence, if the constable believes such articles are concealed on him

where he was when arrested or immediately before arrest, for evidence relating to the offence for which arrested, if the constable believes such evidence is on the premises but

May not remove clothing in public other than outer coat, jacket and gloves but may search a person's mouth

To the extent reasonably required for that purpose

May seize and retain anything found if he believes person arrested might use it to cause injury

May seize and retain anything found (other than items subject to legal privilege) if he believes it might be used to escape, or that it is evidence, or obtained in consequence of the commission of an offence

If these consist of 2 or more separate dwellings, only that part where he was when arrested or was before arrest, or used in common with other occupiers

Nothing above will affect the power conferred by S 43 of the Terrorism Act 2000.

Search Warrants

S 8 POLICE AND CRIMINAL EVIDENCE ACT 1984

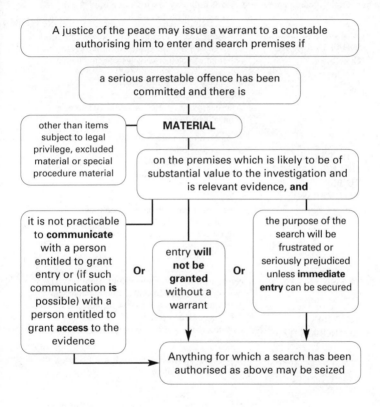

A justice of the peace may issue a warrant to a constable authorising him to enter and search premises if

a serious arrestable offence has been committed and there is

MATERIAL

other than items subject to legal privilege, excluded material or special procedure material

on the premises which is likely to be of substantial value to the investigation and is relevant evidence, **and**

it is not practicable to **communicate** with a person entitled to grant entry or (if such communication **is** possible) with a person entitled to grant **access** to the evidence

Or

entry **will not be granted** without a warrant

Or

the purpose of the search will be frustrated or seriously prejudiced unless **immediate entry** can be secured

Anything for which a search has been authorised as above may be seized

EXECUTION S 16

Must be within **1 month** of issue

Must be at a **reasonable hour** unless the purpose may be frustrated by doing so.

Where occupier or person in charge of the premises is present, constable must **identify himself**, **produce the warrant** and supply him with a copy. If no such person is present, a copy must be left in a prominent place on the premises.

Road Checks

S 4 POLICE AND CRIMINAL EVIDENCE ACT 1984

Under certain circumstances, a PC needs authority to carry out a road check

WHAT IS A ROAD CHECK?	The exercise in a locality of the power conferred by s 163 of the Road Traffic Act 1988, to stop either all vehicles or vehicles selected by any criterion
WHAT TYPE OF CHECK NEEDS TO BE AUTHORISED?	Where it is necessary to ascertain whether a vehicle is carrying: • A person who has committed a serious arrestable offence (other than a traffic or excise offence) and may be in the locality • A person who is a witness to a serious arrestable offence • A person who intends to commit a serious arrestable offence and may be in the locality • A person who is unlawfully at large and may be in the locality
WHO CAN AUTHORISE IT?	Normally a superintendent must authorise it in writing. But it may be authorised by an officer below that rank as a matter of urgency, in which case, as soon as practicable, he must make a written record of the time he gives it and cause a superintendent to be informed The locality at which the check is to be carried out must be specified
HOW LONG MAY IT LAST?	The superintendent or above (not below) must specify a period, not exceeding seven days, during which it may take place (may be renewed in writing). He may direct whether it shall be continuous or conducted at specified times

Stop and Search (Serious Violence)

S 60 CRIMINAL JUSTICE AND PUBLIC ORDER ACT 1994

Serious Violence/Offensive Weapons

If an inspector or above reasonably believes that incidents involving serious violence may take place in his area and it is expedient to give authorisation to prevent their occurrence, or that persons are carrying dangerous instruments or offensive weapons without good reason, he may authorise (in writing) stopping and searching of persons and vehicles in that locality for a period not exceeding 24 hours for offensive weapons or dangerous instruments. The authorisation may be extended for a further 24 hours by a superintendent having regard to the offences which have, or are reasonably suspected to have, been committed. If an inspector or chief inspector gave the initial authorisation, he must inform a superintendent as soon as practicable. A constable in uniform may stop any person or vehicle and make any search he thinks fit whether or not he has any grounds for suspecting that weapons or articles of that kind are present. Any dangerous instrument or article may be seized.

"Dangerous instrument" means instruments which have a blade or are sharply pointed.

"Vehicle" includes ships, aircraft and hovercraft.

Identification Methods

POLICE AND CRIMINAL EVIDENCE ACT 1984. CODES OF PRACTICE, CODE D

Methods

There are a number of methods of identifying suspects. They may be conveniently grouped as identification by:

1. witnesses,
   - ➤ by video,
   - ➤ identification parades,
   - ➤ group identification,
   - ➤ confrontation,
   - ➤ photographs,
2. fingerprints,
3. examination, e.g. to find marks such as tattoos or scars
4. body samples and impressions, e.g. blood or hair to generate a DNA profile,

These will be examined in more depth on the following pages.

General

The provisions of Code C relating to

- persons who are mentally disordered or otherwise mentally vulnerable;
- persons appearing to be under the age of 17 years;
- persons who appear to be blind, seriously visually impaired, deaf, unable to read or speak or have difficulty orally because of speech impediment;
- the definitions of 'appropriate adult', and 'solicitor',

also apply to this Code.

Arranging identification procedures

Normally the arrangements for, and the conduct of, identification procedures, and the circumstances in which they are held, are the responsibility of an officer not below the rank of inspector. However, the arranging and conduct of such procedures may, under supervision, be delegated to other officers or civilian staff. No person involved in the investigation of the case against the suspect may take any part in these procedures.

When an identification procedure must be held

Prior to any formal identification procedure taking place, where a witness has identified, is purported to have identified, expresses an ability to identify, or there is a reasonable chance of him being able to identify, a suspect, and the suspect disputes being the person the witness claims to have seen, an identification procedure shall be held (unless it is not practicable to do so or it would serve no useful purpose).

Selection of the procedure

If a procedure is to be held, the suspect shall initially be offered video identification unless:

- it is not practicable;
- an identification parade is both practicable and more suitable than a video identification; or
- the officer in charge of the investigation considers that a group identification is more suitable than video identification or an identification parade and the identification officer considers it practicable to arrange.

Identification by Witnesses

POLICE AND CRIMINAL EVIDENCE ACT 1984. CODES OF PRACTICE, CODE D

Record of suspect's description
A record must be made of the suspect's description as first given by a witness, before the witness takes part in any of the procedures applicable to cases where the suspect is known.

(a) When the suspect's identity is not known
A witness may be taken to a neighbourhood or place to see whether they can identify the person. The principles applicable to identification by video, identification parades, or group identification (see below) must be followed as far as practicable, e.g. (i) a record to be kept of the witnesses description of the suspect, (ii) the witness' attention is not to be directed to any individual, but this does not prevent him being asked to look towards a group or particular direction to ensure that a possible suspect is not overlooked, (iii) where there is more than 1 witness, they should be kept separate and taken to the area independently, (iv) once there is sufficient information to justify an arrest, the provisions applicable to 'Where a suspect is known and available' (below) shall be followed for any subsequent witness, (v) a record of action taken is to be recorded in the officer's pocket book as soon as possible.

A witness must not be shown photographs, composite likenesses or pictures if the identity of the suspect is known to the police and the suspect is available to take part in video, parade or group identification. If the suspect's identity is not known, the showing of such images must be done in accordance with the procedure for showing photographs (see later).

(b) When the suspect is known and available
If available, the following procedures may be used:

(i) **video** (where a witness is shown moving images of a suspect together with similar images of others who resemble the suspect);
(ii) **identification parade** (where the witness sees the suspect in a line of others who resemble the suspect); or
(iii) **group identification** (where the witness sees the suspect in an informal group of people).

Specific requirements for carrying out each of the above procedures are contained in the following pages.

Arranging identification procedures
Normally the arrangements for, and the conduct of, identification procedures, and the circumstances in which they are held, are the responsibility of an officer not below the rank of inspector. However, the arranging and conduct of such procedures may, under supervision, be delegated to other officers or civilian staff. No person involved in the investigation of the case against the suspect may take any part in these procedures.

When an identification procedure must be held
Prior to any formal identification procedure taking place, where a witness has identified, is purported to have identified, expresses an ability to identify, or there is a reasonable chance of him being able to identify, a suspect, and the suspect disputes being the person the witness claims to have seen, an identification procedure shall be held (unless it is not practicable to do so or it would serve no useful purpose).

Identification by Witnesses – continued

POLICE AND CRIMINAL EVIDENCE ACT 1984. CODES OF PRACTICE, CODE D

Selection of the procedure

If a procedure is to be held, the suspect shall initially be offered **video** identification unless:

- it is not practicable;
- an **identification parade** is both practicable and more suitable than a video identification; or
- the officer in charge of the investigation considers that a **group identification** is more suitable than video identification or an identification parade and the identification officer considers it practicable to arrange.

Notices to suspect

Before any of the above is arranged, the following shall be explained to the suspect, and a written copy given to him, which he will be asked to sign to indicate his willingness to co-operate:

(a) the purpose of the identification;
(b) entitlement to free legal advice;
(c) procedures, including right to have a solicitor or friend present;
(d) that they do not have to consent and co-operate;
(e) if they do not consent and co-operate, their refusal may be given in evidence, and the police may proceed covertly without their consent, or make other arrangements;
(f) in the case of video identification, whether images have previously been obtained, and that they may proved further images instead;
(g) any special arrangements for juveniles, mentally disordered or otherwise mentally vulnerable people;
(h) that if they significantly alter their appearance between being offered a procedure, and any attempt to hold it, this will be given in evidence and other forms of identification may then be considered;
(i) if they change their appearance before an identification parade, it may not be practicable for another to be arranged, and alternative methods may be considered;
(j) a moving image or photograph may be taken when they attend for any identification;
(k) whether, before their identity became known, the witness was shown photographs, etc.;
(l) they or their solicitor will be provided with the description first given by the witness.

(c) When the suspect is known but not available or ceased to be available

In these cases (and in cases involving juveniles when consent of the parent or guardian has been refused or when reasonable efforts to obtain it have failed) **video identification** or, using the same procedures, **still images** may be used. These may be obtained covertly if necessary. Alternatively, group identification may be used. If none of the aforementioned options are practicable, arrangements may be made for the suspect to be **confronted** by the witness in accordance with specific procedures (see later).

Identification by Witnesses – Videos

POLICE AND CRIMINAL EVIDENCE ACT 1984. CODES OF PRACTICE, CODE D

Video identification must be carried out in accordance with the following-

Obtaining the images
Arrangements for obtaining the images is the responsibility of the identification officer, who has no direct involvement in the case.

Composition of images
The images must include the suspect and at least 8 other people who, so far as possible, resemble the suspect in age, height, general appearance and position in life. Only 1 suspect is to appear in any set unless there are two suspects of roughly similar appearance, in which case they may be shown together with at least 12 other people.

The images shall show the suspect and other people in the same positions or carrying out the same sequence of movements. They must appear under identical conditions unless the identification officer reasonably believes that, (a) because of the suspect's failure or refusal to co-operate or other reasons, it is not practicable, and (b) any difference in the conditions would not direct a witness' attention to any individual image.

Identification of participants
All persons shown must be identified by a number. If police officers are shown, any numerals or identifying badges must be concealed. If prison inmates are shown, then either all or none should be in prison clothing.

Suspect's access to images
The suspect, solicitor or friend must be shown the images before they are shown to a witness, but before this, they must be provided with details of the first description of the suspect provided by the witness.

Conducting the identification
Witnesses must not be able to communicate with each other before they see the images, and they must not be told whether a previous witness has made an identification. Only one witness may see the images at a time. There is no limit to the number of times a witness may see the images or any part of them, but they should not make a decision as to identification until they have seen the whole set at least twice. The witness may then be invited to identify the suspect by number of the image. That image is then again shown to the witness to confirm the identification.

Identification by Witnesses – Identification Parades

POLICE AND CRIMINAL EVIDENCE ACT 1984. CODES OF PRACTICE, CODE D

General. Suspects must be given the opportunity to have a solicitor or friend present. The parade may take place either in a normal room or one equipped with a one-way screen (but a screen may only be used when a solicitor, friend or appropriate adult is present, or the parade is being recorded on video). Before the parade, details of the witness' first description must be provided to the suspect. When the suspect is brought to the place where the parade is to be held he shall be asked if he has any objection to the arrangements or any of the participants on the parade. Steps must be taken to remove the grounds for any reasonable objection.

Conduct of the parade. Immediately before the parade, the suspect must be reminded of the procedures and cautioned. All unauthorised persons must be excluded. Before witnesses attend the parade, appropriate arrangements must be made to ensure that they are not able to-

1. communicate with each other or overhear a witness who has already seen the parade;
2. see any member of the identification parade;
3. see, or be reminded of, any photograph or description of the suspect or be given any other indication of the suspect's identity; or
4. see the suspect before or after the parade.

After the parade has been formed everything must be done in the presence and hearing of the suspect or representative (unless a screen is used in which case any communication with a witness must be done in the presence and hearing of the representative, or be recorded on video). The person conducting a witness to a parade must not discuss the composition of the parade, nor disclose whether a previous witness has made any identification. Witnesses shall be brought in one at a time and before they inspect the parade must be told that the person they saw on a previous occasion may, or may not, be present, and that if they cannot make a positive identification, they should say so. They should also be told that they should not make any positive identification until they have looked at each member at least twice. After the witness has properly looked at each member of the parade, they shall be asked if the person they saw on a previous occasion is on the parade and if so, to indicate the number of the person. The witness may ask to hear any member speak, adopt a posture or move. Where the request is to hear a person speak, the witness should be told that the members were chosen on the basis of physical appearance only.

Composition of the parade. It must consist of at least 8 people in addition to the suspect, who should, as far as possible, resemble the suspect in age, height, general appearance and position in life. Only 1 suspect shall be included in the parade unless two suspects have roughly the same appearance, in which case they may appear together with at least 12 other people. The suspect may select his own position in the line and, where there is more than 1 witness, must be allowed to change his position after each witness has left the room. Each position in the line must be clearly numbered. Where separate parades are held, they must be made up of different people. If the suspect has an unusual feature, e.g. a facial scar, which cannot be replicated on other members of the parade, the location of that feature may be concealed on the suspect and all other members, if the suspect agrees, e.g. by use of a plaster or hat. If police officers in uniform form a parade, any numerals or identifying badges shall be concealed.

Identification by Witnesses – Group Identification

POLICE AND CRIMINAL EVIDENCE ACT 1984. CODES OF PRACTICE, CODE D

General. Group identifications may take place either with the suspect's consent or covertly without consent. The location of the identification should take into account any representations made by the suspect or his representative. However, it should be held where other people are either passing by or waiting around informally, in groups such that the suspect is able to join them and be capable of being seen by the witness at the same time as others in the group. The general appearance and numbers of people likely to be present must be considered. Over the period of observation the witness should be able to see a number of others whose appearance is broadly similar to the suspect. If, because of the unusual appearance of the suspect, none of the practicable locations would satisfy this requirement, a group identification need not be held. Immediately after the identification procedure, a colour photograph or video should be taken of the general scene if practicable. Alternatively, if practicable, the identification may be video recorded. If neither of these is practicable, a photograph or film should be taken later, if practicable. If, at the time of being seen by the witness, the suspect was on his own rather than in a group, this will still be a group identification. Before the identification takes place the suspect or his representative shall be provided with the witness' first description.

Identification with the consent of the suspect. The suspect must be given the opportunity for a representative to be present. Those present may be concealed from the sight of individuals in the group if it is considered that this will assist the conduct of the identification. A person conducting a witness to the scene must not discuss the group identification with the witness, nor disclose whether a previous witness has made any identification. Witnesses must not be able to communicate with each other; overhear a witness who has seen the group; see the suspect; or see or be reminded of any photographs or description of the suspect, or given any other indication of the suspect's identity. Witnesses must be brought to the place one at a time. Before they are asked to look at the group they shall be told that the person they saw may, or may not, be in the group, and that if they cannot make a positive identification, they should say so.

Moving groups. If 2 or more suspects consent to an identification, each should be subject to separate procedures, although they may take place consecutively on the same occasion. Once the witness has been asked to observe the group, the suspect may take whatever position in the group they wish.

Stationary groups. If 2 or more suspects consent to an identification, each should be subject to separate procedures unless they are of broadly similar appearance, when they may appear in the same group. If separate identifications are used, they must be made up of different people. The suspect may take whatever position in the group they wish. The witness shall be asked to pass along, or amongst the group and look at each person at least twice.

Identifications without the suspect's consent. As far as practicable these should follow the rules for identification with consent. The suspect has no right to have a representative present. Any number of suspects may be identified at the same time.

Identification at police stations. These should only take place for reasons of safety, security or because it is not practicable to hold them elsewhere. They may take place either in a room with a screen, or anywhere else considered appropriate.

Identifications involving prison inmates may only take place in prison or a police station. If within a prison, other inmates may take part. If an inmate is the suspect, they do not have to wear prison clothing unless the other participants are wearing the same clothing.

Identification by Witnesses – Confrontation

POLICE AND CRIMINAL EVIDENCE ACT 1984. CODES OF PRACTICE, CODE D

Before the confrontation takes place the witness must be told that the person they saw may, or may not, be the person they are about to confront and that if they are not that person, they should say so. The suspect or solicitor shall be provided with details of the first description given by the witness.

The confrontation. Force may not be used to make the suspect's face visible to the witness. The confrontation must take place in the presence of the suspect's representative, unless this would cause unreasonable delay. The suspect shall be confronted individually by each witness, who shall be asked "Is this the person?". The confrontation should normally take place in the police station, either in a normal room or one with a screen so the witness can not be seen by the suspect. If the room is equipped with a screen the suspect's representative must be present, or the confrontation must be recorded on video.

After the procedure each witness must be asked whether they have seen any broadcast or published films or photographs or any descriptions of suspects relating to the offence – and their reply recorded.

Identification by Witnesses – Photographs

POLICE AND CRIMINAL EVIDENCE ACT 1984. CODES OF PRACTICE, CODE D

Responsibility for proceedings. Although an officer of sergeant or above shall be responsible for the procedure, the actual showing may be done by another officer or civilian support staff. The first description of the suspect given by the witness must be recorded before showing the photographs.

The procedure. Only one witness may be shown the photographs at a time. Each witness shall be given as much privacy as practicable and not allowed to communicate with any other witness. They shall be shown not less than 12 photographs at a time, all of a similar type. When shown the photographs the witness must be told that the person they saw may, or may not, be amongst them and that if they can not make a positive identification, they should say so. They should also be told that they should not make a decision until they have viewed at least 12 photographs. The witness may not be prompted or guided in any way.

After the identification. Once a positive identification is made, whether by photographs, computerised or artist's composite or similar likeness, other witnesses should not be shown photographs or likeness, but both they and the identifying witness should be asked to attend an identification by video, parade or group, unless there is no dispute about the suspect's identification. Where a witness has made a positive identification from photographs or other likeness, the suspect and solicitor must be informed of this fact before any subsequent identification by video, parade or group takes place. The photographs used should not be destroyed. They should be numbered and produced in court if needed.

Identification by Other Methods

POLICE AND CRIMINAL EVIDENCE ACT 1984. CODES OF PRACTICE, CODE D

So far we have dealt with identification by witnesses. Now we will consider other methods which may be used.

Identification by fingerprints

For the provisions of Ss 27 & 61 of The Police and Criminal Evidence Act 1984, see under 'Fingerprinting'. References to 'fingerprints' means any record, produced by any method, of the skin pattern and other physical characteristics or features of a person's fingers or palms.

S. 61 of PACE permits the taking of the fingerprints without consent in certain circumstances from any person over the age of 10 years. In such cases reasonable force may be used, if necessary, to take them. Where fingerprints are taken in connection with a 'recordable offence' (see definition under 'recordable offence') they may be subject of a 'speculative search', which means that they may be checked against other fingerprints held by the police or other enforcement authorities. Where the person has not been arrested, charged or reported for such an offence, but is suspected of committing it, the speculative search may only be carried out with the person's consent. Otherwise, consent is not required.

Identification by examination – person detained

S. 54A of PACE deals with persons detained at a police station to be searched or examined. See under 'Searches to Ascertain Identity'. It should be noted that a person detained under a stop and search power is not a detainee for the purpose of these powers. Under certain circumstances the search/examination/photograph may be taken without consent. On occasions it may not be practicable to obtain consent, eg where the person is drunk or otherwise unable to give consent; where it is suspected that the person would attempt to prevent it happening by violently resisting, covering or concealing the mark etc.; or where the parent or guardian of a juvenile can not be contacted in sufficient time. In such cases an inspector or above may authorise the search, etc. Reasonable force may be used if necessary. The thoroughness and extent of the search must be no more than the officer considers necessary to achieve the purpose. Where the removal of more than the outer clothing is required it shall be conducted in accordance with Code C (see under 'Intimate Searches'). It should be noted that intimate searches are not authorised under S. 54A.

(CONTINUED ON NEXT PAGE)

Identification by Other Methods – continued

POLICE AND CRIMINAL EVIDENCE ACT 1984. CODES OF PRACTICE, CODE D

Identification by examination – person not detained

The provisions relating to detained persons apply subject to the following modifications:

1. force may not be used;
2. any photographs taken must be destroyed unless the person is charged, informed he may be prosecuted, prosecuted or cautioned for a recordable offence (see definition under 'recordable offence'), or he consents in writing for it to be retained; and
3. the person must be allowed to witness its destruction or, within 5 days, request a certificate confirming destruction.

Identification by body samples and impressions

'Intimate' and 'non-intimate' samples are dealt with by Ss. 62 & 63 of PACE (see under respective headings). However, whereas S.62 prescribes the circumstances under which intimate samples may be taken, it does not prevent such samples being taken for elimination purposes with the consent of the person concerned. In such circumstances, where applicable, the role of the 'appropriate adult' should be applied (see under 'Identification Methods' earlier). Where hair samples are taken for the purpose of DNA analysis, the suspect should be permitted to choose which part of the body the hairs are taken from. Hairs which are plucked should be plucked individually, and no more should be taken than necessary for a sufficient sample. Before being asked to provide an intimate sample the suspect must be warned that refusal without good cause may harm their case. They must also be reminded of their entitlement to free legal advice.

Chapter 9

Detention and Treatment of Persons

Custody Officers – Qualification

S 36 POLICE AND CRIMINAL EVIDENCE ACT 1984

> Are appointed by the chief officer of police or other police officer directed by the chief officer

WHO MAY BE A CUSTODY OFFICER?

Must be at least the rank of sergeant. However, functions may be performed by any rank if a custody officer is not readily available. Where a person is taken to a non-designated police station (or attends there in answer to S 30A bail), and an officer not involved in the investigation of the offence is not available, any officer may perform the functions of the custody officer. If that officer is the officer taking the arrested person to the police station (or the officer who granted S 30A bail), he must inform an inspector or above who is attached to a designated police station, as soon as practicable, that he is to do so.

WHO MAY NOT BE?

None of the functions of a custody officer may be performed by an officer who is involved in the investigation of the offence for which the person is in detention, except:

A custody officer
- Performing a function assigned to him by the Act or a Code of Practice;
- Carrying out duties imposed by s 39 of the Act;
- Doing anything connected with the identification of a suspect; or
- Doing anything under ss 7 & 8 of the RTA 1988

Custody Records

POLICE AND CRIMINAL EVIDENCE ACT 1984
CODE OF PRACTICE, CODE C

REQUIREMENT

A separate custody record must be opened as soon as practicable for each person who is brought to a police station under arrest or is arrested at the police station having attended there voluntarily or attending a police station in answer to street bail. All information which has to be recorded under this code must be recorded as soon as practicable, in the custody record unless otherwise specified. Such persons must be brought before the custody officer as soon as practicable after their arrival at the station (designated or non-designated) or, if appropriate, following arrest after attending voluntarily. "At the station" means within the boundary of the building or enclosed yard.

When a person is answering street bail any documentation relating to the arrest should be linked with the custody record and any further action recorded on the custody record.

Where a person is transferred to another police station the record or a copy of it must accompany him. The record shall show the time and reason for the transfer and the time of release from detention.

AUTHORITY

In the case of any action requiring the authority of an officer of a specified rank, his name and rank must be noted in the custody record. All entries must be signed and timed by the maker. The requirement to give a name will not apply in cases linked to terrorism or where it is believed that such disclosure might put them in danger. In such cases a warrant or other identification number may be given, and the name of their police station.

ACCURACY

The custody officer is responsible for the accuracy and completness of the custody record

All entries in custody and written interview records must be timed and signed by the maker

Any refusal by a person to sign either a custody or an interview record when asked to do so in accordance with the provisions of this code must itself be recorded

SUPPLY OF COPY

When a person leaves police detention he or his legal representative shall be supplied on request with a copy of the custody record as soon as practicable. This entitlement lasts for twelve months after his release

Responsibility for Detained Persons

S 39 POLICE AND CRIMINAL EVIDENCE ACT 1984

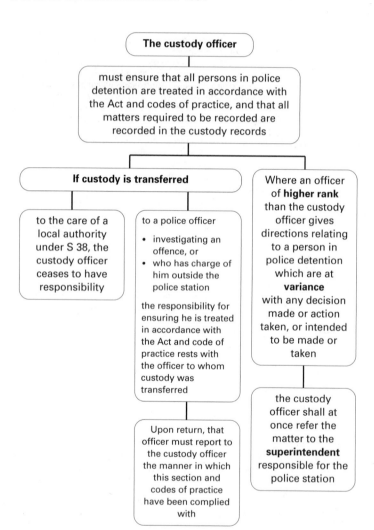

The custody officer

must ensure that all persons in police detention are treated in accordance with the Act and codes of practice, and that all matters required to be recorded are recorded in the custody records

If custody is transferred

to the care of a local authority under S 38, the custody officer ceases to have responsibility

to a police officer
- investigating an offence, or
- who has charge of him outside the police station

the responsibility for ensuring he is treated in accordance with the Act and code of practice rests with the officer to whom custody was transferred

Upon return, that officer must report to the custody officer the manner in which this section and codes of practice have been complied with

Where an officer of **higher rank** than the custody officer gives directions relating to a person in police detention which are at **variance** with any decision made or action taken, or intended to be made or taken

the custody officer shall at once refer the matter to the **superintendent** responsible for the police station

Custody Officers – Initial Action

CODES OF PRACTICE, CODE C

Detained persons – normal procedure

Informing of rights

Where a person is brought to a police station under arrest, or arrested at the police station having gone there voluntarily the custody officer must inform him of the following:

1. the right to have someone informed of his arrest;
2. the right to consult privately with a solicitor and that free independent legal advice is available; and
3. the right to consult the Codes of Practice.

Notices

The detainee must also be given a notice setting out:

1. the above 3 rights;
2. the arrangements for obtaining free legal advice;
3. the right to a copy of the custody record;
4. the caution; and
5. entitlements whilst in custody (this in a separate notice from the rest).

The detainee will be asked to sign for receipt of these notices on the custody record.

Foreign detainees

A citizen of an independent Commonwealth country or national of a foreign country must be informed about his right to consult with the High Commission, Embassy or Consulate.

Questioning and responses

Any comment the detainee makes in relation to the arresting officer's account (but such comment shall not be invited) shall be noted on the custody record. He shall be informed of the grounds for his detention before being questioned about the offence, and any comment in response (but may not be invited) shall be noted. The custody officer shall not question him about the offence, nor about any response as aforementioned. However, any unsolicited comments relevant to the offence should be noted. If the arresting officer is not physically present when the detainee is brought to the police station, the arresting officer's account must be made available to the custody officer remotely or by a 3rd party on his behalf.

Determination of needs

The custody officer shall:

1. ask the detainee whether he would like legal advice or want someone informed of his detention;
2. ask him to sign the custody record in respect to his responses to (1) above;
3. determine whether the detainee needs medical attention, an appropriate adult, help checking documentation, or an interpreter; and
4. record the decision in respect of (3).

Risk assessment

In determining the above needs the custody officer must as soon as practicable carry out a risk assessment which may include consulting others and the PNC. Reasons for delaying the assessment must be recorded. Risk assessment must follow a structured process which clearly defines the categories of risk to be considered, and the results entered on the custody record. The custody officer is responsible for implementing the response to any specific risk, e.g. reducing opportunities for self harm, calling for health care, or increasing levels of monitoring or observation. Risk assessment is an ongoing process subject to review if circumstances change.

Video cameras

If video cameras are installed in the custody area, notices shall be prominently displayed showing cameras are in use. Any request to switch them off shall be refused.

Custody Officers – Initial Action – continued

CODE OF PRACTICE, CODE C

Detained persons – special groups

Interpreters

If the detainee appears to be deaf or there is doubt about his hearing or speaking ability, or ability to understand English, and effective communication cannot be established by the custody officer, he must as soon as practicable call an interpreter for assistance in the normal procedure (see previous page).

Juveniles

If practicable the custody officer must identify a person responsible for the welfare of the juvenile:
• the parent or guardian;
• if in care or otherwise being looked after under the Children Act 1989, a person appointed by the
  authority or organisation; or
• any other person who has, for the time being, assumed responsibility for his welfare.
That person must be informed as soon as practicable of the arrest, the reason for it, and where detained. Juveniles must not be held incommunicado.
If a juvenile is under a court supervision order, the person responsible for the supervision must be informed.

Juveniles and mentally disordered or mentally vulnerable persons

If the detainee is such a person the custody officer must, as soon as practicable, inform the appropriate adult of the grounds for his detention and his whereabouts, and ask the adult to attend the police station to see the detainee. Mentally disordered and mentally vulnerable persons detained under S 136 Mental Health Act 1983 must be assessed as soon as possible by an approved social worker and a registered medical practitioner. Once they have been assessed and arrangements made for treatment and care, they can no longer be detained under S 136. If the medical practitioner concludes that they are not mentally disordered, they must be released from detention.

Compliance with procedure in presence of appropriate adult

If the appropriate adult is at the police station, the normal procedures (see previous page) must be complied with in his presence. If he is not at the police station when they are carried out, they must be repeated when he arrives. The detainee must be advised that the appropriate adult is there to give advice and may be consulted in private. Where either the detainee or appropriate adult request legal advice, the conditions applicable to such provision will apply.

Persons who are blind or unable to read

In these cases (unless the person is not a juvenile, not mentally disordered or not mentally vulnerable) the custody officer shall ensure that a solicitor, relative, appropriate adult, or some other person likely to take an interest in them and not involved in the investigation, is available to help check any documentation. Such person may sign on behalf of the detainee if he prefers.

Persons attending a police station voluntarily

Such persons may leave at will unless arrested, in which case they must be informed at once that they are under arrest and brought before the custody officer who will then treat them in the same way as other detainees. Persons not under arrest but cautioned must be informed of their right to free legal advice and to speak with a solicitor on the telephone.

Legal Advice

S 58 POLICE AND CRIMINAL EVIDENCE ACT 1984 CODES OF PRACTICE, CODE C

Information about rights

Unless a delay has been authorised, all detainees must be informed that they may at any time consult and communicate privately with a solicitor, whether in person, in writing or by telephone, and that free legal advice is available from the duty solicitor. A poster advertising the right to legal advice must be prominently displayed in the charging area.

Dissuading

A detainee may not at any time be dissuaded from obtaining legal advice.

Action to secure legal advice

Unless a delay has been authorised, where legal advice is requested action must be taken to secure it without delay. In any case he must be permitted to consult with a solicitor within 36 hours of the relevant time. If requested the solicitor may be present during the interview.

Access to telephone legal advice

If the right is declined, the detainee must be informed that he may speak with a solicitor on the telephone. The reasons for any continued decline should be recorded on the custody or interview record.

Interviews not to take place without legal advice

Where legal advice has been requested, an interview may not take place or continue until such advice has been received unless a delay has been authorised, in which case the restriction on drawing adverse inferences will apply.

Delays

A delay may be permitted where:

(a) (S 58 PACE): a person is in police detention for a serious arrestable offence and an officer of superintendent rank or above has reasonable grounds for believing that the consequent delay might:
 • lead to interference with, or harm to, evidence connected with a serious arrestable offence, or to other persons;
 • lead to alerting other people suspected of having committed such an offence but not yet arrested;
 • hinder the recovery of property obtained from the commission of such an offence;
 • hinder the recovery of proceeds from a drug trafficking offence; or
 • hinder the recovery of property obtained, or a pecuniary advantage derived, from an offence under Part VI of the Criminal Justice Act 1988 (confiscation orders);

but once sufficient information has been obtained to avert the risk, the questioning must cease;

(b) (Code C): a superintendent or above has reasonable cause to believe that
 • awaiting the arrival of a solicitor who has been contacted would cause unreasonable delay to the process of investigation; or
 • delay might lead to serious loss of, or damage to, property

(c) (Code C): the selected solicitor-
 (i) cannot be contacted;
 (ii) has previously indicated that they do not wish to be contacted; or
 (iii) having been contacted, has declined to attend, and the detainee has been advised of the duty solicitor scheme but has declined to ask for him, in which case an inspector may authorise the interview to take place;

(d) (Code C): the detainee changes his mind about wanting legal advice, in which case the interview may take place if he agrees and an inspector has authorised it.

Legal Advice – continued

CODES OF PRACTICE, CODE C

Solicitor
In this code 'solicitor' means a solicitor who holds a current practising certificate; or an accredited or probationary representative included on the register of representatives maintained by the Legal Services Commission. If the solicitor sends a non-accredited or probationary representative then he shall be admitted to the police station for this purpose unless an officer of the rank of inspector or above considers that such a visit will hinder the investigation of crime and directs otherwise. Once admitted to the police station, the provisions relating to solicitors apply. For matters to be taken into account in reaching this decision, refer to Code of Practice C para 6.13.

If the inspector refuses access to a non-accredited or probationary representative or a decision is taken that such a person should not be permitted to remain at an interview, he must forthwith notify a solicitor on whose behalf the person was to have acted or was acting, and give him an opportunity of making alternative arrangements.

Requirement to Leave
The solicitor may only be required to leave the interview if his conduct is such that the investigating officer is unable properly to put questions to the suspect. If this happens the investigating officer will stop the interview and consult an officer not below the rank of superintendent, if readily available, otherwise an officer not below the rank of inspector, who is not connected with the investigation. That officer will decide, after speaking to the solicitor, whether or not the interview should continue in the presence of that solicitor. If he decides that it should not, the suspect will be given the opportunity to consult another solicitor before the interview continues and that solicitor will be given an opportunity to be present at the interview. The removal of a solicitor from an interview is a serious step and if it occurs, the officer who took the decision will consider whether the incident should be reported to the Law Society. If the decision to remove the solicitor has been taken by an officer below the rank of superintendent, the facts must be reported to an officer of at least superintendent rank who will consider whether a report to the Law Society would be appropriate. In the case of a duty solicitor a report should also be made to the Legal Services Commission.

Records
Any request for legal advice and the action taken on it shall be recorded.

If a person has asked for legal advice and an interview is commenced in the absence of a solicitor or his representative (or the solicitor or his representative has been required to leave an interview) this must be recorded in the interview record.

Notification of Arrest

S 56 POLICE AND CRIMINAL EVIDENCE ACT 1984 CODES OF PRACTICE, CODE C

When a person has been arrested and is held in custody in a police station or other premises, he shall be entitled, if he requests, to have a person told, as soon as practicable (and in any case within 36 hours (48 hours in the case of terrorism acts) from the relevant time) that he has been arrested and is being detained there. These rights are exercisable whenever he is transferred from one place to another. If a person enquires about a detainee's whereabouts, this information shall be given if the detainee agrees.

Delays

A delay may be permitted where:

(a) (S 56 PACE): a person is in police detention for a serious arrestable offence and an officer of inspector rank or above has reasonable grounds for believing that the consequent delay might:
  (i) lead to interference with, or harm to, evidence connected with a serious arrestable offence, or to other persons;
  (ii) lead to alerting other people suspected of having committed such an offence but not yet arrested;
  (iii) hinder the recovery of property obtained from the commission of such an offence;
  (iv) hinder the recovery of proceeds from a drug trafficking offence; or
  (v) hinder the recovery of property obtained, or a pecuniary advantage derived, from an offence under Part VI of the Criminal Justice Act 1988 (confiscation orders).

(b) (Code): the person is detained under the Terrorism Act 2000, Sched 7 or S 41 and may (in addition to any of the conditions in items (i), (ii), (iii), or (v) above) result in:
  (i) hindering the recovery of property in respect of which a forfeiture order could be made under S 23 of the Terrorism Act 2000;
  (ii) interference with the gathering of information about an act of terrorism; or
  (iii) alerting any person, making it more difficult to prevent an act of terrorism or secure the apprehension, prosecution or conviction of a person in connection with an act of terrorism.

If a delay is authorised the detained person will, as soon as practicable, be told the reason for it and the reason shall be noted on the custody record.

There may be no further delay once the reason for authorising it ceases to subsist.

The fact that grounds for delaying notification of arrest may be satisfied does not automatically mean that the grounds for delaying access to legal advice will also be satisfied.

Right not to be held incommunicado (Code C)

In addition to the above provisions, a detainee has the following privileges:

Visits

The detainee may receive visits at the custody officer's discretion. These should be allowed whenever possible, subject to being able to supervise a visit or causing hindrance to the investigation.

Writing materials and telephone calls

He shall be given writing materials on request and allowed to telephone one person for a reasonable time (in addition to the telephone call mentioned above). But these privileges may be denied or delayed if an inspector or above considers either may result in any of the relevant conditions mentioned in (a) or (b) above.

Intercepting contents of communications

Before any letter or message is sent, or telephone call made, the detainee shall be informed that what they say (other than to a solicitor) may be read or listened to and may be given in evidence. A telephone call may be terminated if it is being abused.

Documentation

A record must be kept of any requests made and action taken; letters, messages or telephone calls made or received or visit received; or refusal by the detainee to have information about them given to an enquirer (and the detainee must be asked to countersign).

Treatment of Detained Persons

CODES OF PRACTICE, CODE C

General

If a complaint is made about a detained person's treatment since his arrest, or it comes to the notice of any officer that he may have been treated improperly, a report must be made as soon as practicable to an officer of the rank of inspector or above who is not connected with the investigation. If a possible assault or the possibility of the unnecessary or unreasonable use of force is involved then the appropriate health care professional must also be called as soon as practicable.

Illness

The custody officer must as soon as practicable ensure the appropriate clinical attention is given (or, in urgent cases, send the person to hospital or call the nearest available medical practitioner) if a person brought to a police station or already detained there appears to be ill (mentally or physically), injured, insensible (other than through drunkenness alone) or appears to need medical attention, whether or not the person requests medical attention. The need for clinical attention must also be considered in relation to those suffering the effects of alcohol or drugs.

Infectious disease

If it appears that a person brought to the police station under arrest may be suffering from a significant infectious disease the custody officer should isolate the person and his property until he has obtained medical directions as to where the person should be taken, whether fumigation should take place and what precautions should be taken by officers.

Clinical Examination

If a detained person requests a clinical examination the appropriate health care professional must be called as soon as practicable. He may also be examined by his own doctor at his own expense.

Medication

If a person is required to take or apply any medication in compliance with medical directions prescribed before his detention, the custody officer must consult the appropriate health care professional before the use of the medication. The custody officer is responsible for its safe keeping and for ensuring that he is given the opportunity to take or apply it at the appropriate times. No police officer may administer controlled drugs subject to the Misuse of Drugs Act 1971 for this purpose.

Records

A record must be made of any arrangements made for an examination by a police surgeon, any complaint reported and medical directions to the police.

The custody record shall detail the medicines the person has with him on arrival at the police station and any which he claims to need but does not have.

Conditions of Detention

CODES OF PRACTICE, CODE C

Cells
So far as is practicable, not more than one person shall be detained in each cell. Cells must be adequately heated, cleaned and ventilated. They must be adequately lit, subject to such dimming as is compatible with safety and security, to allow people detained overnight to sleep. No additional restraints should be used within a locked cell unless absolutely necessary, and then only approved restraint equipment which is reasonable and necessary in the circumstances having regard to the detainee's demeanour and to ensure his safety and the safety of others. Particular care must be taken in deciding to use restraints on persons who are deaf, mentally disordered or mentally vulnerable.

Bedding
Bedding should be of a reasonable standard and in a clean and sanitary condition.

Toilets
Access to toilet and washing facilities must be provided.

Clothing
If a person's clothes have to be removed for investigation, hygiene or health reasons or for cleaning, replacement clothing of a reasonable standard of comfort and cleanliness shall be provided. A person may not be interviewed unless adequate clothing has been offered to him.

Meals
At least two light meals and one main meal shall be offered in any period of 24 hours. Drinks should be provided at mealtimes and upon reasonable request between meals. Whenever necessary, advice shall be sought from the appropriate health care professional on medical or dietary matters. Special dietary needs or religious beliefs should be met where practicable. At the custody officer's discretion, meals may be supplied by family or friends at the prisoner's, or their, expense.

Exercise
Brief daily, outdoor exercise shall be provided where practicable.

Juveniles
Should not be put in a cell unless other secure accommodation is not available or is impracticable to supervise or is less comfortable than a cell. A juvenile may not share a cell with an adult.

Force
Reasonable force may be used if necessary:

• to secure compliance with reasonable instructions, or
• to prevent escape, injury, damage to property or the destruction of evidence.

Checks
Detainees should be visited at least every hour. If no reasonably foreseeable risk was identified in risk assessment there is no need to wake a sleeping detainee. Suspects who are intoxicated through drink or drugs or whose level of consciousness causes concern must, subject to any clinical directions given by the appropriate health care professional, be visited and roused at least every half hour, have their condition assessed, and have clinical treatment arranged if appropriate.

Records
Replacement clothing and meals offered must be recorded. If a juvenile is placed in a cell, the reason must be recorded. The use of any restraints, the reason for it and, if appropriate, enhanced supervision whilst restrained, shall be recorded.

Fingerprinting

S 27 & S 61 POLICE AND CRIMINAL EVIDENCE ACT 1984

General principle (S 61)

Fingerprints may only be taken with the appropriate consent, which, if given at a police station, must be in writing.

Taking fingerprints without consent – detained at a police station

Fingerprints of a person detained at a police station may be taken without consent by any constable, or, where a designation applies, by a civilian if:

(a) he is detained following his arrest for a recordable offence, or he has been charged with, or told he will be reported for, such an offence, and

(b) he has not had his fingerprints taken in the course of the investigation by the police (unless they were not a complete set or were not of sufficient quality to allow satisfactory analysis, comparison or matching).

Taking fingerprints without consent – answering bail

The fingerprints of a person who has answered to bail at a court or police station may be taken without consent if the court or an officer of at least the rank of inspector authorises them to be taken. Such authorisation may only be given if the person answering bail:

(a) has done so for a person who has had his fingerprints taken on a previous occasion and there are reasonable grounds for believing that he is not the same person; or

(b) claims to be a different person from a person whose fingerprints were taken on a previous occasion.

Authorisation may be given orally or in writing, but if given orally must be confirmed in writing as soon as practicable.

Taking fingerprints without consent – recordable offence

Any person's fingerprints may be taken without consent if, in relation to a recordable offence, he has been convicted; cautioned (which he admits); or warned or reprimanded under S 65 Crime and Disorder Act 1998.

Information to be given

Where fingerprints are taken without consent the person shall be told the reason before they are taken. The reason shall also be recorded as soon as practicable after they have been taken.

Where fingerprints are taken at a police station, with or without consent, the person shall be told before they are taken that they may be the subject of a speculative search; and the fact that he has been told shall be recorded as soon as practicable after they have been taken.

Custody record

If a person is detained at a police station when his fingerprints are taken, the reason for taking them and, if applicable, the fact that the person has been told of the possibility of a speculative search, shall be recorded on the custody record.

Exclusions

None of the above applies to powers under the Immigration Act 1971, the Terrorism (Temporary Provisions) Act 1989, (except S15(10) and para. 7(6) Sched. 5), or the Extradition Act 2003 (see later).

Fingerprinting of offenders (S 27)

If a person has been convicted of a recordable offence; has not been in police detention for the offence; and has not had his fingerprints taken in the course of the investigation or since the conviction, any constable or, where a designation applies, a civilian, may within 1 month after the conviction require him to attend a police station to have them taken. The person must be given a period of 7 days during which he must attend, and times between which he must attend may be specified. A constable may arrest without warrant any person who fails to comply.

'**Recordable offence**' means convictions for and cautions, reprimands and warnings in respect of any offence punishable with imprisonment; and any offence specified in the schedule to the National Police Records (Recordable Offences) Regulations 2000.

Photographing of Suspects etc.

S 64A POLICE AND CRIMINAL EVIDENCE ACT 1984

A person who is **detained at a police** station may be photographed–

(a) with the appropriate consent; or
(b) if the appropriate consent is withheld, or it is not practicable to obtain it, without it.

A person proposing to take a photograph–

(a) may require the removal of any item or substance worn on or over the whole or any part of the head or face; and
(b) if the requirement is not complied with, may remove the item or substance.

The only persons entitled to take a photograph under this section are constables and, where a designation applies, civilians.

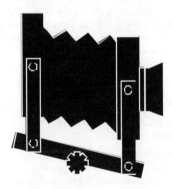

A photograph taken under this section-

(a) may be used by, or disclosed to, any person for any purpose related to the prevention or detection of crime, the investigation of an offence or the conduct of a prosecution; and
(b) after being so used or disclosed, may be retained but may not be used or disclosed except for the above purposes.

Photograph includes any process by means of which a visual image may be produced.

Intimate Searches

S 55 POLICE AND CRIMINAL EVIDENCE ACT 1984

An 'intimate search' consists of the physical examination of a person's body orifices other than the mouth.

Authorisation
If an officer of at least the rank of inspector has reasonable grounds for believing:
(a) that a person who has been arrested and is in police custody may have concealed on him anything which:
  (i) he could use to cause physical injury to himself or others; and
  (ii) he might so use while he is in police detention or in the custody of the court; or
(b) that such a person:
  (i) may have a class A drug concealed on him; and
  (ii) was in possession of it with the appropriate criminal intent (possession with intent to supply, or unlawful export) before his arrest,
he may authorise an intimate search of that person if he has reasonable grounds for believing that it cannot be found without an intimate search.
Authorisation may be given orally (later confirmed in writing) or in writing.

Persons authorised to carry out the search
An intimate search for a drug offence may only be carried out by a suitably qualified person (a registered medical practitioner or a registered nurse).
A search on any other grounds must be carried out by a suitably qual ified person unless an inspector or above considers that this is not practicable, in which case it may be carried out by a constable of the same sex as the person being searched, or, where a designation applies, by a civilian of the same sex.

Venue
An intimate search may only be carried out:
(a) at a police station (but not if for a drug offence);
(b) at a hospital;
(c) at a registered medical practitioner's surgery; or
(d) at some other place used for medical purposes.

Custody record
If an intimate search is carried out, as soon as reasonable practicable after its completion, it must be shown on the custody record which parts of the body were searched, and why they were searched.

Seizure of items found
The custody officer may seize and retain anything which is found on an intimate search:
(a) if he believes that the person may use it-
  (i) to cause physical injury to himself or another person;
  (ii) to damage property;
  (iii) to interfere with evidence; or
  (iv) to assist him to escape; or
(b) if he has reasonable grounds for believing that it may be evidence relating to an offence.

Intimate Searches – continued

CODES OF PRACTICE, CODE C, ANNEX A

The reasons for an intimate search must be explained to the person before it begins.

Juveniles or mentally disordered or mentally vulnerable persons

Intimate searches of such persons may only take place in the presence of an appropriate adult of the same sex, unless the detainee specifically requests a particular adult of the opposite sex who is readily available.

In the case of a juvenile the search may take place in the absence of the appropriate adult only if the juvenile signifies in the presence of the appropriate adult they do not want the adult present during the search and the adult agrees. A record shall be made of the juvenile's decision and signed by the adult.

Police officers carrying out searches

Where an intimate search for items which may be used to cause physical injury, is carried out by a police officer, it must be carried out by a person of the same sex as the person being searched. A minimum of two people, besides the detainee, must be present during the search. No person of the opposite sex to the person being searched (other than a medical practitioner or nurse) may be present, nor may anyone whose presence is unnecessary. The search shall be conducted with proper regard to the sensitivity and vulnerability of the detainee.

Documentation

As soon as practicable the custody officer shall record:

• which parts of the body were searched;
• who carried out the search;
• who was present;
• the reasons for it and why the article could not otherwise be removed;
• the result; and
• if carried out by a police officer, the reason why it was impracticable for it to be conducted by a registered medical practitioner or registered nurse.

Strip searches (means removal of more than outer clothing)

May take place to remove an article which the detainee would not be allowed to keep, and which he has concealed. They must not be routinely carried out.

When strip searches are conducted:
• a police officer must be of the same sex as the person searched;
• must be in an area where it cannot be seen by anyone who does not need to be present, or by the opposite sex (except an appropriate adult);
• if it involves exposing intimate parts of the body, two persons must be present (one must be an appropriate adult in the case of a juvenile or mentally disordered person);
• it must be carried out with due regard to sensitivity and vulnerability and should not involve removal of all clothes at the same time;
• the detainee may be required to hold arms in the air or stand with legs apart and bend forward so a visual examination may be made of genital and anal areas but there must be no physical contact;
• if the detainee refuses to hand over articles found in a body orifice other than the mouth, an intimate search would need to be carried out;
• it must be conducted as quickly as possible and the detainee allowed to dress as soon as the search is completed.

Searches to Ascertain Identity

S 54A POLICE AND CRIMINAL EVIDENCE ACT 1984

Authority to search, etc

An officer of at least the rank of inspector may authorise the search or examination, or both, of a person who is detained in a police station:

(a) to ascertain whether he has any mark that would tend to identify him as a person involved in the commission of an offence; or
(b) to facilitate the ascertainment of his identity,

if he has refused to identify himself; or it is suspected that the person is not who he claims to be.

But a search/examination may only be authorised under (a) above if:

(a) the appropriate consent has been withheld; or
(b) it is not practicable to obtain such consent.

An authorisation may be given orally or in writing, but if orally, it shall be confirmed in writing as soon as practicable.

Photographs

Any identifying mark found may be photographed:

(a) with the appropriate consent; or
(b) if consent is withheld or it is not practicable to obtain it, without it.

Conduct of the search, etc

Any search, examination or photograph may only be carried out by constables, or, where a designation applies, by a civilian, and such force as is necessary may be used.

A person may not carry out a search or examination of a person of the opposite sex. Nor may a photograph be taken of any part of the body of a person of the opposite sex.

An intimate search may not be carried out under this section.

Exclusion

None of the above applies to persons arrested under the Extradition Act 2003 (see later).

Intimate Samples

Ss 62, 65 Police and Criminal Evidence Act 1984

An
INTIMATE SAMPLE

is a sample of blood, semen, any other
tissue fluid, urine, pubic hair or a swab
taken from any part of a person's genitals
(including pubic hair) or from a person's
body orifices (other than the mouth)
or a dental impression

and may be taken from a **person in police detention**

if authorised by an officer of at least the rank of inspector
who has reasonable grounds for suspecting the
person's involvement in a recordable offence and
for believing that the sample will tend
to prove or disprove his involvement

and if the appropriate consent is given in writing

and may be taken from
a person **not** in police detention

if in the course of the investigation two or
more non-intimate samples suitable for
the same means of analysis have been
taken, and have proved insufficient and an
inspector or above authorises it and the
appropriate consent is given

A sample, other than of urine,
may only be taken by a registered medical practitioner
or registered nurse or registered paramedic;
and a dental impression may only be taken
by a registered dentist

Non-Intimate Samples

S 63 Police and Criminal Evidence Act 1984

> ## A **NON-INTIMATE SAMPLE**

is a sample of hair (other than pubic hair), a sample taken from a nail or from under a nail, a swab taken from any part of the body other than a part from which a swab taken would be an intimate sample, saliva, or a skin sample (a record of the skin pattern and other physical characteristics or features of a foot or any other part of the body).

It may not be taken from a person without consent given in writing. But it may be taken without consent by any constable if –

(a) being held in police custody by authority of a court and an inspector or above authorises it (he may only authorise it if he suspects his involvement in a recordable offence, and that the sample will tend to confirm or disprove his involvement),

(b) in police detention for a recordable offence and either (i) he has not had the same type of sample taken from the same part of the body in the course of the investigation, or (ii) he has had such a sample taken but it was insufficient,

(c) whether or not in police detention or held in police custody by authority of a court, he has (i) been charged with, or told he will be reported for, a recordable offence, and (ii) he has not had an intimate sample taken from him (or, if taken, was not suitable for analysis or was insufficient),

(d) convicted of a recordable offence, or

(e) detained following acquittal on grounds of insanity or unfitness to plead.

Exclusion

None of the above applies to persons arrested under the Extradition Act 2003 (see later).

Fingerprints and Samples

Ss 63A, 64 police and criminal evidence act 1984

Fingerprints or samples or the information derived from samples taken from a person arrested for a recordable offence or reported for such an offence may be checked against other fingerprints or samples or the information derived from them contained in records held by or on behalf of the police or in connection with the investigation of an offence.

Fingerprints may be taken without consent from a person aged over ten if the conditions set out above exist, and reasonable force may be used.

Destruction: S 64 PACE requires the destruction of fingerprints or samples as soon as is practicable after the conclusion of proceedings except that samples need not be destroyed if they were taken for the purpose of the same investigation of an offence for which a person from whom one was taken has been convicted or he has consented in writing to them not being destroyed.

Testing for Presence of Class A Drugs

S 63B POLICE AND CRIMINAL EVIDENCE ACT 1984. SCHED. 6 CRIMINAL JUSTICE AND COURT SERVICES ACT 2000. S 5 CRIMINAL JUSTICE ACT 2003.

A sample of urine or a non-intimate sample may be taken from a person in police detention for the purpose of ascertaining whether he has any specified Class A drug in his body if the following conditions are met:

1. the person has been charged
    (a) with a **trigger offence**; or
    (b) with an offence and a police officer of at least the rank of inspector, who has reasonable grounds for suspecting that the misuse by that person of any specified Class A drug caused or contributed to the offence, has authorised the sample to be taken;
2. the person concerned has attained the age of 18 (except in one of the designated police areas mentioned below, where the age is 14); and
3. a police officer has requested the person concerned to give the sample.

The authorisation mentioned above may be given orally or in writing, but if given orally, it must be confirmed in writing as soon as is practicable. (S 63C).

Before requesting the sample the person must be warned that failure to give a sample without good cause may lead to prosecution; and, where authorisation has been given under 1(b) above, informed of the grounds for it. (But if in one of the designated police areas mentioned below, and the person is under 17, the request, warning and taking of the sample must be in the presence of an appropriate adult (see below)).

Where a person is under 18 this section only applies in the designated police areas.

Designated police areas are: Cambridgeshire, Cleveland, Greater Manchester, Humberside, Leicestershire, Merseyside, Metropolitan, Northumbria, Nottinghamshire, West Midlands and West Yorkshire.

Appropriate adult means (a) the parent or guardian (or if in care, a representative of that organisation), (b) a social worker of a local authority social services, or (c) if none of the previous mentioned are available, any responsible person over 18 who is not a police officer or police employee.

Trigger offences. These are the following offences under:

1. the **Theft Act 1968**: S 1 (theft); S8 (robbery); S 9 (burglary); S 10 (aggravated burglary); S 12 (taking vehicle, etc. without authority); S 12A (aggravated vehicle-taking); S 15 (obtaining property by deception); S 22 (handling stolen goods); S 25 (going equipped for stealing);
2. the **Misuse of Drugs Act 1971**, if committed in respect of a specified Class A drug: S 4 (production and supply); S5(2) (possession); S 5(3) (possession with intent to supply);
3. S 1(1) of the **Criminal Attempts Act 1981**, if committed in respect of one of the following offences under the Theft Act 1968: S 1 (theft); S 8 (robbery); S 9 (burglary); S 15 (obtaining property by deception); S 22 (handling stolen goods);
4. the **Vagrancy Act 1824**: S 3 (begging); S 4 (persistent begging).

Testing for Presence of Class A Drugs – continued

CODES OF PRACTICE, CODE C

The following requirements of the Codes of Practice (including Notes for Guidance) should be read in conjunction with the previous page.

Before making the request an officer must remind the person of his rights to: have someone informed of his arrest; consult privately with a solicitor; free legal advice; and to consult the Codes of Practice.

Persons under 17. The making of the request for a sample, the giving of the warning and information, and the taking of the sample, may not take place except in the presence of an appropriate adult (see previous page).

Detention. Custody officers may authorise continued detention for up to 6 hours from the time of charge to enable a sample to be taken.

Documentation. The Inspector's authorisation (if applicable), the warning, and the time of charge and taking the sample, must all be recorded on the custody record.

Taking the sample. Samples may only be taken by (a) a police officer; (b) a person employed by a police authority or police force for the purpose of taking such samples; and (c) a person employed by a contractor engaged by a police authority or police force for such purposes. (SI 2001/2645). **Force** may not be used to take any sample for the purpose of drug testing.

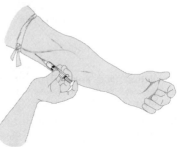

Use of the sample. May only be used for testing for Class A drugs. Must be retained until the person has made his first appearance before the court.

Form of warning. The following words may be used:

"You do not have to provide a sample, but I must warn you that if you fail or refuse without good cause to do so, you will commit an offence for which you may be imprisoned, or fined, or both".

Sufficiency of sample. It must be sufficient and suitable in quantity and quality to enable drug testing analysis to take place.

Limits on Detention

S 34 POLICE AND CRIMINAL EVIDENCE ACT 1984

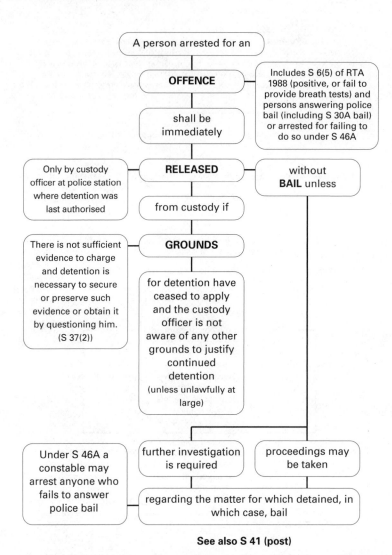

A person arrested for an

OFFENCE

Includes S 6(5) of RTA 1988 (positive, or fail to provide breath tests) and persons answering police bail (including S 30A bail) or arrested for failing to do so under S 46A

shall be immediately

Only by custody officer at police station where detention was last authorised

RELEASED

without **BAIL** unless

from custody if

There is not sufficient evidence to charge and detention is necessary to secure or preserve such evidence or obtain it by questioning him. (S 37(2))

GROUNDS

for detention have ceased to apply and the custody officer is not aware of any other grounds to justify continued detention (unless unlawfully at large)

Under S 46A a constable may arrest anyone who fails to answer police bail

further investigation is required

proceedings may be taken

regarding the matter for which detained, in which case, bail

See also S 41 (post)

Reviews of Detention

S 40 POLICE AND CRIMINAL EVIDENCE ACT 1984

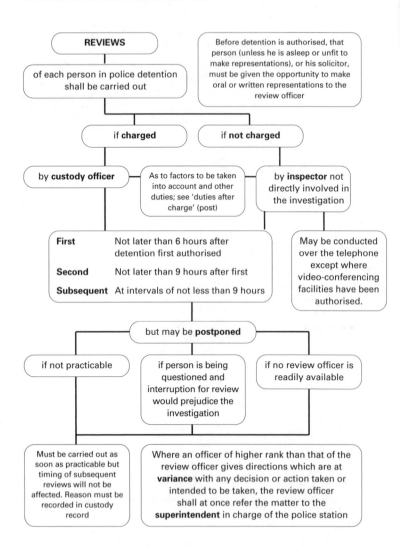

REVIEWS of each person in police detention shall be carried out

Before detention is authorised, that person (unless he is asleep or unfit to make representations), or his solicitor, must be given the opportunity to make oral or written representations to the review officer

if **charged**

if **not charged**

by **custody officer**

As to factors to be taken into account and other duties; see 'duties after charge' (post)

by **inspector** not directly involved in the investigation

First   Not later than 6 hours after detention first authorised

Second   Not later than 9 hours after first

Subsequent   At intervals of not less than 9 hours

May be conducted over the telephone except where video-conferencing facilities have been authorised.

but may be **postponed**

if not practicable

if person is being questioned and interruption for review would prejudice the investigation

if no review officer is readily available

Must be carried out as soon as practicable but timing of subsequent reviews will not be affected. Reason must be recorded in custody record

Where an officer of higher rank than that of the review officer gives directions which are at **variance** with any decision or action taken or intended to be taken, the review officer shall at once refer the matter to the **superintendent** in charge of the police station

Limits on Periods of Detention Without Charge

S 41 POLICE AND CRIMINAL EVIDENCE ACT 1984

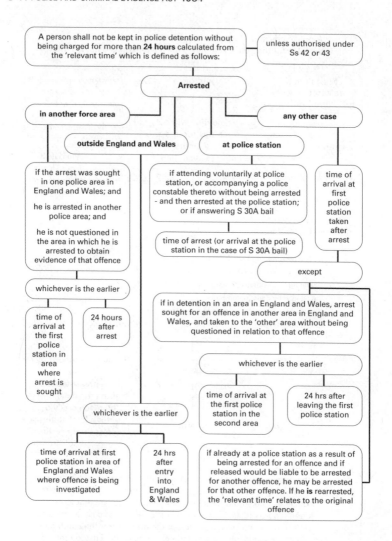

Continued Detention

S 42 POLICE AND CRIMINAL EVIDENCE ACT 1984

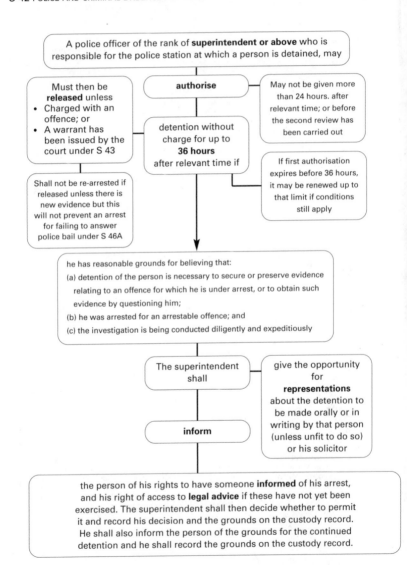

A police officer of the rank of **superintendent or above** who is responsible for the police station at which a person is detained, may

authorise

May not be given more than 24 hours. after relevant time; or before the second review has been carried out

detention without charge for up to **36 hours** after relevant time if

Must then be **released** unless
- Charged with an offence; or
- A warrant has been issued by the court under S 43

If first authorisation expires before 36 hours, it may be renewed up to that limit if conditions still apply

Shall not be re-arrested if released unless there is new evidence but this will not prevent an arrest for failing to answer police bail under S 46A

he has reasonable grounds for believing that:
(a) detention of the person is necessary to secure or preserve evidence relating to an offence for which he is under arrest, or to obtain such evidence by questioning him;
(b) he was arrested for an arrestable offence; and
(c) the investigation is being conducted diligently and expeditiously

The superintendent shall

give the opportunity for **representations** about the detention to be made orally or in writing by that person (unless unfit to do so) or his solicitor

inform

the person of his rights to have someone **informed** of his arrest, and his right of access to **legal advice** if these have not yet been exercised. The superintendent shall then decide whether to permit it and record his decision and the grounds on the custody record. He shall also inform the person of the grounds for the continued detention and he shall record the grounds on the custody record.

Warrant of Further Detention

S 43 POLICE AND CRIMINAL EVIDENCE ACT 1984

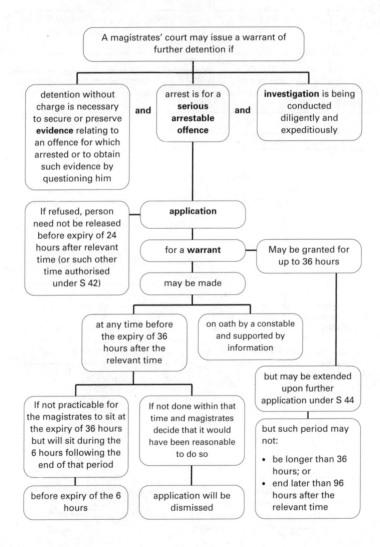

A magistrates' court may issue a warrant of further detention if

detention without charge is necessary to secure or preserve **evidence** relating to an offence for which arrested or to obtain such evidence by questioning him

and

arrest is for a **serious arrestable offence**

and

investigation is being conducted diligently and expeditiously

If refused, person need not be released before expiry of 24 hours after relevant time (or such other time authorised under S 42)

application

for a **warrant**

may be made

May be granted for up to 36 hours

at any time before the expiry of 36 hours after the relevant time

on oath by a constable and supported by information

but may be extended upon further application under S 44

If not practicable for the magistrates to sit at the expiry of 36 hours but will sit during the 6 hours following the end of that period

If not done within that time and magistrates decide that it would have been reasonable to do so

but such period may not:
- be longer than 36 hours; or
- end later than 96 hours after the relevant time

before expiry of the 6 hours

application will be dismissed

Duties Before Charge

S 37 POLICE AND CRIMINAL EVIDENCE ACT 1984

The custody officer at a police station where a person is detained following arrest without warrant, or with a warrant not endorsed for bail (if a juvenile see also following pages)

⬇

shall determine, as soon as practicable after the person's arrival at the police station, whether he has sufficient evidence to charge the person (and may detain him for that purpose).

| If he does not | If he does |

the custody officer must release either with or without bail

the custody officer decides whether to –
(a) release without charge on bail to enable the D.P.P. to make a decision as to whether to charge;
(b) release without charge on bail, but not for the above purpose;
(c) release without charge and without bail; or
(d) charge.

unless he has reasonable cause to believe that detention without charge is necessary to secure or preserve evidence relating to the offence for which arrested, or to obtain such evidence by questioning him.

If released under (a) or (b) above, and at that time a decision whether he should be prosecuted has not been taken, the custody officer shall so inform him.

He may then detain and record the grounds for doing so in the presence of the detained person. At that time he must inform the person of the grounds unless he is-
(a) incapable of understanding;
(b) violent or likely to become so; or
(c) in urgent need of medical attention.

Charging

CODES OF PRACTICE, CODE C

Decision to charge

When the officer in charge of the investigation reasonably believes there is sufficient evidence to provide a realistic prospect of the detainee's conviction, he must cease the interview and shall, without delay, inform the custody officer who will consider whether he should be charged. The custody officer must take into account alternatives to prosecution under the Crime and Disorder Act 1988, reprimands and warnings for under 18s, and national guidance on the cautioning of offenders.

Where a person is detained for more than one offence it is permissible to delay informing the custody officer until there is sufficient evidence in relation to all offences. If the detainee is a juvenile, mentally disordered or otherwise mentally vulnerable, any resulting action shall be taken in the presence of the appropriate adult if present.

Cautioning before charge

When a detainee is charged with or informed they may be prosecuted for an offence (but a warning or NIP under the Road Traffic Offenders Act 1988, he shall be cautioned as follows (unless a restriction on drawing adverse inferences from silence applies):

> "You do not have to say anything. But it may harm your defence if you do not mention now something which you later rely on in court. Anything you do say may be given in evidence."

If a restriction on drawing adverse inferences from silence applies the caution shall be as follows:

> "You do not have to say anything, but anything you do say may be given in evidence."

Serving of notices

When a detainee is charged he shall be given a written notice showing particulars of the offence in simple terms but also showing the precise offence in law, and the case reference number. The officer's name shall also be shown unless the offence is linked to terrorism or the officer reasonably believes that recording his name might put him in danger. If the detainee is a juvenile, mentally disordered or mentally vulnerable, the notice should be given to the appropriate adult.

Statements of other persons

If, after a detainee has been charged or informed he may be prosecuted for an offence, an officer wants to tell him about any written statement or interview with another person relating to such an offence, the detainee shall either be handed a true copy of the statement or have brought to his attention the content of the interview record. Nothing shall be done to invite a reply or comment except to:

(a) caution the detainee, **"You do not have to say anything, but anything you do say may be given in evidence"**; and

(b) remind the detainee about his right to legal advice.

If the detainee cannot read, the document may be read to him. If he is a juvenile, mentally disordered or mentally vulnerable, the appropriate adult shall also be given a copy, or the interview record brought to his attention.

(CONTINUED ON NEXT PAGE)

Charging – continued

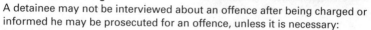

CODES OF PRACTICE, CODE C

Interview after charge

A detainee may not be interviewed about an offence after being charged or informed he may be prosecuted for an offence, unless it is necessary:
(a) to prevent or minimise harm or loss to some other person, or the public;
(b) to clear up an ambiguity in a previous answer or statement; or
(c) in the interests of justice to put to the detainee information concerning the offence which has come to light since he was charged or told that he may be prosecuted;

but before any such interview he must be:
(a) cautioned, **"You do not have to say anything, but anything you do say may be given in evidence."**, and
(b) reminded about his right to legal advice.

Presence of the appropriate adult

Where applicable, the above provisions must be complied with in the presence of the appropriate adult if he is present. If he is not, they must be repeated in his presence when he arrives unless the detainee has been released. There is no power to detain a person solely to await the arrival of the appropriate adult.

Juveniles

Where a juvenile is charged with an offence and his continued detention is authorised after charge, the custody officer must try to arrange for the juvenile to be taken into the care of the local authority to be detained pending appearance in court, unless:
(a) he certifies that it is impracticable to do so; or
(b) in the case of a juvenile over 12, no secure accommodation is available, and there is a risk to the public of serious harm from that juvenile. (See following page).

Except as above, a juvenile's behaviour, the nature of the offence or the lack of secure accommodation will not be grounds for deciding it is impracticable.

If he is not transferred into the care of the local authority the custody officer must record the reasons and complete a certificate to be produced before the court.

Documentation

A record shall be made of anything a detainee says when charged.
Any questions put and answers given after being charged shall be recorded in full on the forms provided, and signed by the detainee. If he refuses it shall be signed by the interviewer and any third parties present.

Duties After Charge

S 38 POLICE AND CRIMINAL EVIDENCE ACT 1984

Requirement to release on bail

Where a person is charged with an offence the custody officer shall order his release either with or without bail, unless:

(a) **if the person is not a juvenile** and it is believed that his detention is necessary:

   (i) because there is doubt whether the name and address furnished is his real one, or that his name and address cannot be ascertained;

   (ii) because he will fail to appear in court in answer to bail;

   (iii) to prevent him committing an offence, where the offence is punishable with imprisonment;

   (iv) to enable a sample to be taken from him to test for class A drugs under S 63B of this Act (see earlier under "Testing for Class A Drugs"), where the person is over 18;

   But this item is substituted in the following police areas: Cleveland, Greater Manchester, Humberside, Merseyside, Metropolitan, Nottinghamshire and West Yorkshire, by the following:

   (iv) except where S 63B does not apply (see earlier under "Testing for Class A Drugs"), to enable a sample to be taken from him under that section.

   (v) to prevent him causing physical injury to any other person or from causing loss of, or damage to, property (but detention not to exceed 6 hours from when charged);

   (vi) to prevent him from interfering with the administration of justice or with the investigation of offences, where the offence is not punishable with imprisonment; or

   (vii) for his own protection,

(b) **if the person is a juvenile** and it is believed that his detention is necessary:

   (i) for any of the above reasons but in relation to the police areas mentioned in the substituted (iv) above, only if the juvenile has attained the age of 14; or

   (ii) in his own interests; or

(c) **if it is one of the following offences,** and he has been previously convicted of any such offence:

   (i) murder;

   (ii) attempted murder;

   (iii) manslaughter;

   (iv) rape; or

   (v) attempted rape

when bail will only be granted in exceptional circumstances.

Factors to be considered in refusing bail

In taking a decision to refuse to grant bail, the custody officer must be satisfied that, if released on bail, the detainee would:

(a) fail to surrender to custody;

(b) commit an offence while on bail; or

(c) interfere with witnesses or otherwise obstruct the course of justice.

Records

Any authorisation for police detention shall, as soon as practicable, be recorded in writing in the presence of the detainee, who shall be informed at that time of the grounds for it (unless the person is incapable of understanding what is being said to him; is violent or likely to become so; or is in urgent need of medical attention).

Juveniles

Where juveniles are to be kept in police detention, they should be removed to local authority accommodation unless the custody officer certifies:

(a) that it is impracticable for him to do so; or

(b) if the juvenile is over 12, that no secure accommodation is available and that keeping him in other local authority accommodation would not be adequate to protect the public from serious harm from him.

Extradition – Treatment of Arrested Persons

EXTRADITION ACT 2003

The following provisions apply where a person has been arrested under an extradition arrest power and is detained at a police station.

Fingerprints and non-intimate samples may be taken by a constable only with written consent (unless an inspector or above authorises it). (S166)

Searches and examination may be carried out by a constable (or person designated by the Chief Constable) if an inspector or above authorises it, to facilitate the identification of the person. An identifying mark so found may be photographed with consent (or without consent if it is withheld or it is not practicable to obtain it). A search, examination or photograph of any part of the body (other than the face) may not be carried out by a person of the opposite sex. This section does not authorise intimate searches. (S167)

Photographs may be taken by a constable (or person designated by the Chief Constable) with consent (or without consent if it is withheld or it is not practicable to obtain it). Any item or substance worn over the head or face may be removed.

Police and Criminal Evidence Act. Sections 54, 55, 56 and 58 apply with modifications as indicated:

(a) S54(4)(b) (searches of detained persons). For "an offence" there is substituted the offence for which extradition is sought.

(b) S55(12)(b) (intimate searches). For "an offence" there is substituted the offence for which extradition is sought.

(c) S56(2)(a) and 56(5)(a) (right to have someone informed when arrested). For "a serious arrestable offence", there is substituted "an offence for which extradition is sought that would be a serious arrestable offence if committed in England and Wales".

(d) S58(6)(a) and 58(8)(a) (access to legal advice). For "a serious arrestable offence", there is substituted "an offence for which extradition is sought that would be a serious arrestable offence if committed in England and Wales".

Index

Index

Index

Index

Index

Index

Index

Index